KU-769-154

VISIONS OF GLORY

A History and a Memory of Jehovah's Witnesses

By the same author

Unlearning the Lie: Sexism in School

Visions of Glory

A History and a Memory of Jehovah's Witnesses

BARBARA GRIZZUTI HARRISON

ROBERT HALE · LONDON

First published in Great Britain 1980
(This edition is an abridged version of the American edition published in 1978)

ISBN 0 7091 8013 6

Robert Hale Limited
Clerkenwell House
Clerkenwell Green
London, EC1R 0HT

Photoset by Art Photoset Ltd., Beaconsfield, Bucks., and printed in Great Britain by Lowe & Brydone Printers Ltd., Thetford, Norfolk.

Contents

This book is for Arnold Horowitz

The author gratefully acknowledges permission to reprint excerpts from the following:

Statement by Dr. Walter Martin in an interview on "The 700 Club" television programme broadcast June 11, 1976, Christian Broadcasting Network.

Faith on the March, by A. H. Macmillan, copyright © 1957 by A. H. Macmillan. Reprinted by permission of the publishers, Prentice Hall, Inc.

Religious Movements in Contemporary America, edited by Irving I. Zaretsky and Mark P. Leone, copyright © 1974 by Princeton University Press. Selections from E. Mansell Pattison, Lee R. Cooper, Lep Pfeffer and Nathan Adler. Reprinted by permission of the publisher, Princeton University Press.

The Divine Milieu, by Pierre Teilhard de Chardin, translated by Bernard Wall. English translation copyright © 1965 by Wm. Collins Sons & Co., Ltd., London, and Harper & Row, Publishers, Inc. Originally published in French as *Le Milieu Divin,* copyright © 1957 by Editions du Seuil, Paris. Reprinted by permission of Harper & Row, Publishers, Inc., and Wm. Collins Sons & Co., Ltd.

The Nazi Persecution of the Churches: 1933–45, by J. S. Conway, copyright © 1968 by J. S. Conway. Reprinted by permission of the publisher, Basic Books, Inc., New York, and George Weidenfeld & Nicolson Ltd., London.

The Rise of American Civilization, Vol. I, by Charles A. Beard and Mary R. Beard, copyright © 1927 by Macmillan Publishing Co., Inc., renewed 1955 by Mary R. Beard. Reprinted by permission of the publisher, Macmillan Publishing Co., Inc.

"The Love Song of J. Alfred Prufrock" from *Collected Poems 1909–1962,* by T. S. Eliot. Reprinted by permission of the publisher, Harcourt Brace Jovanovich, Inc.

In the Service of Their Country, by Willard Gaylin, copyright © 1970 by Willard Gaylin. Reprinted by permission of the publisher, The Viking Press, Inc.

Excerpt from *On Being a Christian*, by Hans Küng, translated by Edward Quinn, copyright © 1976 by Doubleday & Company, Inc. Reprinted by permission of the publisher and Hans Küng.

The Myth of Sisyphus and Other Essays, by Albert Camus, translated by Justin O'Brien. Copyright © 1955 by Alfred A. Knopf, Inc. Reprinted by permission of the publisher, Alfred A. Knopf, Inc., and Hamish Hamilton, Ltd., London.

The Religion of the Oppressed: A Study of Modern Messianic Cults, by Vittorio Lanternari, copyright © 1960 by Giangiacomo Feltrinelli Editore. Reprinted by permission of the publisher, Alfred A. Knopf, Inc.

Acknowledgements

Without the support and generosity of friends and colleagues, and without the gift of time and space provided by the MacDowell Colony, I could not have written this book.

For trusting me enough to share intimate details of their lives, I thank David Maslanka, Walter Szykitka—and others who are unnamed, but not unloved. My debt to them is very great.

For the invaluable information and advice they gave so freely, I thank Bernard and Charlotte Atkins, Leon Friedman, Ralph deGia, Father Robert Kennedy, Jim Peck.

For their creative research and editorial assistance, I thank Tonia Foster and Paul Kelly—and the librarians at the Brooklyn Public Library, who eased their task.

For their perceptive insights and criticism, which helped me to understand not only my subject, but myself and my past, I thank Sheila Lehman, Tom Wilson, Sol Yurick, L. L. Zeiger, and David Zeiger.

No words can express my gratitude to the members of my family who always listened, even when their patience was sorely tried, and who were emotional bulwarks when I was sorely tried: Carol Grizzuti, Dominick Grizzuti, Richard Grizzuti; and my children (who managed, with grace, to live with my obsessions), Anna and Joshua Harrison.

For Father Michael Crimmins, Alice Hagen, and Rose Moss, who gave me a very special kind of encouragement at a very crucial time, I have love and regard.

And finally, I thank and esteem my editor, Alice E. Mayhew, for her good counsel and her good work.

(Throughout this book, I have changed names and identities to protect the privacy of those concerned.)

I
Personal Beginnings: 1944

Jehovah's Witnesses are believers in a fundamentalist, apocalyptic, prophetic religion which has been proclaiming, since the 1930s, that "Millions Now Living Will Never Die." The world will end, they say, with the destruction of the wicked at Armageddon, in our lifetime. Only the chosen will survive. They intensify their preaching efforts in order to increase the number of survivors. They are also increasing their property holdings. [*Yearbook,* 1977,* p. 30]

The Witnesses are a widely varied group of individuals who subject themselves to total conformity in practice, outlook, and belief. To the extent to which they are known—their notoriety follows from their refusal to receive blood transfusions or serve in the army of any country, as well as from their aggressive proselytizing—they are perceived as somewhat eccentric people and dismissed as an irrelevant joke. Little is known of their motives, their anguish, their glorious surges of communal happiness, and little thought is given to the comment their existence makes on society.

In February, 1944, the Supreme Court of the United States affirmed the conviction of Mrs. Sarah Prince of Brockton, Massachusetts, who had been fined for allowing her 9-year-old niece Betty Simmons to distribute the literature of Jehovah's Witnesses on the streets. The Court, by a 5–4 decision, upheld the Massachusetts Child Labour Law under which no girl under 18 (and no boy under 12) could sell magazines or newspapers in a public place; the law could be validly enforced, the Court ruled, against those who allow young children under their care to sell religious literature on the streets.

Hayden C. Covington, legal counsel for the Witnesses, who had, since 1939, come before the Court with sixteen major constitutional issues, contended that the Massachusetts law was in violation of both the constitutional guarantee of religious freedom and the basic rights of parenthood.

On the basis of past decisions, Covington might reasonably have expected to win his case. The Witnesses' bitterly controversial cases had produced twenty-seven Court opinions [See *American Political*

*Abbreviated codes for sources frequently cited are listed on page 229.

Science Review, 1944, 1945], almost all of them ultimately favourable to the Witnesses and many of them strengthening the cause of civil liberties.

In the Prince case, however, Covington's arguments did not prevail. Justice Wiley Rutledge voiced the majority opinion that "neither rights of religion nor rights of parenthood are beyond limitation." "Parents may be free to become martyrs themselves," he said, "but it does not follow that they are free . . . to make martyrs of their children."

Ironically, the Witnesses, bitter foes of the Catholic Church, found support from the only Catholic on the bench, Justice Frank Murphy. In a separate dissent, Justice Murphy insisted that the sidewalk "as well as the cathedral or the evangelist's tent is a proper place, under the Constitution, to worship." [*Prince v. Commonwealth of Massachusetts,* 351 U.S. 158 (1944)]

In 1944, in a small town in the Southwest, a jury returned a verdict of not guilty in the trial of Mary Lou Smith, a 15-year-old girl who had pumped seventeen bullets into her father and brother, killing them both. She had had, defence counsel said, periodic vivid dreams since the onset of menstruation; she was adjudged temporarily not responsible for her acts.

These events are unrelated, except in my mind. I have never met Betty Simmons or Mary Lou Smith, but I feel, somehow, as if we are siblings. They wander, like ghosts, in the baggage of my mind.

In 1944, when I, like Betty Simmons, was 9 years old, I became one of Jehovah's Witnesses. Whatever effects the Supreme Court's ruling may have had on children of Jehovah's Witnesses in Brockton, Massachusetts, it is certain that nobody thought to enforce the Court's ruling in Brooklyn, New York. After my baptism at a national convention of 25,000 Witnesses in Buffalo, New York, in the summer of 1944, I became an ardent proselytizer, distributing *The Watchtower* and *Awake!* magazines on street corners and from door to door, spending as much as 150 hours a month in the service of my newly found God—under the directives of the Watchtower Bible and Tract Society, the legal and corporate arm of Jehovah's Witnesses.

As I had been immersed in water to symbolize my "dedication to do God's will," I became, also, drenched in the dark blood-poetry of a religion whose adherents drew joy from the prospect of the imminent end of the world. I preached sweet doom; I believed that Armageddon would come in my lifetime, with a great shaking and rending and tearing of unbelieving flesh, with unsanctified babies swimming in blood. I believed also that after the slaughter Jehovah had arranged for His enemies at Armageddon, this quintessentially masculine God—vengeful in battle and benevolent to survivors—

would return to earth into an Eden for true believers.

Coincidentally with my conversion, I got my first period. We used to sing this hymn: "Here is He who comes from Eden/ All His raiments stained with blood." My raiments were stained with blood too. But the blood of the Son of Man was purifying, redemptive, cleansing, sacrificial. Mine was proof of my having inherited the curse placed upon the seductress Eve. Mine was filthy. I examined my discharges with horror and fascination.

I was, in equal measure, guilt-ridden and—supposing myself to be in on the secrets of the cosmos—self-righteous and smug. I grew up awaiting the final, orgasmic burst of violence after which all things would come together in a cosmic ecstasy of joy—this in a religion that was totally antierotic, that expressed disgust and contempt for the world.

My ignorance of sexual matters was so profound that it frequently led to comedies of error. Nothing I've ever read has inclined me to believe that Jehovah has a sense of humour; and I must say that I consider it a strike against Him that He wouldn't find this story funny:

One night shortly after my conversion, a visiting elder of the congregation, as he was avuncularly tucking me into bed, asked me if I was guilty of performing evil practices with my hands under the covers at night. I was puzzled. He was persistent. Finally, I thought I understood. And I burst into wild tears of self-recrimination. Under the covers at night, I bit my cuticles—a practice which, in fact, did afford me a kind of sensual pleasure. (I didn't learn about masturbation—which the Witnesses call "idolatry," because "the masturbator's affection is diverted away from the Creator and is bestowed upon a coveted object" [*TW*, Sept. 15, 1973, p. 568], until much later.)

So, having confessed to a sin I hadn't known existed, I was advised of the necessity for keeping one's body pure from sin; cold baths were recommended. I couldn't see the connection, but one never questioned the imperatives of an elder, so I subjected my impure body to so many icy baths in midwinter that I began to look like a bleached prune.

I used to preach, from door to door, that an increase in the number of rapes was one of the signs heralding the end of the world; but I didn't know what rape was. I knew that good Christians didn't commit "unnatural acts"; but I didn't know what "unnatural acts" were. Consequently, I spent a lot of time praying that I was not committing unnatural acts or rape.

Once, having heard that Hitler had a mistress, I asked my mother what a mistress was. I knew from my mother's silence, and from her cold, hard, and frightened face, that the question was somehow a grievous offence. I knew that I had done something wrong, but as usual, I didn't know what.

The fact was that I never knew how to buy God's—or my mother's—approval. There were sins I consciously and knowingly committed. That was bad, but it was bearable. I could always pray to God to forgive me, say, for reading the Bible for its "dirty parts"; for preferring the Song of Solomon to all the *begats* of Genesis. But the offences that made me most horribly guilty were those I had committed unconsciously; as an imperfect being descended from the wretched Eve, I was bound, so I had been taught, to offend Jehovah seventy-seven times a day without my even knowing what I was doing wrong.

I feel now that for the twelve years I spent as one of Jehovah's Witnesses, three of them as a member of the Watchtower Society's headquarters staff, I was living out a vivid dream, hallucinating within the closed system of logic and private reality of a religion that relished disaster; rejoiced in the evil of human nature; lusted for certitude; ordered its members to disdain the painful present in exchange for the glorious future; corrupted ritual, ethics, and doctrine into ritualism, legalism, and dogmatism.

I was convinced that 1914 marked "the beginning of the times of the end." So firmly did Jehovah's Witnesses believe this to be true that there were those who, in 1944, refused to get their teeth filled, postponing all care of their bodies until God saw to their regeneration in His New World.

More than thirty years have passed, but though their hopes have not been fulfilled, the Witnesses have persevered with increased fervour and conviction. Their attitude toward the world remains the same: because all their longing is for the future, they are bound to hate the present. It's impossible to savour and enjoy the present if you are waiting only for it to be smashed by God. There is a kind of ruthless glee in the way Jehovah's Witnesses point to earthquakes, race riots, heroin addiction, the failure of the United Nations, divorce, famine and liberalized abortion laws as proof of the nearness of Armageddon.

The God I worshipped was not the God before whom one swoons in ecstasy, or with whom one contends: He was an awesome and awful judge, whom one approached through his "channel", the "divinely appointed Theocratic organization"—the Watchtower Bible and Tract Society. The Christ in whose name I prayed was not a social reformer, nor was he God incarnate. He was, rather, merely a legal instrument in God's wrangles with the Devil. All the history of the world is seen, by Jehovah's Witnesses, as a contest between Jehovah and Satan.

Hayden Covington once described the beginnings of the world in the Garden of Eden: "It was a legal matter. The [forbidden] tree served as a legal sign, a guidepost between the God-King and man in their governmental dealings with each other. Adam and Eve failed to fulfil their contract." It is a contractual, not an ecstatic, religion.

I rehearse, I jealously preserve preconversion memories; they flash before my mind like magical slides. I treasure a series of intense, isolated moments. I hoard happy images that are pure, unsullied by values assigned to them by others. Afterward, there was nothing in the world to which I was permitted to give my own meaning; afterward, when the world began to turn for me on the axis of God's displeasure, I was obliged to regard all events as part of God's plan for the universe as understood only by Jehovah's Witnesses. Afterward, meanings were assigned to all things. The world was flattened out into right and wrong; all experience was sealed into compartments marked Good and Evil. Before my conversion, each beloved object and event had the luminosity and purity of a thing complete in itself, a thing to which no significance is attributed other than that which it chooses to reveal.

Saturdays I played with the beautiful twins Barbara and Violet, who mirrored each other's loveliness, like Snow White and Rose Red. I thought it was impossible that they should ever be lonely or frightened. I wanted the half of me that had escaped to come back, so that I could be whole, like Barbara-and-Violet.

Sunday afternoons I went to my father's mother's house. I sat at Grandma's vanity table—pink-and-white, muslined and taffetaed, skirted and ribboned—and played with antique Italian jewelry in velvet-lined leather boxes and held small bottles of perfume with mysterious amber residues.

The house of my mother's family, near the Brooklyn Navy Yard, always smelled of fermenting wine and of incense to the saints; its walls and tin ceilings were poverty-brown and -green; but there was always a store-bought chocolate cake waiting in the icebox for my visit.

These are the fragments I jealously preserve like the crêche from Italy (sweet Mary, humble Joseph, and tiny Jesus—always perfect and new) that adorned each Christmas morning.

After my conversion, I began immediately to have a dream, which recurred until I released myself from bondage to that religion twelve years later, when I was 21. In the dream, I am standing in my grandmother's walled garden. At the far corner stands a creature icy, resplendent, of indeterminate sex. The creature calls to me. In my dream its voice is tactile; I feel it flow through my veins like molten silver. I am rendered bloodless, will-less; the creature extends its arms in a gesture that is at once magisterial and maternal, entreating and commanding. I walk toward its embrace, fearful but glad, unable not to abandon myself to a splendid doom. The creature seizes me in its arms and I am hurled out of the garden, a ravaged Humpty-Dumpty flying through dark and hostile space, alone.

I understand that dream to have been telling me my truest feelings, which my conscious, waking mind censored for long hard years. My religion savaged those to whom it offered salvation. For twelve years I lived in fear.

In 1944, the world was at war. Clark had landed with the Fifth Army at Salerno. The covers of news magazines were decorated with Bombs for Hitler. Places named Mindanao and Madang briefly stained the American consciousness. A novel called *Two Jills in a Jeep* appeared on the best-seller lists. Gandhi was in jail. The West Coast having been designated by Executive Order 9066 as a military area, all persons of Japanese ancestry, aliens and citizens, had been evacuated and were confined to camps. The War Production Board had promised civilians that more hairpins would soon be available, but announced regretfully that the shortage of "mechanical refrigerators" was likely to continue. Six million Jews were dead or dying.

Of all these events I had an almost perfect innocence. I perceived the war in terms of daily realities: sand in a regulation red bucket, dark-green air-raid curtains; rubber bands and tinfoil balls and old newspapers competitively offered to my fourth-grade teacher for the war effort. Uncle Tony was Somewhere-in-Burma and would send me the ear of a Jap. Dick Tracy and Uncle Don told us how to recognize Japanese secret agents; but Hirohito was less real than The Shadow (who *knew*), the threat of enemy missiles less to be feared than the creaking door of the Inner Sanctum, and the conflict between the Allies and the Axis of less moment than the continuing debate between me and my friend Lorraine over whether real beauties had auburn hair and blue eyes or blonde hair and grey eyes.

When I became a Witness, I began to take the war seriously. The Witnesses certainly took it seriously. For one thing hundreds of Witnesses—who regard national emblems as "graven images"—were imprisoned for not saluting the American flag. Over 4,000 male Witnesses spent the duration in federal penitentiaries for refusal to join the armed services.

In the midst of wartime fervour, the Supreme Court, in an unpopular decision, found a state regulation requiring schoolchildren, under the penalty of expulsion, to salute the flag invalid. [*West Virginia Board of Education v. Barnette*, 1943] An earlier decision of the Court [*Minersville District v. Gobitas*, 1940] which had resulted in the mass expulsion of Witness children from schools all over America, was thus reversed. The Court ruled that the *Gobitas* case had been "wrongly decided" and that to oblige children to salute the flag was an infringement of the Fourteenth Amendment. Also, in 1943, in the case of *Taylor v. Mississippi*, the Court unanimously set aside the conviction of three of Jehovah's Witnesses under a statute that made it a felony "to teach or preach orally any principles, or distribute any printed matter, calculated to incite violence, sabotage, or disloyalty to state or nation." The Court, refusing to uphold the claim that the Witnesses had created "an attitude of stubborn refusal to salute, honour, or respect the flag or government of the United States and the State of Mississippi," ruled that the Witnesses were not guilty of "evil or sinister purpose."

Unfortunately, the news that the Witnesses were not subversive had not filtered down to P.S. 86 in Bensonhurst. Having to remain seated, in my blue-and-white middy, during flag salute at school assembly was an act of defiance from which I inwardly recoiled. I wanted desperately to be liked—despite the fact that the Witnesses took pleasure in anything that could be construed as "persecution," viewing any opposition as proof of their being God's chosen. Not saluting the flag, being the only child in my school who did not contribute to the Red Cross, and not bringing in tinfoil balls for the War Drive did not endear me to my classmates. I wanted to please everybody—my teachers, my spiritual overseers, my mother; and of course, I could not.

I had learned as a very small child that it was my primary duty in life to "make nice." When I was little, I was required to respond to inquiries about my health in this manner: "Fine and dandy, just like sugar candy, thank you." And to curtsy. If that sounds as if it were from a Shirley Temple movie, it is. Brought up to be the Italian working-class Shirley Temple from Bensonhurst, I did not find it terribly difficult to learn to "make nice" for God and His earthly representatives. Behaving well was relatively easy and a passionate desire to win approval guaranteed that I conformed. But behaving well never made me feel *good*—in part, no doubt, because I couldn't have two sets of good behaviour: one for the Witnesses, and one for my teachers at P.S. 86. I armed myself against the criticism of teachers and peers by telling myself that they were wicked and anyway scheduled for destruction. That didn't work either. I felt as if I were the bad person, unworthy to live forever, yet superior to those who wouldn't consent to listen to my preaching about living-forever-on-a-perfect-earth.

I believed that I had The Truth. One of the things I had The Truth about was the war. In 1944, if one read, as I did, only the literature of Jehovah's Witnesses, one was given to believe that World War II was a plot hatched by Satan and the Vatican to stop the Witnesses from preaching the gospel. The Witnesses' view of the global conflict was, in its own way, as narrow and parochial as my little-girl's view had been. The war was perceived in terms of *their* realities.

All history, as seen by the Witnesses, revolves around them. They are guilty of what theologian Charles Davis calls "pride of history": they "reject temporality as man's mode of existence or else close that temporality against the transcendent; either history has no meaning at all or it means everything." [Davis, *Temptations of Religion* (New York: Harper and Row, 1947)]

The Witnesses were able, without irony, to remark in their 1945 *Yearbook*, "Today men and women are living in marvellous times . . . a most joyful time." Convinced of the *meaning* of the war, they were able to disengage themselves from the bloody *facts* of the war. Between themselves and terror stood their interpretation of Bible prophecy—and numbers: numbers pulled from the Bible books of Matthew, Daniel, and Revelation and contorted into the shape of a chronology to prove that we were living in the last days.

On September 14, my birthday, all over the world—in Dresden, London, Hiroshima—Witnesses opened their day with this obligatory daily text from the 1945 *Yearbook:*

> It is a marvellous day. Though it appears partly dark because of persecution and oppression by enemies, yet Jehovah's clear light of truth is shining and his blessings upon people help to brighten the situation and prevent it from being altogether dark. It is a day by itself, for it precedes the 1000-year reign of his beloved Son. It is a particular day that Jehovah God has reserved for himself for vindicating his name . . . At the evening of his day he will rise up and go forth by his King to give his own testimony to his supremacy and universal sovereignty. Then the day will be light. It will be lightened with the blaze of his glory by his complete victory over all Satan's organization.

In the 1945 *Yearbook*, an account of the Witnesses' worldwide preaching activities for that year, one looks in vain for a mention of the genocide against the Jews—although there is no shortage of detail of the "persecution" of the Witnesses. The *Yearbook* informs us that a ban imposed on the work of the Witnesses by the Government of South Africa was removed in 1943, and the Witnesses rejoice; but apartheid is not mentioned. Social and political realities are ignored except to demonstrate the fulfilment of Bible prophecy.

Even Hitler is dismissed, or seen through their rabid anti-Catholicism as a lackey of the Roman Catholic Church. Vatican City is blamed for the rise of fascism not only in Italy and Germany, but in Argentina as well. The bombing of Britain:

> At times there have been attacks from the air that have made regular Kingdom service extremely difficult. . . . The Lord's protecting care has

been marvellously demonstrated, for none [of the Witnesses] have lost their lives although in the midst of destruction on every hand. . . . On several occasions home Bible-study meetings have been in progress when bombs have struck either the home or nearby dwellings and both the brethren and the newly interested in whose home the studies were being held have had marvellous escapes.

Bombs exist only as obstacles in the path of the monomaniacal preachers of "good news." "At this time it is very difficult to reach some nations, because of the raging war. . . . Every nation under the sun is affected by the war, but God's message concerning the end of this 'present evil world' and the establishment of the New World cannot wait until men get done fighting. . . . This sort of thing has been carried on for generations and ages." Human suffering is understood as "this sort of thing."

In the 1945 *Yearbook* (distributed only among Witnesses, and not among "outsiders" in an "alien world") they hold the mirror to themselves, fascinated by their objectified image. "Why is it," they ask, "that Jehovah's Witnesses are so different from everybody else? It is not because of the way they walk or talk or how they dress or how they act in general. The only thing that makes them different is the way they worship."

And indeed, the way in which they worship *is* different. All of Jehovah's Witnesses are proselytizers. All preach from door to door . . . and fill out, for their local congregations, little yellow slips on which they write the number of hours spent each week at work in the fields of the Lord, and the number of books and booklets "placed" with householders for a "contribution," and the number of return visits. For the Witnesses there is salvation, and comfort, in numbers.

In 1944, according to the 1945 *Yearbook* [p. 56], there were fewer than 65,000 "publishers of the Kingdom news"—that is, Witnesses—in the United States. These publishers distributed 15,298,997 books and booklets, and 7,448,325 copies of the society's magazines—one of them to my father. They made 4,803,084 "back-calls" upon interested persons; one of these interested persons, or "people of goodwill," as they would have it, was my father.

My father was a potential "sheep"; he had not, when a Witness first approached him, demonstrated a "goatlike disposition."

I should explain about "sheep" and "goats": Like any closed society, Witnesses have their own peculiar terminology. They talk to one another in a code that is impenetrable to outsiders. (The year of our conversion, my brother, who was then 4 years old, told a notoriously quick-tempered uncle that one of our cousins was not "In The Truth" but was "of goodwill." My uncle, unused to being diminished by 4-year-olds, slapped him in the face. My brother, reporting to my mother, said he would keep his "integrity" in spite of my uncle's hearty slap.) The Witnesses are able to identify outsiders, or defectors, or hangers-on, by the slightest misuse of code language.

The Witnesses, who disdain metaphysical inquiry and allow for no doctrinal embroidery or fancywork among their members, play with words to keep the illusion that there is something new under their sun. Over the years, they have made small but, to them, important changes in terminology: What used to be called the New World was later described as the New System and is now uniformly referred to as the New Order. Such changes keep the Witnesses alert to potential apostates in their ranks and help preserve them as a cohesive, homogeneous whole. Any departure from the universal language, any verbal eccentricity, starts alarm bells ringing in the heads of Witnesses. (In their publications, Jehovah's Witnesses use a lower-case *w* for witnesses: Jehovah's witnesses. To say *I am one of Jehovah's witnesses,* therefore, is to say not, I am a member of a strange cult with an esoteric name, but I am someone whom Jehovah has chosen to bear witness to His name.)

In their work of dividing the "sheep" from the "goats," Jehovah's Witnesses are often met with resistance they deem goatlike.

When I was 9, I rang doorbells all over Brooklyn. I was almost always alone. Occasionally I rang doorbells with companions of my own age; and we did daft little bits of business to punctuate our high seriousness. Sometimes, sitting on the stairs of apartment buildings, with booklets like "Religion Reaps the Whirlwind!" heaped around us, the girls would "practise" kissing. What a gorgeous dodge! We couldn't kiss the boys—that would have been too frankly sexual, and scary. We kissed each other, clinically; it was science (we thought), not sex. We kept our hot secrets to ourselves. We had no confessors. If, after one of our escapades, we felt guilty, we dealt with our guilt alone—usually by the expedient of ignoring one another, or deliberately fracturing our friendships. We told the adults as little as possible.

Meanwhile, the adults were busy at their own games. Sometimes I was assigned to preach with Crazy Sally as my companion—Crazy Sally, who wore her craziness *à la mode:* peroxided hair glopped on top of her head, shedding hairpins as Ophelia strewed flowers; high heels and white anklets; twin shopping bags; rolling, hyperthyroidic eyes. The grown-ups thought The Truth would save Crazy Sally (35, a virgin whose father, a cop, had shot himself in her bed); they, like Sally, thought the psychiatrists in whose care she'd been were the "instruments of Satan." But they were (I felt) ashamed to be seen with her. So they "gave" her to a child. Me.

I rang doorbells in tenements that smelled of chicken fat; in the vestibules of neat two-storey brick and stucco houses with garish plaster madonnas in the bay windows. I rang the bells of large, quiet houses in Flatbush with wraparound porches and Henry James lawns. Once, a handsome Jesuit—"a wicked representative of *the Vatican*" whom I was obliged to despise, and whose ascetic face and gentle manner I immediately loved—served me iced tea and as we swung together on a porch swing told me, "Saint Augustine says, 'Only love God, and do as you will.'"

Most of the doors were slammed in my face. So many rejections! I told myself they were rejecting Jehovah, not me. (But even now, I feel naked in front of a closed door.)

The Witnesses, gaining access to an ear, or to a door cracked slightly open, assault the householder in a manner both gentle and persistent, with remarkable opening statements like these:

"Good morning. I have come to bring you good news about a perfect new world without crime. Wouldn't you like to live in a world where you didn't have to lock your doors, and where all citizens lived under the law and order of a perfect ruler?"

"I am bringing all your neighbours a message of comfort and hope from the Bible. I see that you have a little child. Wouldn't you like him to grow up in a world where there was no sickness and no death?" (I said that once to a woman with a child in her arms. She said, "My baby is dying of leukaemia.")

"I've come with a message from the Lord." (I said *that* once, and a disembodied voice from behind a peephole said, "Tell the Lord to send it Western Union.")

Given any kind of opening, the Witnesses then recite a tidy little sermon, flipping their New World Translation of the Bible to well-worn passages; offer their literature; and depart—to record the reactions of the householder on a House-to-House record slip. They mark *I* for Interested; *NI* for Not Interested; *GW* for Goodwill; *O* for Opposed; *NH* for Not Home. These scrupulously kept records form the basis for return visits. (In 1956, the year I left the Witnesses—or, according to them, the year the Holy Spirit left *me*—it was estimated that each New York city block was "worked" by the Witnesses in this fashion three times a year.)

On December 24, 1943, my father bought, for 5 cents, a copy of *The Watchtower* magazine from a mild-eyed man standing on a street corner selling *The Watchtower* and *Consolation* magazines and calling out slogans to the oblivious Christmas Eve shoppers. The seller meekly endured the indifference of passers-by. His certitude that he dwelt in the absolute allowed him to enjoy his singularity from the undifferentiated masses who casually disregarded him. It was really more aggressive an act to buy a *Watchtower* magazine than to sell one.

Here is Mario, standing on the street corner, exuding earnestness and the sadness of the isolated whose singularity is a blessing and a burden:

"Read *The Watchtower* and learn about God's Kingdom!"

"*The Watchtower*—announcing God's Theocratic Government."

"Read all about God's purposes for man."

"Read *Consolation*—a journal of fact, hope, and courage."

My father, impulsive and kind, was never oblivious to sadness, and he savoured any evidence of eccentricity as he would a good red table wine. He loved the odd fact; he regarded with affection the quirks of human behaviour. Connoisseur of soapbox orators, mischievous, he loved good-natured contention. He was stubborn in argument and, uneducated and ill informed, frequently irritating; but it was never his intention to draw blood. He bought, from mild-eyed Mario, a copy of *The Watchtower.* And, because he would have considered it an abuse of hospitality not to, he gave Mario our address so that Mario might, as he put it, "Call back to further explain God's purposes."

Several weeks later, we received a visit from Mario, accompanied by his daughter Annie, whose inertia was dazzling. A 17-year-old Frank Sinatra freak, a bubble-gum-snapping bobby-soxer, she followed her intense father with obvious reluctance and remorseless listlessness. She had a crush on a young male Witness and did everything she could to cultivate his interest in her. I, of course, thought 17 was a magical age, a formed, sophisticated age. How slyly she regarded me as I drank in every exotic word of her father's salvation pitch! Annie's condescension to me lent to the evening a *frisson* of special tension.

My mother and father agreed to participate in a "home Bible study." Every Monday night we sat down—Mario; Annie; my 4-year-old brother, Rickie; my father; my mother; and I—to a study of the Witnesses' latest textbook, *The Truth Shall Make You Free.* We took turns reading paragraphs from "the *Truth* book." After each paragraph was read, Mario propounded a question from a glossy question booklet, and one of us volunteered to answer—that is, to summarize the paragraph. Then Mario would read the Scriptures cited in the text to corroborate the Witnesses' exposition, and one of us would undertake to comment on them.

My father found his approach to knowledge antithetical to all his instincts. His casual curiosity had been quickly sated. He had a restless, irritable intelligence that could not be satisfied by rote learning. He had left Catholicism because he found the Catholicism of his immigrant parents gloomy, pedantic, dogma-ridden, and womanish. He had briefly embraced Presbyterianism because the Presbyterian minister was a "regular guy," the Presbyterian church was right around the corner, and Presbyterian hot dog picnics satisfied his gregarious nature. When we moved away from the Presbyterian church on the corner, he left Presbyterianism; the local betting parlour did just as well as a social club, which was all he had really had in mind; and he retreated into his own real nature—cynical, doubting, agnostic, playful, and kind.

He liked to tease God. He soon understood that he could not tease the Witnesses. He argued mischievously; and then, as he understood that his wife and daughter were devouring whole what Mario taught, and were growing swollen with fanaticism that was bound to separate us from him, he argued fiercely; and then, as we became lost to him, he argued wearily.

When, not two months after Mario's first visit, my mother accepted an invitation to attend a meeting of the Witnesses at the local "Kingdom Hall," my father behaved in a way that allowed us to report excitedly to Mario that he had become "an opposer to The Truth."

Every Sunday morning my mother, who was beautiful, baked muffins. Three months after Mario's first visit, she declared her intention to go preaching, Sunday morning, from door to door. Attaching all the fervour of her passionate nature to her new-found, consuming religion, she—who had always been outwardly submissive to my father—declined to bake the muffins. No one else has fought so passionately over muffins in the history of the world. My father—who pronounced himself fed up with all this female nonsense—packed his suitcases to leave home. He didn't leave. He never could bring himself to leave. But we became a bitterly divided household.

What made my mother such an easy mark for conversion? I can only guess, from what I subsequently came to understand about the appeal the Witnesses have for women. For women whose experience has taught them that all human relationships are treacherous and capricious and frighteningly volatile, an escape from the confusions of the world into the certainties of a fundamentalist religion provides the illusion of safety, and of rest. Female Witnesses outnumber male Witnesses 3 to 2. As a child, I observed that it was not extraordinary for women who became Jehovah's Witnesses to remove themselves from their husbands' bedrooms as a first step to getting closer to God. Many unhappily married and sexually embittered women fall in love with Jehovah.

My mother's mother had been a renowned village beauty in her native Abruzzi. Vain, stupid, courted for her beauty, she made a miserable marriage with a man who was her equal in looks and much her superior in intelligence. My maternal grandfather was the last of three male children to arrive at Ellis Island. A patron in the

Abruzzi had paid the steerage passage for the older boys—and kept my grandfather as a kind of indentured servant in return. Grandpa—whose fierce temper was legend—worked for five years as a shepherd; he lived a life of involuntary solitude in a hut. By the time he reached America, his ability to express himself in speech had practically atrophied, so seldom had he had occasion to talk to another human being during the five years of his servitude. Having married my grandmother for her beauty, he noisily lamented his error to the day of her death. Unlike his brothers, he was never more than a labourer, and he railed against his fate with all the strength of a large but thwarted intelligence. My grandmother, a compulsive eater and a diabetic, grew fat; she stunned herself into insensibility with food, and surrounded herself with saints and incense and an army of black-robed churchy friends. Grandpa's rage found expression in violent fits of anger directed against his five children—not one of whom survived childhood without a nose broken by him. My mother's nose was broken when he slammed an iron into her face in a senseless, voiceless seizure of unprovoked rage. Her mother never protected her.

My mother left this house, over which the threat of violence always hung (a house that smelled richly—and claustrophobically—of fermenting wine and incense and all the stale, dark-brown smells of poverty) when she was 19, to marry my father. Whether she loved my father I do not know. After she became a Witness, my mother destroyed every letter they had ever exchanged, every photograph she had ever had taken with him. She no longer wore her wedding ring. My aunts say she used to write my father poetry; if she did, it was burned with the rest of her preconversion past. In my father's sisters' house, there are pictures of my mother as a bride. She looks vulnerable, soft, eager; perhaps it was a trick of lighting, photographer's magic; she looks like a girl in love.

My mother was 20 when I was born. I never knew the tender girl of the studio portraits. I knew a woman hotly involved in family intrigues, a woman who entered my bedroom at night to weep.

She chose "spiritual brothers and sisters" who told her, as her family had, that the world was *other* and evil, alien, and cruel. She found shelter.

What predisposed me toward my conversion? In recent years, when elders of Jehovah's Witnesses have come to call on me, they have usually asked—out of their zeal to assign spiritual cause and effect to all mysterious acts of the spirit, to tame experience by defining it, and to render apostasy less threatening by subjecting apostates to the rigours of private logic—whether, when I was 9, I'd made a conscious decision to serve Jehovah; whether from true knowledge and absolute belief I chose to "dedicate myself to God."

(If they can believe that my water baptism was the act of a dutiful daughter, an aberration of youth rather than an independent act of choice and mature will, they can dispose of me in their minds, categorize and forget me.) Of course I can't answer their question. I choose to believe in free will; but the motives of that little girl who pledged her life to God are necessarily obscure to me.

Nor can the person my brother became help me to understand the person I became. I ask myself how my brother escaped the religion that threw its meshes so tightly over me. Why was he not hounded for years by the obsessive guilt and the desperate desire for approval that informed all my post conversion actions? Partly, I suppose, luck, and an accident of temperament; but also, I think, because of the peculiarly guilt-inspiring double messages girls received as Jehovah's Witnesses. Girls were taught that it was their nature to be spiritual but, paradoxically, that they were more prone to depravity than were boys. In my religion, everything beautiful and noble and spiritual and good was represented by a woman; and everything evil and depraved and monstrous was represented by a woman. I learned that "God's organization"—the "bride of Christ," or His 144,000 heavenly co-rulers—was represented by a chaste virgin. I also learned that "Babylon the Great," or "false religion," was "The mother of the abominations or the 'disgusting things of the earth.' . . . She likes to get drunk on human blood. . . . Babylon the Great is . . . pictured as a woman, an international harlot." [*Babylon,* pp. 576–83]

Young girls were thought not to have the "urges" boys had. They were not only caretakers of their own sleepy sexuality, but protectors of boys' vital male animal impulses as well. They were thus doubly responsible and, if they fell, doubly damned.

I spent my childhood walking a religious tightrope, maintaining a difficult and dizzying balance. I was expected to perform well at schoolwork so that glory would accrue to Jehovah and "his organization"; but I was also continually made aware of the perils of falling prey to "the wisdom of this world which is foolishness to God." I had constantly to defend myself against the danger of trusting my own judgement. To question or to criticize God's "earthly representatives" was a sure sign of "demonic influence"; to express doubt openly was to risk being treated as a spiritual leper. I was always an honour student at school; but this was hardly an occasion for unqualified joy. I felt, rather, as if I were courting spiritual disaster: while I was congratulated for having "given a witness" by virtue of my academic excellence, I was, in the next breath, warned against the danger of supposing that my intelligence could function independently of God's. The effect of all this was to convince me that my intelligence was like some kind of tricky, predatory animal which, if it was not kept firmly reined, would surely spring on me and destroy me.

But sexual guilt and the carefully nurtured fear of intellectual pride, while they may have acted as glues to adhere me to my religion for many dry years, do not (I think) explain my conversion to that religion.

I look for clues; I find very few. I had read precociously and voraciously from the time I was seven. *War and Peace, Gone with the Wind,* and *Little Women* were my favourite books. When my mother learned that I knew what Kotex was, she destroyed all my books, including *Heidi*, because it made me "cry too much." When Mario came with his books and his message, I drank his words as if I were parched. I remember the way the book we studied—*The Truth Shall Make You Free*—looked and felt in my hand. It smelled wonderfully of new glue. Embossed in gold on its azure-blue cover was a circle which embraced a line of smiling people in varied headgear—all with straight, nondescript Anglo-Saxon features; all clasping textbooks in their hands. These, Mario explained, were "people of goodwill from all lands worshipping Jehovah."

The romance of that book, its garish colour plates! Illustrations of Jesus being stoned by the "Jewish religionists" out of the temple; spectacularly un-Darwinian pictures of dinosaurs and lambs roaming the Edenic earth—which resembled the pictures in my school geography book of the Panama Canal Zone; scenes of "free men" (Witnesses) in Nazi concentration camps, their hollow-cheeked faces radiant with the nobility of suffering; illustrations of Jephthah's daughter, girdled in gold, dancing with tambourines in pseudo-Arabian splendour, her father dressed exactly like the Roman warriors in the Metropolitan Museum of Art; representations of a beastlike Nebuchadnezzar (who looked like the Wolf Man), crouched on all fours eating weeds in front of a crumbling Corinthian temple.

"Worldly and religious scientists," I read, "worshipping their own brains and other men, pass by the very source of truthful information, God's word." How, indeed, could "worldly scientists" vie with the wonderful imagery of the *Truth* book—images of creation and destruction; images of water and blood?

According to the *Truth* book, Noah "typified" Christ; Noah's wife "pictured" the bride of Christ (the 144,000 Jehovah's Witnesses who will share Christ's heavenly reign); and Noah's three sons and three daughters-in-law "pictured" the "great crowd of other sheep," Jehovah's Witnesses who will live forever on an Edenic, cleansed earth; the ark "pictured" the new world. (Theologians have accused the Witnesses of "absurd typology." I thought it was marvellous magic—like those Chinese ivory balls one opens to find another ivory ball within, and within that another ball, and within that, another—secrets within secrets.)

Most important, the Flood "foreshadowed" the destruction of the ungodly in our day. "Reckoning each of the six creative days of Genesis to have been of 7,000 years' duration," the Witnesses concluded, in 1944, that "From Adam's creation to the end of 1943 A.D. is 5,971 years. We are therefore near the end of 6,000 years of human history with tremendous events [Armageddon, and the 1,000-year reign of Christ] upon us." [p. 152]

The Witnesses do not distinguish among the lyrical, poetic, mystical, historical, prophetic, and epistological books of the Bible; so from the *Truth* book I learned this hop-skip-and-jump chronology; I zigzagged my way through the Pentateuch to Revelation to Daniel, marvelling at the wondrous way in which this divine jigsaw fitted together.

In 1914 Christ's Kingdom was established in the heavens. (Satan, who had had access to the heavens, presumably to play in the fields of the Lord and have his way with renegade angels, was shortly thereafter restricted to "the realms of the earth"—which accounts for World War I.) This was how the Witnesses (in 1944) arrived at the year 1914: From Luke 21:24 we learned that Jerusalem would be trampled upon by the nations until the "times of the Gentiles" were fulfilled. Now skip to Daniel 7:14, which, according to the Witnesses' reading, proves that Christ was to receive a kingdom that would never be destroyed. When was Christ to receive his kingdom? At the end of the Gentile times—the period in which there was no representative government of Jehovah (such as Israel had been) upon the earth. When had the Gentile times begun? In 607 B.C., when Israel, theocracy, lost her sovereignty and became enslaved to Babylon.

To prove this, we switch to Daniel 3, which contains the account of Nebuchadnezzar's dream of a hewn-down tree, its stump in the earth banded with iron and brass, and of Nebuchadnezzar's seven subsequent years of madness, during which he lived like a beast of the field. (I always thought of the escarole my mother forced me to eat when I thought of Nebuchadnezzar gobbling weeds; it was an "untheocratic" parallel, which I immediately censored.) Nebuchadnezzar was told that "seven times" would pass over him, after which his sanity, and his kingdom—waiting for him like the banded tree—would be restored:

> In the miniature fulfilment of the dream . . . Nebuchadnezzar . . . became like a beast, without human understanding, for seven years, after which he regained sanity and exercised his lordship over the empire. This makes it clear that the "seven times" began with Nebuchadnezzar's overturning of Jehovah's typical theocracy in Jerusalem in

> 606 B.C. . . . The Gentile powers or governments were not exclusive in the field. [pp. 236–38]

In Nebuchadnezzar's case, seven times meant seven literal years. In the *major* fulfilment of the prophecy, however, these "seven times" symbolize the Gentile times.

When would the Gentile times end and Christ take power in heaven? Skip to Revelation 12:6 and 12:14. There we learn that "a time, and times, and half a time" are equivalent to 1,260 days. A time, and times, and half a time are three and a half times. Three and a half times constitute half of seven times; hence seven times equals twice 1,260 days, or 2,520 days. But 2,520 days is equivalent only to 7 years. So skip to Ezekiel 4:6: "I have appointed thee every day for a year." Apply this rule, and 2,520 days means 2,520 years: Since Jerusalem was destroyed

> in the summer of 606 B.C. that year had its beginning in the fall of 607 B.C. and its ending in the fall of 606 B.C. Inasmuch as the count of the Gentile "seven times" began its first year at the fall of 607 B.C., it is simple to calculate when they end. From the fall of 607 B.C. to the fall of B.C. 1 is exactly 606 years. From the fall of B.C. 1 to the fall of A.D. 1 is one year, do not forget. Hence, from the fall of B.C. 1 to the fall of A.D. 1914 is 1,914 years. Add now 606 years and 1,914 years, and the sum total is 2,520 years, ending in the fall of 1914. [p. 239]

It was rather tortuous, one might suppose, for a 9-year-old to work her way through that labyrinthine logic; but though I was never able to understand algebra and never able to grasp the first thing about geometry, I learned my way through that maze. (God was in the heart of the maze.) I did not know that since 1873 the Witnesses had arranged and rearranged pieces of the jigsaw puzzle —which had yielded several different, earlier dates for the apocalypse; nor did I know that there was never any basis in secular history for assuming 607 to be the year of Jerusalem's destruction. I knew only what I was told, and believed it. I can only imagine how insufferable that sure belief made me appear to others—to those who saw only my certainty and knew nothing about my guilt.

Had Armageddon come exactly on schedule, it would have arrived in 1972. ("From Adam's creation to the end of 1943 A.D. is 5,971 years.") In 1944, we were 29 years away from the seven-thousandth year of human history, according to the Witnesses' reckoning. In later years, the Witnesses juggled figures a little and came up with 1975 as the date of the apocalypse: "Six thousand years from man's creation will end in 1975, and the seventh period of a thousand years of human history will begin in the fall of 1975 C.E. [Common Era]. . . . It would not be by mere chance or accident . . . for the reign of Jesus Christ to run parallel with the seventh millennium of man's existence." [*Life*] The Witnesses are now in the process of slithering away from 1975 as they have in the past slithered from other dates. In spite of their modest claim that they do not know "the day and the hour," they have nevertheless led their followers to believe in at least five apocalyptic dates.

Faced with the postponement of their hopes, the Witnesses are instructed to believe that the Watchtower Society is "fallible." God's word, however, is not—and the Watchtower Society is the "sole visible channel" through which God reveals the true meaning of prophecy "in his due time," as the "light grows clearer and clearer." [*Faith*] They are not infallible; they are merely the instrument God uses to make clear His purposes. This would seem to be a distinction without a difference.

The Witnesses continue to grow in number and in strength, even as their chronology continues to falter. Sociologists who have examined the phenomenon of apocalyptic religions have found that almost no religion survives three false dates. [Festinger, Leon, Henry W. Riecken, and Stanley Schachter, *When Prophecy Fails* (New York: Harper Torchbooks, 1955)] The Witnesses are a striking exception. What accounts for their staying power? "Hope deferred," says the Psalmist, "maketh the heart sad." One might reasonably expect the Witnesses to grow weary with waiting.

Why this tenacity of belief? What needs does this religion gratify? Why do people choose abandonment of personality, a harsh, disciplinary, self-negating religion? Why do women, in particular, choose an all-consuming religion; why, in particular, do they choose suffering—renunciation of sexual and family ties in exchange for a love affair with a vengeful God?

Does the fear and loathing of the physical world spring from deformed psyches? Or is it explainable in terms of a leap into a belief so rigorous and rigid that a world view has been imposed, through external discipline, upon passive personalities?

I can answer some of these questions by reflecting on my experience. And some of the answers may be ascertained through the testimony of others who have left what used to be their spiritual home; what these survivors have to say is more eloquent than abstract analysis.

But it is necessary also to look at the history and the doctrinal and organizational evolution of this sect.

To examine one prophetic, apocalyptic cult is to explore the existential experience to which human society is bound at any given moment. Jehovah's Witnesses may be regarded as people seeking religious renewal and liberation in order to heal deep personal psychic wounds—people who contain and channel their craziness in a "crazy" religion; but the *form* their religion takes may also be seen as a response to social and cultural realities. To look closely at the psychology of a single all-consuming religion is necessarily to examine human nature, while to understand its ideology and to trace its historical genesis and development is to gain insight into the contradictions, necessities, and turmoil of the society and culture that gave it life. [See Lanternari, Vittorio, *The Religions of the Oppressed* (New York: Mentor Books), pp. v-viii]

Jehovah's Witnesses wilfully place themselves outside the mainstream and relish their role as outcasts; nonetheless, they borrow from the worst of mass culture and, it will be seen, tend to reinforce the status quo. Terrified of dissolution and real-life change, sedate, orderly, law-abiding, they are a reactionary force, tending to blunt not only revolution, but social reform.

Demonstrably racist and sexist, they nevertheless draw most of their members from the ranks of the oppressed: oppressed people respond to the assurance that the day of the Lord is at hand, when all manner of blessings shall be their reward and the evil oppressors shall be blotted out. In search of an ultimate solution, they give themselves over to a dull submission to a tyrannical force.

Jehovah's Witnesses are a microcosm of mankind trying desperately, often pitifully, to find possibility, hope, and grace in a moral wilderness. This is their story (and mine).

II

Organizational Beginnings: (1873–1912) Charles Taze Russell

> Since 1873 we have been living in the seventh millennium . . . the lease of Gentile dominion. "The Times of the Gentiles" will expire with the year 1914; and . . . the advent of him whose right it is to take the dominion was due in 1874. . . . 1874 is the exact date of Our Lord's return. . . . Only twenty-four years of the harvest period remain, the close of which will witness the end of the reign of evil and the ushering in of the glorious Millennial day; and within this period the dark night of the world's greatest tribulation must find place.—Charles Taze Russell, *Studies in the Scriptures,* Volume III, *Thy Kingdom Come* (1891), pp. 211, 305–06.

Science and secularism, industrialism and invention flourished.

Everyone believed in progress.

Worship of the aristocratic Calvinist God did not flourish. The masses—farmers and workers—were exalted. The doctrine of a favoured few was irreconcilable with the mythologizing of the masses. The 1840s, '50s, and '60s in America were

> an age of mass movements—an age of lectures, public schools, circuses, museums, penny newspapers, varied propaganda, political caucuses, woman suffrage conventions, temperance reform, proletarian unrest, labour organisation, Mormonism, Millerism, . . . mesmerism, phrenology . . . Madmen and women, men with beards, Dunkers, Muggletonians, Come-outers, Groaners, Agrarians, Seventh-Day Baptists, Quakers, Abolitionists, Unitarians. . . .
>
> The revolution in technology, the reconstruction of the social order under the impact of the machine industry, the advance of science into the domain of cosmogony, the economic independence brought to the nation by increased wealth, the ferment of political equality, the changing status of women, the clash of parties over domestic issues, and the new contacts with foreign countries reset the intellectual stage for speculation about life and for all forms of imaginative literature. [Beard, Charles A. and Mary R., *The Rise of American Civilization,* Vol. I, pp. 728, 757, 761, (New York: Macmillan, 1927)]

In 1859, Darwin, disregarding accepted biblical chronology, asserted the antiquity of man and the earth. Rejecting the belief that each species was the result of an original divine act, he proclaimed the mutability of the species and the survival of the fittest.

Cornerstones of Christian faith—original sin, the Virgin Birth, salvation by faith, the resurrection of the dead—were challenged by the new rationalism. The intellectual life of America was stirred by fresh currents of inquiry and criticism. [See Beard, p.733.]

"Higher criticism" threatened the established churches. Established Protestant sects were thrown into turmoil. As the frontier expanded, new sects proliferated. Enthusiastic evangelical revival meetings became boisterously expressive of strange dreams and wondrous portents. Two-Seed-in-the-Spirit Predestinarian Baptists fought with Free-Will Baptists. Schisms tore the churches apart. Presbyterians split into four or five divisions.

In 1843, William Miller had confidently announced the second coming of Christ, and his followers earnestly awaited their salvation and the end of the world. The world did not end; but second-adventists continued to flourish.

Protestantism was splintering, becoming free-wheeling, effervescent, drunk on the wine of individualism. Only in the industrial cities, among new immigrants, did the centre hold: Roman Catholics continued to acknowledge the ecclesiastical authority of their Church.

In 1860, the U.S. census reported that one-third of the population was sustained by "manufacturing industry." Workers had left the soil for the cities. By the middle of the 19th century, the old planting aristocracy had been replaced by Abbots, Laurences, Astors, and Vanderbilts. The 1860s saw the rise of trade unions. During the 1870s, the Rockefellers assumed command of their oil empire. The immense concentration of wealth and power, the consolidation of industry and railways, and the shift of economic power of financiers led to bloody fights between labour and employers.

Charles Taze Russell, founder and first president of the Watchtower Bible and Tract Society, was a child of his time. He believed in progress. He looked around him, saw class warfare on the horizon, and declared that "the old order of things must pass away, and the new must supersede it . . . the change," he predicted, "will be violently opposed by those advantaged by the present order." In his second volume of *Studies in the Scriptures* (consisting of seven volumes, which achieved a circulation of 10 million copies in thirty-four languages), Russell wrote that "revolution world-wide [would] be the outcome, resulting in the final destruction of the old order and the introduction and establishment of the new." His feeling that a wonderful new world order was at hand was reinforced by what he perceived to be the fulfilment of Daniel 12:4: "But thou, O Daniel, shut up the words, and seal the book, even to the time of the end: many shall run to and fro, and knowledge shall be increased."

A fevered visionary who would not allow the world to confound him, who wished above all to have everything cohere, and who sought to impose logic and a pattern on the disparate elements of his time, Russell looked at class conflict and steam cars; fertilized what he saw with the rich products of his imaginings, an idiosyncratic reading of the Bible chronology that was inventive and convoluted, a gorgeously eccentric interpretation of history, and some borrowings from Madame Blavatsky's heady mystical theories on the "inner meaning" of the Great Pyramid of Egypt—and came up with a fancy new religion.

The Witnesses say they are "the most ancient religious group of worshippers of the true God . . . Abel was . . . the first." Abel sacrificed the firstlings of his flock to Jehovah; Russell sacrificed a haberdashery business.

Charles Taze Russell—later known as "Pastor" Russell—was born on February 16, 1852. The second son of Scotch-Irish parents, Joseph L. Russell and Ann Eliza Birney Russell, he was raised a Presbyterian; at an unspecified later date he joined the Congregational Church because of its "more liberal views." His mother died when he was 9, the year the Civil War began.

In 1863, the year of the Emancipation proclamation, 11-year-old Russell, according to Watchtower sources, entered a business partnership with his father, for which he himself drew up the contract under which the business was brought into being and managed. By the time he was 15, he and his father had succeeded in establishing a chain of men's-clothing stores radiating out from Pittsburgh. According to the Witnesses, Russell eventually closed out his business for a quarter of a million dollars. [*JWDP*] According to the *American Encyclopedia of Biography*, 1968, Russell "sold shirts to make a living until he got his first congregation."

It is said that Ann Russell dedicated Charles Taze to God when he was born. It is also said that Pastor Russell's father frequently found his son, when Charles was as young as 12, poring over a Bible concordance in the family store.

It is a strange picture: young Russell keeping the business books by day and reading The Book by gaslight in the small hours of the morning—but not so strange, after all, when one considers the Mellons, Carnegies, and Rockefellers of Russell's time, millionaires who regarded the Deity as the Great Paymaster who kept all his good children (good equalling rich) on His dole.

As a youth Russell seems to have been obsessed with hellfire and torment; he also apparently saw himself as the instrument of men's salvation. An early associate of Russell's tells us that 14-year-old Charles Taze would go out Saturday nights "to where men gathered . . . to loaf, and would write Bible texts on the sidewalk with coloured chalk. . . ." [*Faith*, p. 17]

When Russell was 17, he suffered a revulsion against the concept of eternal punishment and against the doctrine of predestination. He deserted the sidewalks and immersed himself in a study of Oriental religions (his later infatuation with the Pyramids may have been a holdover from this time). But Eastern religion did not satisfy him. Never a man to do things by halves, he renounced religion at the age of 17. One detects more than a hint of megalomania in his renunciation, which, as he saw it, would necessarily affect not only himself, but all of "suffering humanity": "I'm just going to forget the whole thing and give all my attention to business. If I make some money I can use that to help suffering humanity, even though I cannot help do them any good spiritually." [*Yearbook*, 1975, p. 35].

Russell's crisis of faith lasted a year. In 1870, when he was 18, "shaken in faith regarding many long-accepted doctrines . . . a ready prey to the logic of infidelity" [*Ibid.*], Russell entered a dim meeting hall in Allegheny where Second Adventists congregated to find out what this small group believed that would be more convincing than the teachings of the established churches. The sermon he heard was enough to bring him around to a belief that Jehovah had truly inspired the Scriptures and to prove to him the link between the Apostles and Prophets.

From 1870 to 1875, Russell, together with six young men of his acquaintance, studied the Bible. Russell's small schismatic band was soon convinced that Jehovah had blessed them with increasing light and truth. [*Yearbook*, 1975, p. 36] They had come to believe that the second coming of Christ would be invisible: Russell pronounced himself deeply disappointed in the teaching of the Second Adventists, who believed in the visible return of Christ and the destruction of the earth and its inhabitants in 1873 or 1874. To Russell these predictions seemed naive, not to say crude, and he felt they could only bring scorn on the faithful who awaited the Kingdom. Russell—who seems always to have regarded himself as the cynosure of all eyes and never to have doubted that his spiritual odyssey was of compelling significance to all of mankind—promptly acted to remove the reflected reproach he felt contaminated him and to set the record straight. In 1873, when he was 21, Russell wrote a booklet called "The Object and Manner of the Lord's Return"; he published 50,000 copies at his own expense.

This was the year of the great industrial panic, the year Carnegie embarked on his steel mergers in Russell's native Allegheny. In 1870, Rockefeller founded his dynasty with Standard Oil. In 1872, Victoria Woodhull ran for President as the candidate of the People's Party.

None of these events is alluded to in the Witnesses' biographical references to Russell. As far as the Witnesses are concerned, all of these events are the detritus of human history. What was significant about the last half of the 19th century is that "as the conclusion of the system of things approached, the Most High God, Jehovah, acted to identify the 'wheat' [the sons of God—*them*] in a pronounced way." [*Ibid.*, p. 33]

In January, 1876, Russell came across a periodical called *The Herald of the Morning*, published by N. H. Barbour of Rochester, New York. Barbour, like Russell, believed that the object of Christ's return was not to destroy the physical earth, but to "bless all families of the earth." [*Ibid.*, p. 36] Barbour and Russell shared the belief that Christ would come invisibly, like "a thief in the night," and that Adventists erred when they expected to see the Lord in the flesh. When he found this kindred soul, Russell affiliated his Pittsburgh Bible Class—which by this time had grown to 30 members—with Barbour's slightly larger Rochester group. He contributed money to the *Herald* and became its co-editor. In 1877, when he was 25, Russell sold out his business interests and began to travel from city to city, delivering sermons. Charles Taze Russell was thereafter known as Pastor Russell.

Pastor Russell prohibited collections at his meetings and depended, according to the Witnesses, on unsolicited contributions after all his money was exhausted. How Russell managed to "exhaust" a quarter of a million dollars—if indeed he did, or if he'd had it in the first place—was to become a matter of fierce contention between him and the woman he later married and a subject for speculation during the lawsuits and counterlawsuits that kept him in the public eye during the last quarter of the 19th century.

In 1877, Russell and Barbour jointly wrote and published *Three Worlds, and the Harvest of This World*. The biblical chronology set forth in that volume, and in Russell's subsequent books, is labyrinthine. One despairs of making it explicable. Indeed, I feel justified in conjecturing that many of Russell's followers must have accepted his sanguine conclusions without comprehending his premises.

Russell preached that the 6,000 years of man's existence on earth had ended in 1872—Victoria Woodhull also foresaw an end to "man's" rule in 1872, but she meant by that something quite different—and that the seventh millennium had begun in 1873. The glorified Christ became invisibly present in 1874. Shortly after 1874 had begun the "antitypical Jubilee," an event "foreshadowed" by the ancient jubilees observed under the Mosaic Law. For forty years, the "saints," God's consecrated ones, would be "harvested," until, on October 1, 1914, the Gentile Times would end. On October 1, 1914, the evil worldly system would collapse, God would save His everlasting day, and there would be a general "Restitution" for all mankind—but not before the "living saints" (Russell and his followers) would be suddenly and miraculously caught away bodily to be with their Lord, in 1878.

In October, 1914, of course, the world was two months into the bloodiest war of its history—and Russell, not having been "caught away," was very much alive and in the flesh. As a recent publication of Jehovah's Witnesses remarks, somewhat laconically, "Something must have been miscalculated." [*God's Kingdom of a Thousand Years Has Approached,* 1973, p. 188]

It is interesting that Russell himself wrote [*SS,* Vol. III, *The Time Is at Hand,* 1905, p. 243]: "For it be distinctly noticed that if the Chronology, or any of these time-periods, be changed but one year, the beauty and force of this parallelism [with the Jewish Jubilee cycles] are destroyed. . . . If the Chronology be altered but one year, more or less—it would spoil the parallelism."

As we have seen, the parallelism has been destroyed with a vengeance. Russell, playing with exactly the same Scriptures (Daniel, Ezekiel, Matthew, Luke, Revelation) as current Witnesses, came up with totally different dates. Only 1914 remains a fixed date, and it has been assigned a different meaning.

Russell's calculations are not easy to unravel; they are, however, not without a certain quaint interest. In *Thy Kingdom Come* (Volume III of *Studies in the Scriptures*, 1891), he calls attention to the 2,300 days of Daniel's prophecy and, by legerdemain, comes up with 1846 as

> the time when God's sanctuary would be cleansed of the defiling errors and principles of Papacy. . . . We have noted the fulfilment of the 1,260 days, or the time, times, and half a time of Papacy's power to persecute, and the beginning, in 1799, of the Time of the End. We have seen how 1,290 days marked the beginning of an understanding of the mysteries of prophecy in the year 1829, culminating in the great movement of 1844 known as the Second-Advent movement when . . . the wise Virgins went forth to meet the Bridegroom, thirty years prior to his actual coming. . . . We have remarked, with special delight, the 1,335 days, pointing . . . to 1874 as the exact date of our Lord's return. [pp. 305–06]

Eighteen forty-six . . . 1799 . . . 1829 . . . 1844 . . . 1874; 1,260 days . . . 1,290 days . . . 1,335 days . . . No wonder the Witnesses won't allow "outsiders" access to the *Studies in the Scriptures* (which are very hard indeed to come by). Even they, who justify all past error on the ground that Biblical dates are "ingeniously hidden" and cannot be ascertained until God sees fit to shed His light on the "mathematically precise" meaning of prophecy, must prefer not to have to expose to ridicule all of Russell's peculiar reckonings. They certainly prefer to forget that their founder dragged Napoleon Bonaparte into his calculations:

> . . . the exact date of the beginning of the "Time of the End" . . . is shown to be Napoleon's invasion of Egypt, which covered a period of a year and five months. He sailed May, 1798, and, returning, landed in France October 9, 1799. . . . Napoleon's work, together with the French Revolution, broke the spell of religious superstition, . . . awakened the world to a fuller sense of the powers and prerogatives of manhood and broke the Papal dominion. . . .

Russell was eclectic. Having convinced himself that Napoleon was clearly portrayed in prophecy as "the man of destiny," he revised history to bend it to his theological will.

The Witnesses today no longer read the French Revolution into the Book of Revelation; and the meaning of the Book of Daniel, into which Russell read the fanciful interpretation that the King of the North pictured "the Roman Empire's representative," and the King of the South pictured "a representative of Egypt's kingdom," has been amended. In current Witness theology, the King of the North "pictures" "the Communist bloc of nations," and the King of the South is "manifestly the Anglo-American World Power." [*TW*, Feb. 1, 1976, p. 94]

But the Witnesses still hold that Russell's writings were the vehicle God used to reveal His divine will and to separate the peoples of the earth into the sheep and the goats.

Some things have not changed. The Witnesses are still ferociously anti-Papist, and the appeal to the disenfranchised that characterized Russell's work (Russell believed that there would be a conflict between "the classes and the masses") underlines the work of his successors, although it has taken different form; and the peculiarly American flavour of this religion, which translated American technology and class struggle into quasi-mystical terms, remains.

America gave birth to this religion; and it remains in essence American. The law-and-order God of the Witnesses is Middle American. The Witnesses are international and claim not to be chauvinistic; the American Revolution is now dismissed, as is the French Revolution, as irrelevant to God's purposes. Still, one wonders. Witness workers in British headquarters were forbidden, in the 1950s, to take their ritual morning tea break on the grounds that it was "untheocratic" and counterproductive; I can't help feeling that what was being objected to was that it was un-American. Even when they are clad in saris and loincloths, muumuus and kimonos, there is something ineffably missionary-Midwestern about the aura they project. The Witness dream of Eden is a dream of American suburbia—with a few people in foreign dress to lend exoticism to the proceedings.

Russell fortified his chronology with cranky evidence from "God's Stone Witness—the Pyramid." "The Great Pyramid [is] a part of [God's] instrumentality for convincing the world of his wisdom, foreknowledge and grace. . . . located in the geographical centre of the land surface of the world, the measurements of the Great Pyramid represent the earth and God's plan for the earth's salvation. . . . In it are contained prophetical and chronological teachings." [*SS*, Vol. III, pp. 317, 326]

Russell believed that the measurements of the Pyramid proved that 1914 would be the end of the world order. He read more things into the Entrance Passage of the Pyramid than an art critic might read into an Abstract Expressionist painting.

"The Great Pyramid witnesses, not only the downward course of man in sin, but also the various steps in the divine plan by which preparation is made for his full recovery from the fall, through the way of life, opened up by the death and resurrection of our Lord Jesus." [*SS*, VI, *The New Creation*, p. 356]

Among the more extravagant claims Russell made for the Great Pyramid were that the Pit of the Pyramid symbolized the descent of the nations into anarchism and that the ventilating tubes or air passages of the Queen's Chambers suggested that "the condition of human perfection, when reached [after the Restitution], may be made an everlasting state." [*Ibid.,* p. 370] The Pyramid, Russell further asserted, was absolute proof that the theory of evolution was untrue.

Pittsburgh newspapers reported that on the night of the Memorial of Christ's death in 1878, Russell was found on the Sixth Street Bridge dressed in a white robe, waiting to be wafted to heaven.

Russell told reporters that on that night of glory-be that was not to be, he was home in bed. "However, some of the more radical ones might have been there," he said, "but I was not." [*Faith*, p. 27]

(Parenthetically, it's worth noting that the only holiday Witnesses celebrate is the Memorial of Christ's death—and they "celebrate" it by listening to a speech. Neither Christ's birth nor His resurrection is marked on their gloomy calendars.)

After the saints were stranded on the Sixth Street Bridge, Russell "re-examined" Scripture and decided that the true significance of the year 1878 was that from that time on, none of the saints would "sleep in death," [*Ibid.*, p. 27] but would, upon death, immediately be resurrected, to life in heaven with Christ.

Russell's colleague Barbour was not satisfied. In a bitter article written for *Herald of the Morning*, Barbour argued that "Christ's death was no more a settlement of the penalty of man's sins than would the sticking of a pin through the body of a fly and causing it suffering and death be considered by an earthly parent as a just settlement for misdemeanour in his child." [*Ibid.*, p. 28] So Barbour and Russell split. This was to be the first of many schisms. None of the schismatic sects has flourished.

Russell, who saw the Lord's hand in everything that pertained to him, including his finances, withdrew financial support from *Herald of the Morning*, understanding it to be the Lord's will for him to start another journal. In 1879, together with five other contributors, he funded *Zion's Watch Tower and Herald of Christ's Presence*. Russell was editor and publisher of the *Watch Tower*, which had a first-issue printing of 6,000 copies. [*Ibid.*, p.28]

Between 1879 and 1880, Russell and his associates founded thirty congregations—called "ecclesias"—in Pennsylvania, New Jersey, Massachusetts, Delaware, Ohio, and Michigan.

Today, the 40,155 congregations of Jehovah's Witnesses are governed from the Brooklyn headquarters of the Watchtower Bible and Tract Society. [*Yearbook,* 1977] The Witnesses describe their structure as "theocratic"; it is more accurate to call it totalitarian. During the 1880s, ecclesias of Russellite Bible Students voted congregationally on some matters and elected a board of elders who were responsible for directing congregational matters. Today elders of congregations are appointed by the eighteen-man governing body in Brooklyn (an all-white, all-male group with a median age of 60); elders and governors form a self-perpetuating elite.

There were, in 1976, 2,248,390 Jehovah's Witnesses, all active proselytizers, in 210 countries. [*Yearbook*, 1977, pp. 30–31] In 1881, when Zion's Watch Tower Tract Society was established as an unincorporated body with Russell as its manager, there were 100 proselytizing Russellites, known as "colporteurs." By 1885, the number had grown to 300 colporteurs. [*Yearbook*, 1975, pp. 39–40] By 1914, there were 1,200 congregations of Russellites.

The unincorporated Zion's Watch Tower Tract Society, the printing organization to which Russell ("with others") is supposed to have contributed $35,000 of his fortune, was incorporated as Zion's Watch Tower Tract Society in 1884. [*Yearbook*, 1975, p. 40]

Russell was the president of the organization that is today known as the Watch Tower Bible and Tract Society of Pennsylvania. Mrs. Russell was a director of the Society and served as its secretary and treasurer for some years. [*Yearbook*, 1975, p. 66] According to its charter, "The purpose for which the corporation is formed is, the dissemination of Bible Truths in various languages by means of the publication of tracts, pamphlets, papers and other religious documents and by the use of all other lawful means which its Board of Directors, duly constituted, shall deem expedient for the furtherance of the purpose stated." [*JWDP*, p. 27]

By 1889, the Watch Tower Society had begun to amass property. A four-storey brick building in Allegheny, known as the Bible

House, was built and legally held in title by the Tower Publishing Company. [*Yearbook*, 1975 p. 42] A holding company for his private interests, the Tower Publishing Company (which Russell used, at one time, to publish literature for the Watch Tower Society at a price agreed upon by the board of directors—of which he was president), built the Bible House "at a cost of $34,000." [*JWDP*, p.27; *Yearbook*, 1975, p. 42] In 1898, ownership of the Tower Publishing plant and real estate was transferred by donation to the Watch Tower Society. The board of the Watch Tower Society evaluated the Allegheny property and equipment at $164,033.65. [*Yearbook*, 1975, p. 42] (There were at this time 400 preachers associated with the Watch Tower Society.) The Allegheny building remained the Society's headquarters for twenty years.

Russell's critics charged him with financial flimflammery, arguing, on circumstantial evidence, that he was manipulating publishing houses and property to assure himself of an outlet for his prolific writings for his personal enrichment. The Pastor was beset with troubles, assailed from within and without his organization. His wife became his bitterest and most outspoken enemy. Lawsuits and civil investigations brought him notoriety—welcome notoriety; he wore it like a mantle of righteousness. The more trouble, the more he was able to insist that the Devil was out to crush him; his scandalous behaviour was transformed, by his followers, into proof of his holiness. Every time new litigation was brought against him, each time he was reviled, each time something horrible befell him as a result of his own conduct—things humiliating enough to send most men fleeing to obscurity—he puffed himself up and offered it as proof that, like Jesus, he was persecuted as a Messenger of Truth.

I am like a jellyfish; I float around here and there. I touch this one and that one, and if she responds I take her to me, and if not I float on to others.—Attributed to Charles Taze Russell by Mrs. Russell [Court transcript, Court of Common Pleas, Pittsburgh, Pennsylvania]

In 1894 Maria Frances Russell was—as far as the world could see—her beleaguered husband's staunchest ally. In 1897, Mrs. Russell fled from her husband, later declaring, "Even a dog has more rights than I had."

In the early 1890s, some of Russell's associates attempted to wrest control of the Watch Tower Society from him. They charged him with financial dishonesty and with aberrant, autocratic behaviour. The Pastor, they asserted, not content to lay down doctrinal law for his followers, was so greatly intruding upon the private lives of the Bible Students as to tell them whom they might or might not marry. Russell, it was stated, was "in a deplorably sinful state—dishonest, a traitor, a liar." [*ZWT*, June 11, 1894]

Russell issued a countercharge that there was a "conspiracy" in his own office and in his own household—a "special and cunning attack made by the great enemy"—"to shatter the body of Christ." [*Ibid.*]

Matters came to a head in 1894. There were rumours of marital discord between the Pastor and his wife, who was a regular contributor to *Zion's Watch Tower* and an associate editor of that magazine. Mrs. Russell, it was stated, together with all of Russell's household and office workers, was under compulsion to lie for him. According to one of Russell's closest associates, a Mr. Rogers, Mrs. Russell was often observed "weeping bitter tears over Brother Russell's sins." [*Ibid.*]

Maria Russell undertook to speak in her husband's behalf. For eighteen days she visited congregations in ten cities to staunch the flow of rumours and to defend her husband. She represented her husband as a just, noble, and generous man, maligned by "false teachers" of "damnable heresies," wolves in sheep's clothing.

This is a partial account of her vindication of the man she was later to charge with extreme cruelty:

> [A Bible Student] told that my husband forbids people to marry, and as proof of this related how he once sent Mr. Bryan a three day's journey into the country at an expense of twelve dollars, in order to prevent a wedding. I answered . . . that Mr. Russell never forbade anyone to marry, and that not a living being could truthfully say that he or she had been forbidden; but that I knew that when his opinion was *specially asked* he gave the Apostle Paul's advice (I Cor. 7:25–35). . . . It was to my husband's credit that he spared neither trouble nor expense in order to let a sister in Christ know something of what he knew of the *character* of the man she was about to marry; that, thus informed, she might the better judge for herself whether or not he would make a desirable husband. [*Ibid.*]

This ambiguous statement, which might just as easily have led Bible Students to conclude that Russell did indeed seek to influence the personal decisions of the "sisters," served to convince the majority of Russell's followers that he was acting in the best interests of his flock.

Maria Russell's arguments in defence of her beleaguered husband may have been impassioned; they were hardly conclusive. They were, however, successful. Women in Russell's ecclesias all over the country reported having dreams in which their beloved Pastor Russell was scourged and flagellated, but shielded by a protecting angel. Female Russellites seemed to be in the grip of hysteria: one Bible Student reported that she had had a "prophetic" dream in which "someone in the congregation hurled a stone at the head of the preacher, which struck him in the mouth, from whence the blood flowed profusely." In her dream, she "ran to his aid and tried to wipe away the blood, which only flowed the more."

It is doubtful that Mrs. Russell's rebuttals of the charges brought against her husband were, in themselves, enough to persuade anyone that the Pastor was blameless. It would seem, rather, that *anything* Mrs. Russell said in Russell's defence would suffice for those whose investment in their religion was so great that to leave it would cause a gaping hole in the fabric of their lives. The "persecution" the faithful endured served to reinforce their conviction that they were a tiny band of comradely brothers and sisters united in a common cause against the wolves howling at the gates of their belief.

Mrs. Russell, implicitly acknowledging that her husband was not entirely without fault, wrote that the truth was contained "in imperfect earthen vessels; but . . . the very frailness of the vessels only manifests the more clearly that the excellency of power is of God and not of us." [*Ibid.;* see *Yearbook,* 1975]

Three years later, in 1897, after eighteen years of marriage, Maria Frances Ackley Russell made a public about-face. She left her "imperfect earthen vessel," fleeing to relatives in Chicago to gain protection from the man who she claimed was committing gross improprieties with other women and who, furthermore, was trying to have her incarcerated in a lunatic asylum.

In 1903, Mrs. Russell filed for legal separation in the Court of Common Pleas in Pittsburgh, Pennsylvania. The case came up for trial in 1906 before Justice Collier and a jury; it was a sensational case—a Victorian gothic, with intimations of perversions, imprisonments, madness; and it was resolved in Mrs. Russell's favour. Pastor Russell fought Mrs. Russell's demands for separation and alimony for five years, initiating libel suits against newspapers and a minister along the way. On March 4, 1908, Mrs. Russell was granted a divorce. In 1909, she appealed for an increase in alimony, and Russell moved out of the jurisdiction of the Pittsburgh courts, transferred all his assets to the Watch Tower Society so that he could declare himself penniless, and moved his staff and his operations to Brooklyn, New York, to avoid being jailed for failure to pay alimony. Finally, in 1911, the courts, on appeal, ruled conclusively on behalf of Mrs. Russell, Justice Orlady of the Superior Court of Pennsylvania stating, with barely concealed anger, that Pastor Russell's "course of conduct toward his wife evidenced such insistent egotism and extravagant self-praise that it would be manifest to the jury that his conduct toward her was one of continual arrogant domination that would necessarily render the life of any sensitive Christian woman a burden and make her life intolerable."

The Witnesses have in recent years published an expurgated

version of Pastor and Mrs. Russell's difficulties—a story which for many years they kept scrupulously shrouded. It pleases the Witnesses now—perhaps we have the resurgence of feminism to thank for it—to hold up Maria Frances Ackley Russell as an object lesson: Vanity, thy name is woman. Their interpretation of events [*Yearbook*, 1975; pp. 65–75; see also *WT*, June 15, 1972, and *JWDP*, p. 45] is that shortly after her tour in defence of her husband, Mrs. Russell, "an educated, intelligent woman" (the adjectives are pejorative), attempted to usurp the Pastor's rightful place and asserted herself concerning the material intended for publication in *The Watch Tower*. For this she was compared to Moses's sister Miriam, who tried to usurp her brother's place as the leader of the Israelites but who was prevented because of Jehovah's displeasure.

The man whose financial treatment of Mrs. Russell Justice Orlady characterized as "radically different from the standard imposed upon him by the law, and recognized by all the courts of this country" wrote in 1906,

> I was not aware of it at the time, but learned subsequently that the conspirators [of 1894] endeavoured to sow seeds of discord in my wife's heart by flattery, "woman's rights" arguments, etc. However, . . . I was spared the humiliation of seeing my wife amongst those conspirators. . . . As matters began to settle down, the "woman's rights" ideas and personal ambition began again to come to the top, and I perceived that Mrs. Russell's active campaign in my defence, and the very cordial reception given her by the dear friends at that time . . . had done her injury by increasing her self-appreciation. . . . I was continually harassed with suggestions of alterations of my writings. I was pained to note this growing disposition so foreign to the humble mind which characterized her for the first thirteen happy years.

"*For the past three years you have been gradually forcing upon me the evidence that we both erred in judgment when we married—that we were not adaptable to each other. . . . I conclude that no one is adapted to me—except the Lord. I am glad that He and I understand each other and have confidence in each other.*" Letter of July 8, 1896, from Pastor Russell to his wife, Exhibit No. 3, Court Transcript, Superior Court of Pennsylvania.

In an undated letter, Pastor Russell wrote her of his pleasure in the memory of her devotion—her inability to live without him, her longing to die first. And, indeed, he tells her, he feels the same, but it is her "fall," her "everlasting loss," that gives him the greatest pain rather than the thought of his own lonely future.

The official Watchtower version has it that Mrs. Russell became ill in 1897, and her husband gave her much cheerful and kind attention to "touch her heart and restore it to its former loving and tender condition." [*Yearbook*, 1975] Having thus applied balm to her wayward spirit, Russell, in the presence of an official Bible Students Committee, gained his wife's agreement not to interfere in his management of *Zion's Watch Tower:* "I then asked her in their presence if she would shake hands. She hesitated, but finally gave me her hand. I then said, 'Now, will you kiss me, dear, as a token of the degree of change of mind which you have indicated?' Again she hesitated, but finally did kiss me and otherwise manifested a renewal of affection in the presence of the Committee." Russell was so good as to allow his wife to lead a weekly meeting of the "Sisters of the Allegheny Church." His amplitude of spirit was to no avail. Mrs. Russell left her long-suffering husband in 1897, after her illness; and he dutifully made arrangements for her financial support, providing her with a separate home and all that a reasonable woman could ask.

The court transcripts tell a different story of a woman sick and afraid, abandoned in an empty four-storey mansion, bewildered, agitated, cut off from help. It is a penny-dreadful story, full of Victorian vapours and horrors; but the pain of a woman being pushed into insanity, tormented by vindictive messages sent to her in the guise of husbandly love through her husband's intimate, is undisguised in the purple prose of her defence lawyer and the majestic prose of a judge splendid in his wrath. There is something impressive about the peculiar genius of a man who could inspire adoration and worship—particularly among women—while judges and courts threatened him with jail sentences and exposed him as a sophist and a fraud.

Pastor Russell stood ready to take on the whole world; he loved to be hated equally as he loved to be loved. He always had to stand stage centre, whether the audience threw eggs or roses. Only indifference was terrible to him.

Mrs. Russell's testimony on cross-examination by Attorney Porter (Court of Common Pleas):

Q. Did [Mr. Russell] say anything to you . . . while you were sick, as to what was the nature of your sickness?

A. He said it was a judgment on me from God.

Q. For what?

A. I wasn't in harmony with him.

Pastor Russell's testimony under cross-examination by Attorney Porter:

Q. Did you or did you not tell her that her sickness was the judgment of God on her for her failure to obey you?

A. I did not.

Q. You didn't do that?
A. No.
Q. Nothing of that kind?
A. No, sir. I did say some things like that.
Q. What did you say?
A. Miss Ball, who was her special friend, and who I knew would tell her, I told her in my opinion, this was a judgment from the Lord on her.
Q. And you intended Miss Ball to tell her that?
A. Yes, sir. I wished her to. I thought she ought to know it.
Q. (By the Court): Was that the time she had erysipelas?
A. Yes, sir.
Q. Did you believe that was the judgment of the Almighty?
A. I think so.
Q. Where did you get that authority?
A. Well, whether my judgment is good or not—

Mrs. Russell testified that the Pastor frequently "kissed and fondled" Rose Ball, the "special friend" who was used to convey her husband's messages to her sickroom. She testified that being informed, in this way, and by this messenger, that her sickness was "a judgment" caused her to have a serious relapse.

Q. (By the Court): That is your idea of good treatment?
A. That was my idea. I was treating the lady the very best, there couldn't have been a kinder treatment given to anybody in the world, and I know I couldn't say this to her myself, she wouldn't take it from me, and I thought that it might prove beneficial to her, and I prayed at the time that this sickness might result to her advantage, and I hoped it would.

The Witnesses today use the same defence that Pastor Russell proffered and Justice Orlady discredited, that the Russells kissed and made up in the presence of a committee convened to witness Mrs. Russell's capitulation to her husband's demands that she cease "interfering" in his management of *Zion's Watch Tower*.

The court records tell a different story:

> [Pastor Russell] called an assembly of his followers to this city for a secret meeting at the so-called Tabernacle; and another similar meeting on Sabbath evening, the fifth instance. These meetings were attended by about sixty people, a number of whom were from a distance. The respondent confesses that at the meeting he stated that his wife was weak-minded and under the spell of a Satanic influence which proceeded from her sisters. This statement was nothing more or less than a genteel way of stating that his wife's mind was unbalanced,

and notwithstanding the fact that Mrs. Russell was within the building at the time this meeting was held, she was locked out under the direction of the respondent.

In addition to this statement, which he made to this assembly, Mrs. Helen Brace testified, and it was not denied, that his wife was suffering from mental aberration. We find also in a letter to Mr. Brown (Exhibit No. 5), just three days after that meeting of September 5, 1897, a similar statement, as in his letter he tells Mr. Brown that his wife's mind is poisoned and that she is semi-hypnotized by his sister. "Weak-minded," "mind-poisoned," under "Satanic hypnotic influence," "mind unbalanced" were the expressions that he used to many people concerning his wife. The only charitable excuse he could find for her is that she was passing through a critical time of life, which was not true, but which, had it been true, would have made his conduct toward her only the more brutal. . . .

But this is not all, the very next day after that meeting of September 5, 1897, respondent sent insulting and threatening letters to libellant's relatives and intimate friends, warning them under threats of legal proceedings and suits for damage, not to harbour libellant or have any communications whatever with her. He had already turned his whole congregation against her by the meetings of September 4 and 5, 1897, from which she was excluded, and now, September 6, 1897, is endeavouring to cut her off from the last natural ties, her own relatives and a few loyal friends.

It is painful to imagine Maria Russell before that Committee—obliged to kiss the smiling, smarmy man who held her up to shame. Furthermore, as in any witch trial, there are strange sexual overtones in Charles Taze Russell's behaviour. An intriguing Freudian puzzle is contained in Attorney Porter's brief:

Pastor Russell "went about among her associates and told them *she was under the hypnotic influence of Satan in the form of her sister, who was his father's second wife.*" [Italics mine.]

Russell had married his stepmother's sister and then accused his father's second wife of being a manifestation of the Devil.

Whatever the pathology that led Russell to such stunning abuse of Mrs. Russell, his contention (which is perpetuated by the Watchtower Society today) that their difficulties stemmed from her militant desire to take over his publication was given little credence by the Court.

There seems no doubt that Pastor Russell would brook no interference with his management of religious affairs. There is little doubt in my mind that the Russells' disagreements over editorial policies were not the cause of their breakup, but a symptom of Pastor Russell's spiritual malaise. Russell stated his antiwoman views, which repelled Justice Orlady: "I am convinced that our difficulty is a growing one generally; that it is a great mistake for strong-minded men and women to marry. If they will marry, the strong-minded had far better marry such as are not too intellectual and high-spirited."

Mrs. Russell, according to testimony not contradicted by her husband, was so far removed from a status of equality that she complained, "Even a dog has more rights than I have." "You have no rights at all that I am bound to respect," replied Mr. Russell.

Another part of the testimony which Russell did not trouble to contradict makes it very hard indeed to think of Maria Russell as a Castrating Suffragette.

> When leaving home for the far West, she helped him get ready, and then putting her hand on his arm, she said: "Husband, you are going far away. There are lots of railroad accidents, and we might never meet again. Surely, you don't want to leave your wife in this cold, indifferent way."

But he did. He pushed her away, slammed the door in her face, and departed.

Outside the courtroom, Russell exercised himself in frenzies of self-justification; inside the courtroom, he assumed a pose of Olympian disdain.

Russell, the evidence shows, refused to extend to his wife even the minimal courtesies. It was to the ultimate good fortune of Maria Russell that her husband was a ceaseless letter writer: maintaining a stony silence in person, the man who had once written on sidewalks to inform unbelievers of God's wrath fired off letters to the poor woman to whom he would not deign to speak. Fortunately for Mrs. Russell, she was not so gaga as to destroy the evidence.

In a letter of July 9, 1896, Russell wrote: "To avoid misunderstanding, let me say, under the circumstances it properly devolves upon you to make the advances on the line of social amenities between us. It would be improper for me to take the initiative in the matter of amenities such as, 'good morning,' 'good night,' etc." (Exhibit 2, Superior Court)

Reviewing the evidence, Justice Orlady ruled in Mrs. Russell's favour with barely concealed anger:

> The indignities offered to [Mrs. Russell] in treating her as a menial in the presence of servants, intimating that she was of unsound mind and that she was under the influence of wicked and designing persons, fully warranted her withdrawal from his house, and fully justified her fear that he intended to further humiliate her, by a threat to resort to legal proceedings to test her sanity. There is not a syllable in the testimony to justify his repeated aspersions on her character and her mental condition, nor does he intimate in any way that there was any difference between them other than that she did not agree with him in his views of life and methods of conducting business. . . .

> . . . His course of conduct towards his wife evidenced such insistent egotism and extravagant self-praise that it would be manifest to the jury that his conduct toward her was one of continual arrogant domination that would necessarily render life of any sensitive Christian woman a burden and make her conditions intolerable.

No charge of adultery was brought against Charles Taze Russell by his wife. In the trial of 1906 before the Court of Common Pleas, Maria Russell testified that Rose Ball—the bearer of messages to Mrs. Russell's sickroom—had once told her that Pastor Russell said: "I am like a jellyfish. I float around here and there. I touch this one and that one, and if she responds I take her to me, and if not, I float on to others." Russell denied the story. Judge Collier charged the jury: "This little incident about this girl that was in the family, that is beyond the ground of the libel and has nothing to do with the case because not being put in it or allowed to pass."

The press did not allow the jellyfish story—or Russell's relationship with "this girl that was in the family," Miss Ball—to pass. Russell brought suit against *The Washington Post* and the Chicago *Mission Friend* for promoting the jellyfish story and for charging him with promiscuity and immorality; he won both cases.

His followers adored him. Their piety was not affronted by his peccadilloes; they relished, it would seem, the mingled odours of sanctimony and spice.

When Mrs. Russell applied for an increase of alimony in 1900 in the Pennsylvania courts, Russell divested himself of his personal assets and removed himself and his headquarters staff to Hicks Street in Brooklyn, New York. He purchased Plymouth Church, which had been completed in 1868 for the Plymouth Congregation of which Henry Ward Beecher was pastor. The Watch Tower Society also bought Beecher's four-storey brownstone parsonage at 124 Columbia Heights, a building that overlooked what has been called the most glorious urban view in the world—the New York skyline and the Brooklyn Bridge. The Beecher residence became the home of the headquarters staff of 30-odd Russellites; the remodelled Hicks Street building became known as the Brooklyn Tabernacle.

When the Pennsylvania courts ordered Russell to pay alimony to his wife, he filed a plea that he had nothing with which to pay, as he had transferred all his property, evaluated at $317,000, to the Watch Tower Bible and Tract Society. The courts had answered that the transaction was a fraud upon his wife and that Russell still controlled the Pittsburgh property, inasmuch as he still controlled the Society. (He had, upon transferring his assets, required the issuance to him of one voting share for every $10 contribution. Russell thus acquired enough voting shares to give him control of the annual elections.) Referring to one transaction involving a sheriff's sale of property worth $20,000 for less than $200, the Court of Common Pleas said, "The purpose of this whole transaction was to deprive the wife of her dower interest and was a fraud on her." Evidence was produced in the alimony case to show that Russell had accumulated a fortune through stock speculation and donations from his followers. His substantial properties, it was alleged, were carried in the name of various holding companies which he controlled. Maria Russell's attorneys, who spent many months investigating Russell's finances, alleged that the United States Investment Corporation, a holding corporation, had become the owner of Russell properties. The company's charter showed that its capital stock was divided among Russell and two associates—one of whom was Ernest C. Hennings, a director of the Watch Tower Society and the husband of Rose Ball.

Russell remained unruffled throughout these disclosures. For one thing, his loyal followers, who remained convinced that their Pastor was the Messenger of the Millennium and not a Prophet of Mammon, greeted him, upon his return from a European trip, with a gift of $9,000 to pay back alimony. For another, Russell had small entertainments to distract him.

Russell contended, as do the Witnesses today, that the move from Pittsburgh to New York (which Judge MacFarlane called "in bad taste, at the very least") was planned some time before Mrs. Russell's request for increased alimony, as was his transfer of $20,000 to the Watch Tower Society: "We are all working in the interest of the Lord," he told a reporter from the *Brooklyn Eagle.* He declared that it was easier to sell books and pamphlets from Brooklyn than from Pittsburgh, because there were "hundreds of thousands of very very intelligent people in Brooklyn. . . . Believe me, we are doing it all for the Lord."

Brooklyn, so often the butt of bad jokes, has seldom received such oily praise. When I told a resident of Brooklyn Heights, the elegant, moneyed section of Brooklyn where the Watch Tower Society holds property tax-assessed in 1971 for $14 million, of Russell's panegyric to the very very intelligent people of Brooklyn, he said: "Tell the Witnesses for me that we're at least intelligent enough to know that any religion that puts plastic flowers in its windows can't possibly be the true religion. . . . Can't the Lord provide fresh flowers?"

This is a ghoulish, syrupy chocolate bonbon, *Who-Is-the-Mysterious-Veiled-Lady-Who-Brings-Roses-to-Rudolph-Valentino's Grave?* anecdote told, deadpan, in the Witnesses' 1975 *Yearbook:*

> At C. T. Russell's funeral at Pittsburgh in 1916 . . . "an incident occurred just before the services . . . that refuted lies told in the paper

about Brother Russell. The hall was filled long before the time for the services to begin and it was very quiet, and then a veiled figure was seen to walk up the aisle to the casket and to lay something on it. Up front one could see what it was—a bunch of lilies of the valley, Brother Russell's favourite flower. There was a ribbon attached, saying, 'To My Beloved Husband.' It was Mrs. Russell. They had never been divorced and this was a public acknowledgment."

If the Veiled Lady was indeed Maria Frances Russell, she'd had a sudden and complete change of heart. In 1913, Mrs. Russell testified against her former husband at a public meeting of the (New York) Board of Tax Commissioners investigating Russell's finances; she testified against him once again in a libel suit he initiated (and lost, on procedural grounds) against a Canadian minister, J. J. Ross; and in 1914—two years before Russell's death in a railway car near Pampa, Texas—she issued a detailed denial that any reconciliation between her and Russell was in process. In a letter addressed to the Rev. DeWitt Cobb of the Second M. E. Church of Asbury Park, New Jersey, Maria Russell wrote:

> For sixteen years we have walked far apart in every sense of the word, and paths so divergent give no assurance of coming together. If Mr. R.'s followers are circulating such a report, they have manufactured it out of their imaginings.

Maria wrote that one of Russell's female followers, "an entire stranger" to her, represented Russell as sick in body and penitent in soul. Maria said that her intention all along had been to oppose unrighteousness, and that she would consider it her Christian duty to save Russell's soul from sin and the consequences of sin; she would go to the dying man, she said, with forgiveness, and with her prayers.

> That would be, however, only at his express request and acknowledgment of the wrongs he had done, for the time was (when I was with him) that he did not want my prayers, and said so. [*Brooklyn Eagle,* July 6, 1914]

III

Waiting for the World to Die

Woman is merely a lowly creature whom God created for man as man's helper.—*Let God Be True* (Watchtower Bible and Tract Society, 1946), p. 24.

I slept fitfully the night of the day I read the account of Maria Russell's court testimony. I understood how strong a hold that woman—consigned, by the Witnesses, to an eternity of lovelessness—had on my imagination. Once I thought I heard her voice. "Don't leave me," she said. "Help me." I don't believe in "voices" (words like Yin, Yang, Zen, astral projection, and What-is-your-astrological-sign? send me fleeing from a room as quick as you can say UFO); I put it down to overtiredness.

My brain flashed an unwelcome signal to me. I resurrected the warnings I'd read, over and over, for years and years, in *The Watchtower* and *Awake!* magazines. Make mock of Jehovah's Witnesses, the warnings said, and demons will take over your mind. I reminded myself that it would be extraordinary if I didn't, occasionally, get nightmarish nudges from a programmed past (as one might experience pain in an amputated limb), dismissed all thoughts of "demon influence," felt maudlin pity for the bludgeoned little girl I'd been, and fell into a troubled sleep.

I dreamed of God as the last link in the food chain, the Ultimate Predator, the Final Devourer. I dreamed He swallowed women up alive. I saw an endless procession of Pastor Russells offering up women as sacrifices, and I saw the women greet their bloody consummation with a smile.

The official stance of the Witnesses toward women has been consistent. It derives from Paul: "The head of every man is Christ; and the head of the woman is the man; and the head of Christ is God." [I Corinthians 11:3] Sometimes, in their zeal, they achieve black-comedic effects: In *Aid to Bible Understanding*, a 1971 Watchtower publication, we are told that a female zebra—whose "characteristic or quality [is that she craves] sexual satisfaction from any quarter"—symbolizes "Israel unfaithfully seeking after pagan nations and their gods." [p. 202]

Russell set the tone. In *Studies in the Scriptures,* Volume VI, *The*

New Creation, published in 1911, after his divorce, he professed to see sex as an evil necessity, a messy marital obligation that was part of the marriage contract rather than a pleasure and a joy. "Sexual appetites," he said, "war against the spirit of the New Creation."

A woman with strength of mind was more to be despised than one who had the good sense to remain as passive, humble—silly—as God, in His wisdom, had made her:

> Depraved and selfish [women], disposed not only to rebel against an unreasonable and improper headship, but even to dispute any and every proposition, and to haggle and quarrel over it . . . while not claiming to be the provider for the family, nevertheless [attempt] directly or indirectly, to usurp the authority of the head of the home. . . . Should . . . a wife gifted with superior talent, judgment and abilities . . . be regarded as the head of the family, and the husband as the helpmate? . . . No. . . . No woman should marry a man beneath her in character and talents.

It may be that Charles Russell had Maria in mind, and he probably had himself in mind when he wrote that a husband was "thoroughly justified in considering himself deserted, and in taking up a separate home to which he could take such of the children as had not been thoroughly poisoned by the mother's wrong course" if his wife exercised "petty tyrannies" to make his home "a veritable purgatory." [*Ibid.*]

When I became a Witness, in 1944, marriage was frowned upon. In 1941, at a convention in St. Louis, Missouri, J. F. Rutherford, Russell's successor, combining evangelistic fervour with vaudevillean flair, said that a woman was nothing more than (as Kipling had put it) "a rag and a bone and a hank of hair." Marriage, it was implied, was "selfish"; it kept one from entering the full-time service of the Lord.

I remember a family of Greek Witnesses: an imposing matriarch; a pale, insignificant father; two daughters, Olivia and Thea—one beautiful, the other plain. (Plain Thea played the opening and closing hymns on the upright piano at meetings in the Kingdom Hall; everyone felt sorry for her—and liked her better, and treated her more kindly than they did Olivia.) People gossiped about Sister L., the mother: She'd been overheard telling her beautiful daughter, as they watched a bridal party pass by, "See that bride? That's what I want for *you*." Olivia, it was rumoured, whenever a male Witness from headquarters was invited to her family's private house for supper, would plant herself in front of a window with an open Bible in her hand—a picture of spiritual and physical beauty to entice men.

The fact that the L.'s lived in a private house was not insignificant. In our largely working-class South Brooklyn congregation, very few people lived in private houses. Class animosity was never allowed to rise to the surface—brothers and sisters, we all "loved" one another—but class animosity would find expression in whispered conversations about somebody or other's not being sufficiently "theocratic." It was remarkable how many people who lived in private houses were "un-theocratic."

My mother and her friends judged other Witnesses (in spite of the constant exhortations to be non-judgmental) on the basis of their profligacy. If you used heavy cream or Kleenex, you were self-indulgent, a Bad Person. We were both suspicious and envious of anyone who had more money than we had. We asked God to forgive us our failures of love. We maintained our do-gooder, passive mentality, behaving "nice" in front of the people we mistrusted. Aggressive behaviour was not allowed us. We never fought it out like gentlemen. Inside, we seethed, we burned. We turned our hostility against the alien world.

We all knew men and women who'd "given each other up" in order to serve Jehovah. We regarded them with a kind of awe. For us younger Witnesses, they were the soul of romance.

Our South Brooklyn congregation was not far from Bethel, Watchtower headquarters. We felt about young male "Bethelites," whose characteristics we lovingly rehearsed, as other young girls might feel about glamorous, unattainable movie stars. They moved through our lives, and in our fantasies, like gods. They were not permitted to marry if they wished to remain at Bethel. Often they dated girls from local congregations—took them to a roller-skating rink, danced the tango after dinner in parents' homes. When I was 13, a beautiful young man with a Southern accent that turned me to jelly took me to see Jane Wyman and Lew Ayres in *Johnny Belinda* at the Brooklyn Paramount, and then we walked across the Brooklyn Bridge, holding hands and talking about God. *He* talked; I, practised in the art of humility and not knowing how to combine humility with something called "personality," which the Witness girls endlessly discussed, listened, occasionally uttering a monosyllabic response. He never took me out again: there were other girls who knew better than I how to combine "submissiveness" with charming artifice. But even for those popular girls who had "personality," there was always an underlying sadness. Young women charmed; but their charms could not seduce. They had a powerful rival—God.

When two Witnesses did marry—usually after months of clandestine meetings and hot, claustrophobic secrecy—we spoke of them wonderingly, critically. We were jealous, and couldn't admit it. They had violated an ethic that was all the stronger because it was not an absolute imperative; they had broken an unwritten law.

We watched to see how great the evidence of their "selfishness" would be: Would they pioneer (work as full-time proselytizers) together? Would they have children right away? If they did pioneer, their having married would be—with more or less charity—more or less forgiven (although, of course, we knew they were doing *it*. No one, then, talked much about *it*). If they had children immediately, they gained a reputation for foolish or "immaturity"; how could one, selfishly, have children in a world so close to dying? If they neither pioneered nor had children, it was clear that they had married for "selfish purposes"—to do *it*. Some Witnesses, marrying, felt compelled to say they were marrying "for companionship" —the implication being that they were not doing *it*, or at least not doing *it* a lot.

As the years passed, the Witnesses' attitude toward marriage slowly changed. By the time I was at Watchtower headquarters, in the early 1950s, missionaries were drifting back across the seas, reuniting, marrying without stigma. Male Bethelites were permitted to marry provided that they, and their prospective mates, had served at Bethel headquarters for ten years. (The first beneficiary of this change of regulations was the man who amended the regulations—Nathan H. Knorr, third president of the Watchtower Society.) Young men and women are now warned against the dangers of premarital intimacy. They are encouraged to keep themselves pure for Christian matrimony. They may now marry with impunity. (It is still regarded as somewhat foolhardy to bring children into a dying world. Children are, after all, unpredictable, potential rebels; they divert emotional and financial resources away from God—and from "his organization.")

The Witnesses' response to changing sexual mores in the sexually permissive 1960s and '70s has guaranteed that they will not lose all their young people to whimsy or wilfulness or spontaneity—that is, to depravity: to the evil world where all sexual appetites are indiscriminately gratified. Better to marry—within the organization —than to burn with worldly sexual libertines.

The Witnesses tend now, as they move toward the mainstream, to reinforce the nuclear family and traditional family roles.

Still, Paul's saturnine attitude toward marriage—"It is better to marry than to burn" [I Corinthians 7:9]—informs their views. *The Watchtower* suggests that while sexual desire "can seem quite compelling" in a young adult, "time might show that the Christian could make a success of singleness without being tormented by desire." [*TW*, Nov. 15, 1974] *The Watchtower* advises its readers to wait till they are "past the period of primary surge of desire . . . to evaluate" the decision to marry or not to marry. Singleness is still thought to be the better course.

Responding to external realities, the Witnesses choose now to emphasize the horrors attendant upon premarital intimacy, the vileness of "unnatural acts." And their language is no less stringent than one would expect from people who look upon the Sistine Chapel and see, in that unrivalled magnificence, "pornography . . . rampant." [*Aw,* Jan. 8, 1975]

Masturbation is "unnatural." Mentally deranged people are notorious masturbators. *The Watchtower* can't resist a jibe at the Catholic Church: "Many mentally disturbed priests and nuns are chronic masturbators." Unemployed persons and prisoners masturbate. If a Witness masturbates in a "state of semi-conscious sleep," Jehovah will no doubt forgive him or her; but for added insurance, it would be wise to speak to an elder or (if you are a woman) to a mature sister. [*TW,* Sept. 13, 1973]

It is wrong to look at somebody passionately, or to touch anybody passionately. It is a serious violation of God's will to "excite each other sexually by putting . . . hands on each other's private parts." Fornication refers not just to sexual union between unmarried persons, but "to lewd conduct such as one might find in places of prostitution." [*TW*, Oct. 1, 1973] Avoid the occasions of sin: "Ice-skate, play tennis, have a restaurant meal together, visit some museum or local point of interest and beauty." Surround yourself with people.

Oral and anal sex—within marriage, and performed by consenting adults—are perversions: male and female homosexuals indulge in these practices. You don't have to perform a homosexual act to qualify as a homosexual: if you have homosexual fantasies, you are a homosexual in your heart—and God sees your heart.

I couldn't have been more than 12 when my friend Milly, a Witness who was two years my senior—and light-years ahead of me in sophistication and daring—invited me to her house after a morning of proselytizing and proposed that we "talk dirty." Talking dirty led inevitably to bed, where Milly showed me "how babies nurse," "how grown-ups do it," Milly slid her finger along my vagina—a favour I was too scared, too rigid, to return. I told her I was scared; I said we shouldn't do it. "Dumb," Milly said. "You don't get pregnant from a girl on top of you." Too scared to protest that that wasn't what I was scared of—Jehovah's wrath was what I was scared of—I allowed myself to be seduced. I didn't enjoy it.

Later, as I was walking home, a man called to me from a parked car. "Do you know where Suzie lives?" he asked. "I'm sorry, no," I said. "That's too bad," he said, "I wanted to suck her pussy." Hearing him but not hearing him, I repeated, "No, I'm sorry." "Have you ever been laid in a car?" he asked. I *did* hear that, and I ran, convinced that this was a punishment, that I was a dirty, wicked girl who invited lewd comments. I was tortured by the certainty that *they*—God, the elders, my mother—all *knew* and were allowing me to suffer the agonies of waiting before they revealed my wickedness to the world.

Not all Witnesses are successful in their struggles against their sexual nature. When I was interviewing Witnesses at a district convention at Aqueduct Race Track in 1974, I found that while few women were willing to admit that sex, or the Women's Movement, posed any kind of problem for them at all, male Witnesses frequently acknowledged that the prohibition against premarital sex might conceivably create conflicts. Not all Witnesses have become their personae; occasionally, at Aqueduct, most often with men, a hint of jocularity and frivolity entered conversations. It was almost immediately aborted, as they remembered that I was not one of them.

At the convention at Aqueduct, I did find, in the midst of certainty, among 25,000 pain-evaders and happiness proclaimers, two men who stood out like birds of paradise: Bo Jacks, dressed in poison-green silk, pimp straw hat, platform shoes; and Ron Bookers, resplendent in a white ruffled, sequined shirt. On their partially exposed black-is-beautiful 18-year-old chests hung gold chains and medallions surrounded by sparkling stones. They admitted to being in trouble. Their confusion was refreshing; it felt like something precious. They were trying hard to be Jehovah's Witnesses; their mothers had raised them to be Witnesses, but, "Yeah, sometimes it's hard. . . .

"Sex? That's the hardest thing in the life. It's hard. You know, I'm not gonna say I never had sex, 'cause you know I do, but I try, you know, to keep it to a certain extent where I can stop. I really want to get married. Therefore it would be legal, I wouldn't have to do it behind doors. You know, you can get kicked out of the Witnesses for having sex. . . . They find out 'cause somebody tell on you or you tell on yourself; it's suppose' to be you tell on yourself. See, the sisters won't have nothin' to do with me, 'cause their parents told them, don't mess with a brother 'less he dressed up in a suit and tie. Well, that's not my thing. Who I have sex with, they call them 'worldly people.' But I wouldn't marry one of them.

"I'm trying. I'm really trying."

As Middle American as apple pie (but not quite so Middle American as to enshrine Mom on her kitchen-pedestal), the Watchtower Society reacts to "New Wedding" ceremonies with irritation. Witnesses exchange vows in the Kingdom Hall meeting place, after an elder of the congregation gives an "upbuilding talk" on the appropriate behaviour of husbands and wives.

The groom: "I ——— take you ——— to be my wedded wife, to love and to cherish in accordance with the divine law as set forth in the Holy Scriptures for Christian husbands, for as long as we both shall live together on earth according to God's marital arrangement."
The bride: "I ——— take you ——— to be my wedded husband, to love and to cherish and deeply respect, in accordance with the divine law as set forth in the Holy Scriptures for Christian wives, for as long as we both shall live together on earth according to God's marital arrangement." [*TW*, May 15, 1974, p. 275]

Although women bear the brunt of door-to-door proselytizing, there are no female elders in congregations of Jehovah's Witnesses. There are no women in the governing body of the Witnesses, or on the board of directors of the Watch Tower Bible and Tract Society or its sister corporations.

When there are no qualified male members present in a congregation, a woman may perform duties otherwise reserved for men; she must, however, in that event, and if she is teaching others in the presence of her husband or another male, "wear some form of head covering besides her hair, which she normally always has," [*Aid*, p.275]

A Christian husband is instructed to be mindful of the "limitations and vicissitudes" of his wife and to "consider the opinions, likes, and dislikes of his wife, *even giving her the preference when there is no issue at stake.*" [*Aw*, April 22, 1972, p. 11; italics mine]

Are the women happy? They profess to be happy.

Irving I. Zaretsky and Mark P. Leone *(Religious Movements in Contemporary America)* believe that women in evangelical religions gain a position of their own in the community without reference to their husbands. (A female Witness who has an unbelieving mate is told to "accept his headship" *except* in regard to worship. She is to defer to him in all other matters, but not to permit his indifference or opposition to deter her from going to religious meetings, proselytizing, or instructing her children in the faith.) Religion, Zaretsky and Leone suggest, becomes an acceptable form of activity for women who cannot operate in the secular world because they lack the necessary education or certification. Their religion becomes the "avenue that short-circuits a whole set of life-problems."

For disaffected women whose experience has taught them that all human relationships are threateningly volatile, capricious, and unreliable, the Witnesses provide an answer. Relate to God. God is a safe lover, a constant lover, a consuming lover. For women who are mired in oppressive poverty—and for a smaller number of guilt-ridden affluent women—the Witnesses provide an answer: Jehovah's New World will eradicate poverty; He will redistribute the wealth. Explicitly antifeminist, the Witnesses nevertheless provide a vehicle for downtrodden women—their religion allows their voices, drowned by the voices of the menacing world, to emerge. Women whose self-hatred is pathological find a congenial home among the Witnesses; they are told that it is desirable to be persecuted, Godly to be hated, proof of goodness to be considered worthless by the world. Women who fear and hate the world are secure in the knowledge that God will smash the evil world for them. They find hope in a world without hope.

Here are some of their voices (these are the voices in which they speak to non-believers):

"I had searched for years to find answers, and the Witnesses are the only people who have answers for the world situation. I think I would have been the kind that would be on the soapbox complaining about my taxes if it were not for the Witnesses; now I understand that *I* can't do it—God will."

"I used to be involved in lots of different organizations and clubs, but not any more. Now I stay home and study the Bible with my children."

"My liberation came when I realized there was no future in higher education because this whole system is dying. I wasn't involved in drugs like a lot of the people who are in The Truth now. The opposite of dropping out—being popular—is just as dangerous: I was the captain of twirlers, vice-president of the art club, on the senior-class board, on the community-action committee—you name it. Now I know that I was just calling attention to myself. . . . But when I got The Truth, I left college and I stopped all those worldly activities to preach full time. . . . My classmates jeered at me. But we're told we're going to be hated by this world, and it's better to be persecuted than to be popular."

A 40-year-old woman, her green eyes shining with the rich gleam of lunacy, all ruffles and bows and corkscrew curls, a neat approximation of an Ivory Snow queen: "I'll wait for God's kingdom to get married. Men in our organization have headship. It works nicely; families keep together. . . . Dating? It's been such a long time. I won't go out with worldly men. But I keep busy and occupied. I preach. I work for a doctor; I like to read books about cancer. I don't watch R-rated movies or read dirty books. I never think of sex. . . . Do you think of it a lot? Probably you do. I don't judge people, though."

A 20-year-old woman who believes herself to be dying of leukaemia invites me radiantly to join her "in finding real peace and security by becoming one with Jehovah's people. I'm dying," she says, sweetly smiling, "but I will be resurrected on a perfect earth. Live with me!"

These are the voices the outside world hears. In the daily realities of the women's lives, one hears a murmur of different voices.

They have fun together. They sing together; they dance together (they may be the only people left, outside of Roseland, who dance the cha-cha-cha). They tell each other mildly risqué jokes (never in the presence of men). Sometimes they hold hands together when they preach together. They read and underline *The Watchtower* together, as a form of communion. Drawing courage from one another, they are subtly subversive of its text—particularly when the text refers to their relationships with believing or unbelieving mates: they giggle together about how they can avoid sex without giving the appearance of being delinquent in "rendering their marriage dues." If their husbands oppose their religious will, they huddle together for warmth. They gossip together like girls about the men they'll marry in the New World. If, as I frequently heard women complain when I was a Witness, their husbands were lax in "assuming headship," if their husbands would not "take the lead" —placing in their hands the real power in the family while their husbands wore the face of authority—they would talk about ways of subverting their own strength; or they would heave sighs together, in a sisterhood of tea and sympathy and soon-to-be-alleviated grief.

I have asked Witness women why, if women are not inferior to men, they are not elders, ministers, shepherds of the flock. I have been answered, "I don't know. I believe in the inherent wisdom of the Bible. We don't have to justify our position with biology or anthropology. God is our Creator and our Regulator; He knows what's best. Our responsibilities are worked out by God; we don't make decisions."

The Witnesses encourage women to exercise a degree of autonomy over their own bodies. Contraceptives are acceptable. Women are encouraged to breast-feed babies (and made to feel slightly guilty if they do not); recent Watchtower publications have endorsed giving birth in one's home.

Abortion, however, is, under any circumstances, murder—even when birth might jeopardize the pregnant woman's life. Diabetes, hypertension, and other grave cardiovascular diseases are not reasons to abort, nor does the danger of giving birth to a defective or deformed child constitute justification for abortion: Jehovah can always undo the damage in His coming New Order. [See *TW*, March 15, 1975, p. 191–92.]

Artificial insemination by an anonymous donor is regarded as a form of adultery; both the wife and her consenting mate will be penalized by expulsion from the congregation. In cases in which a husband's sperm is introduced artificially to impregnate his wife, "They would have to resolve any personal questions of propriety as to the manner of acquiring the semen." [*Aw*, Aug. 8, 1974, p. 22]

The Witnesses' feelings about rape can be summed up in the familiar: She got no more than she deserved. Virtuous women don't *get* raped. They might get killed, but they don't get raped. And if it isn't the rapist's victim's fault, it's the rapist's *mother's* fault. Rape is on the increase because "Satan the Devil together with his demons is influencing the minds of mankind" as we approach the end of the world. However, "Womankind must share the blame."

Women are discouraged from learning to defend themselves; they must scream. Indeed, their only recourse is to scream—if they do not scream, and the rapist has his way with them, *they are guilty of fornication or adultery*. If they do scream and get raped anyway, they're in the clear. If they scream and get killed, God will resurrect them. Watchtower publications have testimonials of women who screamed and got off safely; one woman screamed first—and then told her would-be rapist the story of Noah and the Flood. The rapist and she disagreed about how many years Noah had preached before the flood: he said two hundred, she said forty.

A Witness woman believes she is special, different; she "maintains her integrity in an alien world." She needs the society of "the friends" to validate her existence; and each deprivation she endures draws her closer to "God's organization". When the Watchtower Society forbade Witnesses to celebrate Christmas, or birthdays, the response of one elderly woman was "We felt we were privileged to know things others were ignorant about." When I told my Bethel roommate that I was leaving religion, she said, with anguish, "But where will you *go*?" Her anguish was for me; it was also for herself—my defection terrified her, it threatened her security. The only way Witnesses can deal with defectors is to abort their love for them immediately.

Talented women frequently throw away their talents—which serve the Devil and gratify the flesh; or they subordinate their talents to the relentless demands of their religion. Happiness has not come from economic and social rewards, so they seek ultimate happiness, the crown of happiness only the Lover-God can bestow. Worldly success is dust and ashes without the revivifying flame of God's love. The Witnesses have a stunning ambivalence toward worldly success. On the one hand, they profess to despise it, as they profess to despise materialism and the acquisition of wealth. On the other hand, its glitter fascinates and enthralls them.

Teresa Graves, the television actress who used, in her pre-conversion days, to wriggle on to *Laugh-In* with words like RING MY CHIMES and WHITE SALE painted on her beautiful black body, became one of Jehovah's Witnesses. Her job, she said, came second. She found it difficult to reconcile herself to her affluence.

Unlike most of the never-never-land people in Beverly Hills, she remembered there was a Watts down there beneath the swimming pools and the smog; and her social consciousness, combined with a sense of impotence, led her straight to an ultimate solution: She spent as much as 100 hours a month proselytizing, the only door-to-door television star.

Watchtower and *Awake!* magazines frequently have articles contributed by actors, artists, and musicians (always anonymous) who gave it all up for Jehovah (they are usually women); or by Witnesses whose worldly successes left them, unaccountably, fragmented and depressed.

A highly placed television network executive, a former member of New York Media Women, a feminist consciousness-raising and political-activist group [*TW*, July 1, 1974, pp. 387–93], transferred "the feeling of solidarity, of trust, of love . . . 'sisterhood,'" from the Women's Movement to Jehovah's Witnesses when it became apparent to her that Women's Liberation "did not have the answers." "Confused, disillusioned, and saddened" by ideological quarrels within the Movement, depressed that "many of the women I had admired and who were taking over the leadership were lesbians," discouraged because many men walked out on feminist women to find more "feminine" women, disturbed because women were deserting their families and putting down motherhood and child-rearing as atavistic and bourgeois, she opted for a movement that would tolerate no ideological dissension, that answered all her questions definitively, and that delivered her from her terror of sexual differences, of sexual and personal choice. She instructed her lawyers to drop the $2-million lawsuit she had filed against the network after she was fired in 1971, allegedly because she had refused to date her boss, and rested her case with the Judge who will resolve all injustices.

Secular work is only a means to support the Witnesses' preaching. Art does not nourish or sustain or ennoble. Everything must be utilitarian, practical—at the most, decorative. Michelangelo was a pornographer. The Cathedral at Chartres is a Devil place. Their God will destroy all man's art at Armageddon; not a poem or a song man has made will survive that burning day.

A friend of mine who was a Witness for three troubled years tells me that she quit going to Witness meetings because "They made me pinch my Joey. . . . They scolded him from the podium when he was only three years old to make him quiet," Sara says, "and they said he couldn't play with his crayons, he had to keep still and listen to the *Watchtower* discussion or he wouldn't live forever in the New World . . . so I was humiliated, and I pinched him to shut him up;

and then I felt guilty—because how could a good mother pinch her son for God?"

When it is assumed that human nature is basically evil, that a child inherits the sinful nature of his first parents, Adam and Eve, the expression of idiosyncratic views, self-assertion, and rebellion are perceived as a smack in the face of a wrathful God. It falls to the parents—God's surrogates—to bring the evil impulses of the child under holy control. If a 2-year-old doesn't eat his carrots, it is not his parents he is offending, it is God. His instincts must be squashed, because they are evil; his spirit must be broken, because pride leads to a Lucifer-fall. The child is controlled and dominated—in the name of a God of love. The child is disciplined in the name of a judgmental God, from Whom all rewards and punishments flow.

Poor Sara. She was convinced that at a convention of 50,000 people, her Joey was the only unruly child. She may well have been right: meetings and conventions of Jehovah's Witnesses are remarkable for the stillness—the unnatural stillness, the lobotomized good behaviour—of Witness children. Their voices are not heard. The Witnesses are the best child-squashers and -controllers I know.

The instructions Charles Taze Russell issued for raising children [*SS*, Vol. VI] are as saccharine as the lace valentines of his day; but Russell's flowery language disguises an iron determination to repress all the child's true feelings: "Is my little boy feeling happy this morning? Does he love papa and mama and sister and brother and doggie?" [p. 552] No verbal or physical aggression is permitted the child; aggression is interpreted as hostility toward God.

Russell instructed parents to "apply suggestion" to their children. There was nothing to be gained and everything to be lost, in Russell's view, by allowing a child to relate directly and individualistically to his environment. The child must relate only to God (and to His representatives); the material world exists only to provide moral lessons.

While dressing a child, Russell advised, "talk about the pretty wee birdies and about the big sun looking in at the window and calling all to get up and be good and happy, and learn more lessons about God." On a rainy day, call the child's attention to "the beautiful rain which God has provided for giving the flowers and trees and grass a drink and a bath to refresh them . . . and for cattle and for us to bathe in and be clean." [p. 550]

The reverse side of Russell's cheery optimism was the admonition to withdraw affection if the child flouted God's or his parents' imperatives: "I know you didn't mean to be bad, but you will get no good-night kiss tonight. You have failed to please us again. I am so sorry my little daughter failed again, I do not doubt your good intentions, dear." [p. 553]

To play, in Russell's view, was to be immoral: a "desire to be amused" led, in due time, to a craving for "the theatre and the nonsense of the clown." [pp. 556–57] Idleness was a sin and a shame. If the mind and the imagination were kept a blank slate, Russell believed, the child's handwriting would cover it soon—with "unclean thoughts, the contemplation of obscene pictures." [p. 542] Of course Russell was afraid of leisure: it is true that only in leisure can vice flourish; it is also true that only in leisure can art flourish.

The greatest danger for a Witness child, as for an adult, is to think autonomously. To reason independently is an affront to the God whose ways are higher than our ways, the God one may never question. Fortunately, say the Witnesses, they have been provided with "a visible instrument or agency on earth" through which Christ provides "spiritual food" to his "slaves." [*LGBT*] That agency is the Watchtower Bible and Tract Society, which, though it makes no claim of infallibility, nevertheless excommunicates anyone who comes to conclusions independent of its own.

(I knew that I was intractable, that I was "hardhearted" and had probably caused God's holy spirit to abandon me, when I found, to my sorrow, that "God's organization" could not explain God to me. When I was a girl, I thought—and the guilt and shame attendant upon this aberrant thought shrivelled my soul—that Jehovah was like Mr. Rochester or the absent father in *The Turn of the Screw*: a felt presence that moved darkly through my life, His motives often inexplicable, His word law, His love mysteriously withheld.)

When everything is given (by "God's organization"), nothing more is required. It was thought to be worse than redundant—it was thought to be a mark of contempt for God's "channel"—for a young Witness to go to a college or university:

"In sending [a child to college] at the present time," Russell wrote, parents "should feel a great trepidation, a great fear, lest this outward polish in the wisdom of the world should efface all the polish of faith and character and heart which they as the parents and proper instructors of the child had been bestowing upon it from infancy and before."

Since Russell's time, nothing has changed. Parents are still reminded that they must render an account to God, Who has placed in their hands the responsibility to convey His desires to children. They are God-appointed guardians and God-appointed moral censors; and their homes reek with the stale smell of religiosity—religion by rote, dogma uninformed by the energy of spiritual passion.

David Maslanka, a young composer who was raised as a Witness, tells me that his childhood "was like a dark, airless chamber illuminated by rainbow-coloured fantasies. My mother was a 'suspect' Witness," he says: "the other Witnesses thought she was off centre, flirting with spiritualism. So they wouldn't allow their kids to play with me. I blamed my mother and I pitied her; and I felt that evil forces were working within me, too. I lived in almost absolute isolation. I used to pray someone would invite me to sit next to him at meetings; no one ever did. I felt despised. When I was 11, my mother was excommunicated because of dabbling with the occult; and, since I had burned my bridges by refusing to have worldly friends, there was nobody at all I could talk to, nobody at all." David still finds it hard, so scarring was that brief and bitter experience, to talk freely: in his intensely passionate music, great blocks of glorious coloured sound alternate with great blocks of dark, Rousseauvian silence. His music reminds me of ruined Mayan temples thrusting out of the jungle density and stillness, stone upon stone rising from dark decay, sheer will conquering a ripe darkness illuminated with rainbow flashes of blinding light.

Many Witness kids were forbidden to play with me because I was judged to be too smart for my own good—for *their* own good (and, I suspect, because my mother's beauty and her highly effectual proselytizing evoked jealousies that could not be expressed). I remember once, feeling sophisticated and daring, using a bobby-soxer word—*devastating* ("This fudge sundae is devastating"); and a Witness mother pounced—she had been waiting. "Only Jehovah can *devastate*," she said fiercely, the fire of the Inquisition burning in her eyes. And she forbade her daughter, my best friend, to play with me. I was 10 years old. I have never forgiven her cruelty, the tears I shed on her account.

The Witnesses have not seen fit to change their views on education. Why bother with Devil-knowledge? Why imperil your standing with the all-knowing God? To what practical uses can a college education possibly be put? For the Witnesses, all knowledge must be practical, utilitarian: At the Watchtower Bible Missionary School of Gilead, established in 1942 for full-time preachers, no humanities are taught, and no creative arts. Future missionaries are taught "a course in college arithmetic; instructions on shipping and use of Society's forms and reports; manner of dealing with government officials; the required international law; a course in English and grammar . . . the essentials of the needed foreign language." No academic credentials are necessary for enrolment; the principal training given to the tuition-free students is "Bible research and public Bible speaking, and the understanding of Theocratic organization instructions." [*JWDP*, p. 204] Confrontation with metaphysical, philosophical, theological, or moral problems is avoided, as are sociology and psychology. Freud and Marx might never have lived. When morality is legislated, there is no reason to discuss its nuances—there are no nuances. (One reference work, *Aid to Bible Understanding*, a concordance published by the Watchtower Society, devotes as much space to "greyheadedness" as to "goodness.")

I have, as a consequence of this attitude toward "worldly wisdom," known Witnesses who have not read a single book or magazine not published by the Watchtower Bible and Tract Society for twenty years. I am still amazed at my own youthful temerity: defiantly, when I was at Bethel headquarters, I smuggled *New Yorkers* into the building, locking myself into an unused guest room to read them. *Raise High the Roof Beam, Carpenters!* Salinger, I then thought, would know me, would understand me; and I loved (love) him for that.

Of course I did what I was told and did not go to college. In high school, I took a commercial and then a "cooperative" course—going to school and working in the office of a tool-and-die factory on alternate weeks. I was the despair of my teachers, who pleaded with me to take college-preparatory courses. I protested, rebutted, denied; but in the unredeemed, unredeemable part of my God-possessed heart—that tiny corner which denied Him access—I longed to do what I explained I could not, in good conscience, do. If anyone had picked me up bodily, bound and shackled me, and deposited me on any campus in the Western world, I would have considered it a deliverance; Mephistopheles could have had my soul for the price of a course in Freshman English. I ached—wanting so much to be one of them, despising my own longings—when I saw book-laden college students. I seldom allowed my mind to know what my heart was doing. Vice was the Flatbush Avenue bus. I rode the Flatbush Avenue bus, pretending to be on my way to Brooklyn College, hoping that someone would mistake me for one of those privileged people free to learn and to explore. And all this time, I believed that I still believed; I preached with fervour and conviction.

The Watchtower [April 1, 1975, p. 217] quotes the Australian *Journal of Personality,* March 1973: "A disproportionately large number of highly creative children were Jehovah's Witnesses. Four children from the total sample of 394 were members of this sect, and all four showed high creative ability. The girl who gained the highest total score on the Torrance [creativity] tests, and the girl who was the only child, male or female, to be included in the top 20 percent of all five performance measures, were both Jehovah's Witnesses." On the face of it, this seems difficult to reconcile with the fact that college students from authoritarian fundamentalist religions have been found, in psychological testing, to have "constricted and rigid cognitive and perceptual functioning on projective and intelligence tests, lower scholastic achievement, lack of creative responsitivity with conventional routine aesthetic attitudes, . . . and generally poorer overall adjustment and achievement in comparison with students in matched groups." [E. Mansell Pattison, Z&L, p. 424] On reflection, however, the Australian statistics yield to another interpretation. The children tested were 12 years old. Sexuality rigorously repressed in puberty conduces to a strongly coloured fantasy life. The imagination of very young Witnesses is fuelled and fired by the rich imagery of destruction and creation with which they live. It is not surprising that the tension produced by the clash between force-fed dogmatic certainty and inner confusion, and the friction created by the rub of the socially isolated against the world, may be, for a time, *creative* tension.

On April 18, 1951, the State of Illinois went to court to take temporary custody of a child of Witness parents in order to administer a blood transfusion to the dying infant. Six-day-old Cheryl Labrenz was the victim of a rare medical syndrome that was destroying her red blood cells. The doctors' consensus was that the baby would die without blood transfusions. Cheryl's parents, Darrell and Rhoda Labrenz, paid no heed; they were concerned, they said, with their infant's eternal welfare. They were prepared to see her die, knowing that Jehovah would resurrect her and give her everlasting life—and that they would be consigned to everlasting death if they did not adhere to God's laws prohibiting the ingesting of blood. Cheryl became a ward of Court for the time necessary to administer the life-saving transfusions.

The Labrenz case was the first of many in which minor children became wards of the Court so that blood transfusions, prohibited by the governing body of Jehovah's Witnesses since 1944, could be administered.

An absurdly literal reading of the Mosaic injunction not to "eat blood," together with Paul's instructions (Acts 21:25) for Christians to "keep themselves from things offered to idols, and from blood, and from strangled, and from fornication," is bolstered by the Witnesses with the declaration that blood transfusion dates back to the ancient Egyptians (anything pagan is sinful) and by the seemingly contradictory fact that "the earliest reported case was a futile attempt to save the life of Pope Innocent VIII in 1492." [*Yearbook*, 1975, p. 222] (If the Church—whose genius it is to absorb and assimilate pagan practices so as to make Christ accessible to all people—does it, it can't possibly be right.)

It cannot be said that the Witnesses are not willing to endure grave discomfort, or to die for their beliefs. I have known Witnesses who scurried frantically from doctor to doctor, postponing vital operations in an often futile attempt to find a practitioner who would agree to operate without transfusing blood. (I have also been told, in confidence, by doctors that they did at the last moment—when it was apparent that the patient's life was at stake—administer blood transfusions unbeknownst to the Witness, in default of the agreement not to do so.) On the other hand, Watchtower publications are full of testimonials of people who were told that they would die without transfusions—and who, refusing transfusions, nevertheless lived. During World War II, male Witnesses imprisoned under Selective Service draft laws went so far as to refuse to be vaccinated, regarding vaccination, not logically, as being no different from blood transfusion. Hugh Macmillan [*Faith*, pp. 188–90], the elder assigned to visit and counsel imprisoned Witnesses, set them straight. He told the young men in solitary confinement that "All of us who visit our foreign branches are vaccinated or we stay at home. Now, vaccination," he said, with dubious logic, "is not anything like blood transfusion. No blood is used in the vaccine. It is a serum." He advised the jailed Witnesses to act as the prophet Jeremiah had. Jeremiah had told the governmental authorities of his time, "I am in your hands; do with me as you wish; if you put me to death, innocent blood will be on your hands." "They have you where they could vaccinate an elephant," Macmillan said, "and they will vaccinate you all" whether you agree to it or not. "If evil resulted," he told the prisoners "the government would be held responsible" by God. The blood of the innocent would be on Caesar's hands. The Witnesses agreed not only to accept transfusions, but to write a letter of apology to prison officials "for the trouble they had caused." My sympathy is with the Witnesses who were willing to endure solitary confinement and withdrawal of all jail privileges and who listened to the voice of their conscience. Individual conscience, however, was overruled by the voice of authority. The jailed Witnesses were forced to violate their consciences, which told them that vaccine would pollute the bloodstream they had been taught to regard as sacred.

I grudgingly admire the brave silliness of adult Witnesses who are willing to risk the consequence of death by refusing to receive blood. They are analogous, in my mind, to would-be assassins of bad men—who are just as brave, just as silly, just as futile, and whose orientation is similarly futuristic. But how can one admire an adult who makes that life-or-death decision for a child? It is apparently a monstrous, unnatural act. But one must remember the brainwashing to which the Witnesses are constantly subjected; they are not monstrous child-haters; they are sad men and women with an obsession that overrules natural necessities and concerns.

They are surgically prepared by their overseers even to amputate their grief: "Because of the wonderful hope of the resurrection, a Christian is not overwhelmed with tears and grief. His sorrow is not as great or as deep as that upon those who have no knowledge of the hope the Bible gives." [*Aw,* May 8, 1975, p. 23]

To suppress natural grief is to invite disaster. The Witnesses are psyched up to deny their grief. But I have seen Witnesses give way to an excess of grief that was terrifying. I knew a young mother who lost two small children in one year—one was run over by a car; the other died of pneumonia. The child who was struck by a car might have been saved by blood transfusions. In her fear and terror, his mother—who had been taught to make sense of the world, and who could not make sense of this senseless slaughter—held him dying in her arms while she argued with doctors about blood transfusions. When her daughter died, six months later, she entered an unnatural calm, a false and dreadful stillness. She began to tell fellow Witnesses that she was sure her children were in heaven, that they visited her comfortingly in her dreams. The Witnesses, frightened by her apostasy—she could reasonably expect, according to their dogma, only to see her children resurrected to an earthly life, heaven being reserved for 144,000 older Witnesses—chided her for expressing heretical views. They scolded; they did not comfort. And yet the people who withheld comfort from a woman driven mad by grief weren't monsters either. They were afraid of her because her grief threatened the security of their belief. She wasn't *supposed* to abandon herself to grief. So they chose to see her grief as Devil-inspired apostasy.

People believe their own myths; unfortunately, they can't always live them. The Father Knows Best ideal toward which the Witnesses reach—happy families sitting down to a pre-breakfast Bible discussion, working together in the door-to-door field ministry, sitting together in scrubbed and pleasant rows at meetings—is a soothing invention.

It is true that conversion to "The Truth" may result in major behavioural changes that can equip marginal people for life in the real world—the world that has bruised and defeated them: alcoholics stop drinking; addicts get off junk; men who are unemployed find work—with a little help from "the friends" (the Witnesses tend to use *lazy* and *unemployed* as if they were synonyms); women who were sloppy housekeepers, once taught that cleanliness is part of Godliness, become living advertisements for *Küche, Kirche, Kinder*; and children, rigorously controlled, do not (as long as they remain Witnesses) smoke, dope, litter, fornicate, or rebel.

These accommodations appear, on the surface, to improve family life; mechanistically, they do. But changing the outer man (or woman) does not—although change does sometimes work from outside in—annul or change the inner personality configuration that made them Witnesses in the first place. They are dependent for approval and sense of worth on external authority; their sights are fixed on a future that will dispel the pain of the present and make up for the deprivations of the past. They are, in an expression borrowed from the 1950s (in which decade they seem permanently mired), outer-directed.

At conventions, where there is indeed great communal tenderness, they radiate happiness. They look like picture-book families, kindergarten-primer families. But the maggots of their frustrations and discontents—their fear and distrust of the material world, of the present—often eat into their apple-pie lives. Depression among Witnesses is widespread, as are tight-lipped repressed familial animosities for which there is no appropriate outlet.

They seek, by their busy-ness—each family is instructed to have one full-time preacher—to lock up their discontents in an attic of their minds. Frequently their discontents flare up in odd ways. I have observed families quarrelling over such how-many-angels-can-dance-on-the-head-of-a-pin issues as "Will our cats live through Armageddon and live forever in the New World?" (I'm not making that up. One woman who insisted that her cats would live forever was threatened by her husband with public reproof from an elder.) You might wonder who would seek to ask such a question. Someone who has only the future. That people do ask one another such questions, and have bitter fallings-out over them, is proved by this depressing exercise in unreality, a speech at a recent convention of Jehovah's Witnesses in New York: "Brothers, do not ask, Will some form of money be used in the New System? What about machinery, such as car, TV, computers? Will we have them after Armageddon, in God's New Order? Shall I save up money now to buy them? Shall I buy a new car and a new TV so I can start off on the right foot in the New System?" Such speculations are food and drink—and fuel for contentious arguments—among people who have no more questions to ask, since all their questions have been answered.

The Watchtower assures its readers that to testify against a family member whose behaviour is antithetical to its instructions is a viable way of protecting the "moral fibre" of God's organization. "Yielding to the influence of a close family member . . . to disregard God's law can only spell disaster. . . . Relatives . . . could cause one to fail in giving God exclusive devotion . . . Anyone . . . taking on undue importance in our lives can lead to our not being exclusively devoted to God. . . . because the object of a person's craving diverts affection from God and in this way becomes an idol." [*TW*, June 15,

1975, pp. 381–82] Every member of one's household is a potential enemy, a potential threat.

Witnesses are instructed to be "examples" to one another in godly conduct. To objectify oneself, and others, as "examples," to be obliged to regard oneself and others as the personification of a doctrinaire idea rather than as complex, complicated human beings is a reduction of humanity that may lead—has led—to schizophrenia, and certainly to depressive behaviour.

These are excerpts from a five-minute play ("demonstration") written to be performed at congregations of Jehovah's Witnesses:

> Because the God of this world is not Jehovah, this is not a happy world, reeking with disillusionment and bitterness, permeated with hatred and jealousy, saturated with disappointment and heartache. But, true to his promise, Jehovah has taken a people out of this wretched world—a people for his name—Jehovah's witnesses. And because they have accepted Jehovah as their God, these people are happy—truly happy. They enjoy peace of mind, receive rich blessings continually from the hand of their God and look to the future with anticipation.
>
> We would like you to meet the Spencer family—a happy, theocratic family.
>
> First, there's Brother Spencer. Bill Spencer. Bill is a friendly fellow, and he knows the importance of there always being a warm, friendly atmosphere around the home. "After all," he says, "what's a home, if it isn't friendly?" Bill has enthusiasm too. Especially when it comes to Kingdom activity. In fact, it's his enthusiasm that helps keep the family so active and alive. He knows this is his Scriptural obligation.
>
> Next, we'd like to have you meet Gladys, his wife. Nice woman, Gladys. Works hard, like a theocratic wife should. Bill takes the lead; she follows. The more you get to know these two and the way they work together so beautifully, the better you like them. Gladys is one who has always had dreams about the future. You know how most women are: A home in the country, a little garden, two or three children running around the place and all that. Funny thing about those dreams, though. Since coming into the truth, all of a sudden they're not important any more. Oh, she thinks about the new world all right. Guess we all do. But she realizes she has a job to do now, and she enjoys every minute of it.
>
> And one of her big jobs is helping train their son, Jimmy. There he is now. He causes them a few anxieties now and then, but generally speaking, he's a good boy.
>
> They have overcome their problems—by following the advice of the Scriptures and Jehovah's organization.

[Scene I of the play has Bill and Jimmy and Gladys sitting at the breakfast table, discussing a Bible text (Jimmy: "We speak the truth to the people. The religious leaders tell lies to the people in church") and reviewing, from the *Yearbook*, the work of the Witnesses in the Philippine Islands. In Scene II they all go out preaching from door to door together; and before they go together to a meeting at the Kingdom Hall, Jimmy sets the table for the meal his mother has cooked, in a "spirit of joyful cooperation," and they discuss their morning's preaching activities. There then follows a monologue by Bill Spencer, discussing the nature of his happiness.]

> The holy God expresses his purpose for good toward his servants by providing them with opportunities to experience progressive states of happiness from one period of joyful existence to another.
>
> How true that is. Since knowing Jehovah it has been just one progressive state of happiness after another.
>
> Before knowing Jehovah our happiness depended on things that might not last until tomorrow. *And we never were really happy*. We were always hoping for something better. And if we found that what we hoped in wasn't going to come, everything seemed so useless.

[Bill explains that before his conversion, he had looked forward to "getting a job as a doctor at the Glenwood Hospital out on Long Island." There were no openings at Glenwood. So, showing, it would seem to the ungodly eye, a remarkable lack of enterprise and imagination, Gladys and Bill did office work ("And I had worked so hard to learn the medical profession!") while the bills piled up and they quarrelled, and little Jimmy, a fifth-grader, threw his clothes on the floor and neglected to learn how to read, and they were altogether miserable. Then a Witness came to call. Bill studied the Bible with him. Gladys wasn't having any. Jimmy continued to throw his clothes on the floor and to forget how to spell his name. In Scene III, Bill offers his woes to his Bible instructor. The Witness tells him how to deal with the recalcitrant Gladys and the delinquent Jimmy.]

> Well, I wouldn't try to force her into anything, Bill. If you see that you're getting nowhere by trying to reason with her, then don't try. There have been many cases like yours. The Apostle Paul even wrote about split families like that. But he advised that you should just continue to fulfil your marriage obligations and that perhaps in time, with love and consideration and tact, you may win over your mate to the truth. So I'd say, just be a good husband to her and let her see that this message has done something for you, has given you a hope, something to live for, and she may wonder about it in time and want to know more about it.
>
> Show love to your son; instead of hitting him or hollering at him, take him aside and kindly explain to him what he should do and why; there should be some improvement. And also bring God into the picture and tell him what God requires of little boys and what they will receive if they are good.

[Bill decides to give up his career—"my doctor's profession"—because "there are higher principles in life." He begins "to exercise Christian principles in the home, . . . Christian love toward

Gladys" (who has not been consulted about his "doctor's profession") "and Jimmy. After a while they begin to notice this and it begins to have its effects." Bill is happy. Jimmy wants to live in the New World, so he learns to read and picks his clothes up off the floor. Bill buys his wife a mixer, and his kindness inspires her to ask him about his new-found religion. She likes what she hears and decides she wants to live in the New World too. Jimmy sets the table instead of sassing.]

> Bill: So Jehovah provided me with another source of happiness. Then it was like learning the truth all over again. But this time it was even more thrilling than before. I was giving to someone else—Gladys. My wife. It made me happier than words can express. We studied hard. The more Gladys learned, the more she wanted to learn. Then we began teaching Jimmy, too. We began attending meetings together. All three of us. This was real progress. And then we even began going out in the service together. In only a few months we developed into a real happy, theocratic family.
>
> We were serving Jehovah. We even got rid of all our bills, without the doctor's profession. . . . I never knew that one person could experience so much happiness. . . . "Happiness is the people whose god is Jehovah."

And we never were really happy. The man, no longer a Witness, who wrote this idyll was married to a Witness for three years before he could tell his wife that he was gravely troubled by profound doubts. When he admitted to doubt (he felt he was putting his life in her hands), her response, unanticipated, incredible to him, was that she herself had not believed for two of the three years they had lived together; her faith was a dry husk. During those years of doubt—of torment (the fact that the pap they listened to was corny, tacky, does not lessen the authenticity of their suffering)—they had been in the full-time ministry, living a Gladys/Bill exemplary life; and they were unable to share their core feelings with each other. They divorced their feelings from their actions, and their marriage was a charade. They were strangers afraid of damaging each other. They were each other's "examples." Sex was lousy. They spent their honeymoon playing draughts, and things never progressed much beyond that point. Each assumed the other to be frigid.

Pain is multiplied when one member of a marriage is not a Witness. Because women outnumber men among the Witnesses, the likelihood is that the unbelieving mate will be the husband. The believing woman is told that she may be the instrument of her husband's salvation. This places an intolerable burden upon her: She cannot but feel superior to the man who is scheduled for destruction, while at the same time she must act as if the man who despises or is indifferent to her beloved Jehovah is, by Divine arrangement, the head of her household. She is constrained from leaving her mate, even if he is abusive; she is, in effect, the caretaker of his soul.

A woman asking whether she might justifiably secure a legal separation from a husband who beat her was told, in the columns of *The Watchtower* (May 1, 1975), of another Witness whose alcoholic husband abused her—beat her, slapped her, kicked and punched her—for twenty years: "The Bible's truth enabled her to endure and to be a happy Christian." This happy Christian had frequently to barricade the entrance of her barn, cowering with her eleven children, when her husband arrived with blood lust in an alcoholic rage. After twenty years of this, her husband, according to *The Watchtower*, quit drinking, "improved in controlling his temper," and began to accompany her to meetings. "Marriage mates should strive to remain together despite marital problems resulting from human imperfection." [*TW*, May 1, 1975, pp. 286–87]

Can a woman live like this with any degree of self-respect? Women live with men they hate. Because there is no comfort for them anywhere else—so they have been told, by their mentors, whom they do respect—they become increasingly dependent upon the Watchtower Society. They are God's foundlings, turning to "His organization" for the warmth and support the Watchtower Society has assured them is available nowhere else.

Opposition from their mates allows women to feel martyred and to gain status within the organization. Their increased worth within the organization compensates for their domestic suffering.

I think of the years I spent feeling contemptuous of my dear father, of his impotence in the face of the contempt of his wife and daughter. He was our head, our master, we were told, in all things but worship. But our whole life was worship! His nominal "headship" was as empty as our treacly declarations of submission. My beautifully gregarious father could have no friends of his own in our house: they drank and made dirty talk and defiled. *Our* friends were always there, at his table, in his living room, preaching at him or indifferent toward him, glaring at him when he helped himself to food, a small revenge, as we were saying grace. His presence was tolerated.

He argued pugnaciously with the Witnesses, who provoked him to impotent rage by fielding all his questions with rote reiteration of Bible texts; his rage increased geometrically as they refused to be provoked to answering rage, never sacrificing their studied demeanour to the urgency of passion or of anger. My father thought that was inhuman; "Stone-wall Jehovahs," he called them. "Your God is no better than Hitler," he said. "The whole world is a concentration camp—everybody's going to the ovens but you." "We love you," they replied. "We want to help you." But their love was for my mother; she grew sleek and beautiful with it, while my father raged.

My father once wanted to take me to the country for a weekend; and I—wretched child that I was—refused to go unless I could take my Watchtower study books with me. We were both adamant; neither of us would yield. My brother tells me how my father spent that weekend: driving wildly, blindly along mountain roads, courting his own destruction. I had won.

One Christmas Eve, when I was alone with my father, who was drinking dully, steadily, there was a poltergeist phenomenon in our kitchen—cups and saucers and plates and pots spun wildly around and settled with a thunderous crash while he went on drinking. It was as if the universe had wheeled drunkenly in protest and settled at his feet. (I do not think I am imagining this. I think I had an awful hunger for my father's love.)

My mother was my "sister" in the faith—and God's surrogate. How she wanted and needed a perfect, "theocratic" child. So often I displeased her. Days of heavy silence were her reproach. In her silence and mine she wrote letters to me, when we lived together, and posted them, and handed them to me when the mailman came, her face averted from my gaze. They were the words she could not say. (Now we have no more words.) And we were rivals for the love of God, and allies against my father. And rivals for the love of men. Every man who came to see me was seduced by my mother's lofty spirituality, by the faint fragrance of suffering and martyrdom that accompanied her. I was imperfect, available flesh; she, removed from the arena of sexuality, was pure, untouchable spirituality. It was never any contest. (All this my father watched.) I admired her, I envied her, I was jealous of her—my mother, my sister (we are each other's failures). I have wanted so often to tell her I love her; the words are locked in my throat. I lack charity. I have wanted to hear her say she is sorry (for our loss, our defeat, for failing me). I have wanted to tell her I am sorry (for our loss, our defeat, for failing her). But we have no more words.

I was over 30 before I felt I had any right to my father's love. He gave it freely when I asked; I had only to ask. When my father lay dying, we thought, of a massive coronary, I said, reaching down to touch his wired chest, "Daddy, I'm so glad the last years have made us friends." "We were always friends, Bobbie," he said. "It was just that we didn't always know it." I felt as if I had entered my childhood at last, reclaimed what I had wantonly thrown away. I had sacrificed him for God, stolen from him and from myself the best love I had to offer and to receive. My friendship with my father has been healing, redemptive; it has made me whole. He has forgiven me those sorry years. That amplitude of spirit humbles me.

At a convention of Witnesses, I watched a Bible "drama" that was meant to illustrate the danger of rebellion against Jehovah. The highlight of the production came when a small child, whose mother and father had been among 14,700 Israelites destroyed by Jehovah for insurrection against Moses, sobbed wildly for his dead parents: "Oh, Mommy, oh, Daddy, why did you do it? Why did you sin against Jehovah?" A voice from the wings thundered: "Don't cry, my dear, though your heart is breaking. . . . We must not mourn for those who are punished. We must not cry for those Jehovah kills." That drew ecstatic applause.

As I left the convention grounds, feeling pity and anger, and remorse, I ran into a free-lance photographer whose extraordinarily beautiful and gentle face invited confidence. "They're telling people to rejoice in the destruction of their own families!" I said to him. But it turned out that he, a former acid-head from a poor Cuban family, was, although "not a baptized Christian," studying the Bible with the Witnesses. "I don't know," he said. "The world is so bad. . . . If I didn't have this, what's my purpose in life? What am I doing with my life? The world is full of such bad things. Corruption and all. People aren't kind. . . . The Witnesses made me give up my beard. I liked my beard, but the elders told me it was wrong, and I figured, Christ gave his life up for people he didn't even know, so what's a beard?"

"But how do you feel when you know old friends of yours, maybe even members of your family, are going to be destroyed at Armageddon?" I asked this sweet, shy man. In a dead voice, he gave me the history of the world—Adam and Eve, the ransom, the signs foretelling the end of the world. His face had nothing to do with his words. His face was creased and earnest with suffering. "No," I said. "Please tell me what you *feel.*" "Well," he said, "I try not to think about it too much. Well, really . . . sometimes I think . . . other people are human beings too. I guess I feel some pain. I'm struggling to accept it. . . . It'll be nice when the earth is clean, when there isn't any more death and suffering. Jesus was kind . . . I try to think that even though certain people I love are going to perish, I have to be happy because God says I should. Though sometimes, like when we have family gatherings, and I have so much fun, you know . . . I think . . . well, it hurts. I think about it a lot. Like, my mother . . ." And he began to cry.

IV

Accumulating Wealth While the World Refuses to Die

I sought a prophet and I found a businessman! Instead of a humble seeker after truth, I found the cleverest propagandist of the age, a man before whom Mary Baker Eddy, Madame Blavatsky, . . . and Joseph Smith pale into puerile ineffectiveness. . . . I found not a blazing zealot . . . . but a shrewd old man . . . When it comes to raising money, most pastors, board secretaries and financial representatives of benevolent causes can sit at Russell's feet—William T. Ellis, *The Continent* (National Presbyterian Weekly), week of Sept. 30, 1912.

We have no church organization in the ordinary sense of the word, no bondage of any kind, no obligation to pay, either to the parent society or anybody else, either ten per cent or any sum. . . . No solicitations for money in any way are authorized by this Society; . . . every amount, therefore, that has come into our hands, and been used, has been a voluntary donation from a willing heart. . . . One million dollars have been spent in the service of present truth this year.—Charles Taze Russell, 1914 Annual Report, *The Watch Tower*, December 1, 1914, Vol. XXXV, No. 24, p. 5591 (371–72).

It is not uncommon to find a charismatic leader being sued for sexual, financial, or legal breaches which he feels are his due right as a superior being.—E. Mansell Pattison, "Faith Healing and Glossalia," Z&L, p. 432.

In 1911, the market price for wheat was 59 cents to $1 a bushel. In Charles Taze Russell's Hicks Street Tabernacle, "miracle wheat" was being sold for $60 a bushel, or $1 a pound.

In 1904, K. B. Stoner, a 70-year-old veteran of the Confederate Army, farming in Fincastle, Virginia, discovered an unusual strain of wheat growing in a little garden patch behind his house. Stoner's experimentations led him to the conclusion that the uncommonly heavy wheat, when planted thinly, in Virginia soil, yielded as much as 1½ to 2 times as much grain as ordinary wheat. It was bruited about that the "miracle wheat" had appeared in Stoner's garden as a result of Stoner's asking the Lord for a miracle. Stoner later laconically denied that he and the Lord were in collusion to increase the yield of grain.

Stoner sold his wheat for $5 a bushel—five times the market price of regular wheat.

Russell's Tabernacle sold "miracle wheat" for $55 more a bushel than Stoner.

The "miracle wheat" came into the hands of the Watch Tower Society when the president of the United Cemeteries Corporation of Pittsburgh gave J. A. Bohnet, a director of the Watch Tower Bible and Tract Society, "permission" to plant the Stoner wheat on his land and expressed his willingness to donate the crop to the Watch Tower Society. Inasmuch as the United Cemeteries Corporation—of which Russell was a trustee—was later found to be a dummy corporation for Watch Tower assets, this was hardly an act of disinterested charity. It was a very carefully nurtured "miracle" indeed.

The *Brooklyn Eagle* charged Russell with exploitation, taking raucous delight in his "bunco game." The *Eagle's* investigative reporters' diligence led to an examination of the $60-a-bushel wheat by the Department of Postal Inspection, the Polytechnic Institute, and the Department of Agriculture. The consensus of chemical analysts was that the Stoner-brand "miracle wheat" was better than some and not so good as others. An official of the Department of Agriculture, in a letter published by the *Rural New Yorker*, declared that the "miracle wheat" did not merit the extravagant claims made for it.

Tests showed, in fact, that Fultz wheat—which was selling for $1 a bushel—yielded, under ordinary circumstances, twice as much as the $60 miracle wheat: Fultz seed yielded 66 bushels to Stoner's 33.

Russell once again sang his persecution song: The pastors of the city are jealous of me, he said. "Other people than my own," said Russell, "wouldn't believe that this wheat contains extraordinary qualities. It is too much of a miracle for them to comprehend." Russell cited the prophet Ezekiel—"I will call for corn and increase it"—and delivered himself of the opinion that the "miracle wheat" was "a sign" that the Lord was fulfilling the prophecy that the desert would bloom like a rose. Directors of the Watch Tower Society, possibly with a view to litigious trouble ahead, sought to temper Russell's extravagant claims. The original advertisement in *The Watch Tower* had stated that the yield of "miracle wheat" ought to be from 10 to 15 times that of ordinary wheat; but one "Brother" Dockey informed an *Eagle* reporter that "no guarantee is offered that 'miracle wheat' possesses powers of extraordinary yield." As things heated up and the *Eagle* continued, scarcely containing its glee, to deride Russell (who very carefully allowed his fellow directors to act as agents for the sale of the wheat, promoting the picture of himself as an objective, non-profit-making observer of God's bounty), Watch Tower spokesmen issued slithery disclaimers: "The advertisement in *The Watch Tower* does not say that miracle wheat is worth $1 a pound," said the general counsel for the Watch Tower Society. "It says simply that Brother Bohnet is willing to sell it at that price. It is purely a donation sale, for the benefit of the society."

On September 23, 1912, the *Eagle* ran a cartoon called "Easy Money Puzzle." It showed a fat gilded banker standing on the steps of the "Onion Bank" calling to a sinister, sloppy pedlar with a top hat and a scraggly beard sneakily carrying off a parcel of loot. "You're wasting your time," the banker said. "Come on in here!" The cartoon's caption read, "If Pastor Russell can get a dollar a pound for Miracle Wheat, what could he get for Miracle stocks and bonds in the old Union Bank?" (The Union—"Onion"—bank was liquidated in 1912; the bank was unable to pay more than half of what it had held in trust for its depositors. The *Eagle* had been in large measure responsible for the exposure of "ill-smelling" securities which led to the bank's downfall.)

Russell sued the *Eagle* for libel, demanding $100,000 in damages for "injury to his reputation, good name, fame and standing."

The *Eagle*'s defence was that the sale of "miracle wheat" was a scheme intended to benefit the Watch Tower Bible and Tract Society, of which Pastor Russell had complete control, and that its articles and cartoons were justified by the facts: "The plaintiff has held himself out to be a teacher of other people, a public leader, and the public press has a right to criticize him or his doctrines."

The case was brought before Justice Charles H. Kelby and a jury in the Kings County Supreme Court.

Several farmers testified—their testimony avidly received by Russell's followers, who jammed the courtroom—that "miracle wheat" produced up to twice the yield of ordinary wheat when planted thin.

It was thin testimony, and skimpy cause for rejoicing. The *Eagle*, in its defence, called a government agronomist, who testified that the Department of Agriculture had tested "miracle wheat" under carefully checked conditions and found it to be a good-yielding wheat, but no better than other varieties. In competitive testing, he said—bolstering his testimony with certified copies of the public records of the Department of Agriculture—it had ranked eighteenth in one test, tenth in another, and third in a test when it was thinly sown.

There were several bizarre aspects to the trial. One amusing grace note was that Russell's vanity prompted him to have his attorney protest that Russell's beard was not, as in the cartoon, scraggly at all, but kempt. Russell's doctrines—held, by the Court, to be relevant to the libel—were held up for ridicule. One dogma, in particular, brought delight to the pastor's antagonists. This was the

Pastor's conceit that "old worthies" such as King David, Moses, Solomon, *et al.*, were due for resurrection before 1914 to rule as princes in the earth. One of the juicier allegations made against the Watch Tower Society was that it had coerced an insane man, Hope Hay, into contributing $10,000 to its funds. William E. Van Amburgh, secretary-treasurer of the Watch Tower Society, acknowledged that Mr. Hay was in an "insane asylum" and that the Watch Tower Society was footing his bills, but denied that Mr. Hay had not given his money of his own free will.

Russell did not take the stand; he conveyed all his messages through attorney J. F. Rutherford (who was to become the second president of the Watch Tower Bible and Tract Society, after Russell's death). "What the character of the plaintiff is," the *Eagle*'s attorney told the jury, "you can infer from the fact that he did not take the witness stand and let you look in his eyes as he told of his past life. He did not give you and me the chance to question him as to . . . why he left Pittsburgh, why he came here, and what he intends to do when he leaves here."

The burden of Justice Kelby's charge to the jury was that as a matter of law, the cartoon was libellous in itself unless justified by the evidence. The burden of proof, Kelby charged, was upon the *Eagle*: "Truth is always a defence in a libel suit, but the defendant must prove the truth is as broad as the charge."

The jury of twelve men was out for less than forty-five minutes before it returned a verdict of not guilty in the *Eagle's* favour.

The evidence that weighed most heavily with the jury was that of Mr. Van Amburgh.

The Watch Tower Society has, from time to time, advised "children of light" to act as cunningly as serpents when they deal with "children of darkness." Van Amburgh was a singularly unwily serpent; every time he opened his mouth, the *Eagle*'s attorneys milked him of information that destroyed the credibility of Russell's organization. Every word he said contributed to the jury's impression that the Watch Tower Society was a sophisticated financial corporation masquerading as primitive Christianity on a non-profit-making crusade.

It is not surprising that although Russell's attorneys pleaded that a finding in favour of the *Eagle* would be tantamount to calling a simple man of God "a crook," the finding went against Russell. He had been "smitten," he said, like Our Lord and like St. Paul. "I, like them," he proclaimed, "have been refused the law's protection. I murmur not."

Indeed he did not murmur. He bellowed and bawled and contrived to turn his disgrace to his advantage. Maintaining the pose of injured innocence, he said, flatly, that he had had "nothing whatever to do" with "miracle wheat." It seems unbelievable that his followers should have swallowed that: but Russell took care to frost his bald statement with the anticlerical declarations they loved: The *Eagle*, he said, had in reality been "the champion of certain clerical enemies of mine."

"Presumably because there were seven Catholics on the jury," Russell said, "the *Eagle*'s attorney was prompted to refer to the Sisters of Charity and their noble work as nurses without referring to the fact that those nurses are well paid and that the hospitals, in large measure, are supported by state taxation." Russell's organization was pure, according to his arguments—which also took into consideration the Church's wealth—precisely because it did *not* engage in acts of charity; the Church, he implied, used charity as a cover for sneaky thievery.

Nor did the Protestants escape: For defending the *Eagle*, he said, "the Protestants on the jury were led to hope for escape from eternal torment through the 'pearly gates of heaven,' welcomed with the words, 'Well done,' for giving the *Eagle* the verdict. Neither I nor my attorneys could offer such inducements conscientiously."

"I am the more encouraged," said the man who implied that Protestants on the jury had voted against him because of the *Eagle*'s attorneys' enticing them with the promise of entry into the "pearly gates of heaven," "because I realize that the great Day of Blessing, the great Thousand Year of Messiah's Kingdom, is near at hand, is dawning now. Soon Satan, the 'Prince of Darkness,' will be bound. . . . No longer will darkness be permitted to masquerade as light, and the light be slandered as darkness."

The Witnesses view organized charity as a scheme to draw men's attention away from the salvation that lies only in the coming Kingdom of God; they are self-congratulatory because they are not engaged in charity as normally (but not necessarily legally) defined. Witnesses are taught to believe that all forms of charity are corrupt (charities line the pockets of bureaucrats or the clergy) and redundant (God, not the American Cancer Society, will cure cancer).

The Watchtower Society comes to the aid of congregations that have been struck by natural calamities—earthquakes, hurricanes, floods; it is not, however, in favour of "promiscuous charity."

The Witnesses pride themselves on not gathering in "rice Christians." To be a relief recipient one must have impeccable credentials as a Witness. In the United States and overseas, the Watchtower Society has no funds for hospitals, shelters, clinics, or rehabilitation services. The deserving poor get fed. Years after I ceased being a Witness, I lived, for eight years, in India and in

Guatemala. I was overwhelmed by the beauty and generosity of Mother Teresa in Calcutta—to her, all the dying belong to God—and by the untiring efforts of Maryknoll priests and nuns to keep babies from dying of roundworms; I was in awe of priests and missionaries, who, unheralded, in isolated poverty holes, kept people alive, regardless of their religious beliefs.

I have a clear memory (which, unfortunately, I cannot document) of the excommunication of two Witness missionaries, in the late 1940s, who had taken it upon themselves, without a directive from the Watchtower Society, to introduce to starving agrarian workers in South-east Asia better ways of growing rice. Their actions were construed as a dereliction of duty—their duty was to preach the gospel. The Witnesses have consistently taken the position that the greatest act of charity is the preaching of the gospel; they have no mandate to engage in "social reform."

Through individual acts of charity, Witnesses sometimes proffer assistance to members of the congregation who are in financial need. Because the Watchtower Society itself sets aside no funds for charity, giving is spontaneous and always the responsibility of the individual. It is truly impressive to watch the Witnesses come to the aid of a member of "the family" who is in need. Sick or elderly Witnesses get their shopping and cooking done for them. The Witnesses put themselves at one another's service (and place themselves in one another's debt). Whatever skills they have, they use to one another's advantage.

But some people get more help than others. A subtle caste system obtains. It is human to wish to select one's own company. But, taught to love one another diffusely, the Witnesses cannot consciously admit that they find some of their brothers and sisters more attractive than others. So they judge people on the basis of how "theocratic"—how active and effective in the field ministry—they are. And they tend to exclude those who seem slightly "off."

One disaffected ex-Witness describes the mechanism of this rejection and discrimination:

> There was an old lady with horrible garlic breath and a retarded son. The Witnesses avoided her. But since they were taught that we are all equal in God's sight, and equally lovable, they couldn't take the responsibility for disliking her. They'd say, "What will people of goodwill think about her? She'll turn people away from The Truth." So they felt justified in ignoring her. She was poor and unattractive, and she had an even more grossly unattractive son. She had a dogged determination to be a Witness, but an imperfect grasp of Witness theology. It was a deadly combination.

When I lived at Bethel, I saw, or heard of, these failures of charity.

A young woman who had been a full-time field worker (a "pioneer") came to Bethel headquarters after her husband had died of a sudden heart attack and her son had, accidentally it was supposed, hanged himself. She was put to work in the laundry room, operating a giant press. She was a perpetually smiling, sweet, singularly unassertive woman who seemed to have put her personal tragedies behind her. One day, her glasses slipped off and were smashed in the press. She began to howl and scream and cry that immemorial cry—"Why *me*?" Her roommate reported that she cried "Why me?" in her sleep. She was judged unstable. She was given a Greyhound ticket to her parents' home in the North-west.

An old man, who had been at Bethel for thirty years, grew senile. His senility took the form of his muttering obscenities at the dining-room table. He was given two "warnings," which his hardened arteries obviously couldn't assimilate, and then ordered to leave. He had no resources, financial or emotional. He was last seen begging in downtown Brooklyn.

In both these cases two factors are at work: The Watchtower Society has no charitable institutions to handle emotionally disturbed or mentally ill persons; and disturbance and illness are seen as evidence of the Lord's displeasure. There is no place for people in trouble to go.

Needless to say, Jehovah's Witnesses have no lock on arbitrariness, arrogance, or unkindness. Every religious order has its horror stories. But because there is no institutionalized charity among the Witnesses, giving is individual, and not giving may be justified on theological grounds. (I am blurring definitions purposefully: I mean *giving* in the sense of spontaneous goodness, Christian love; and I mean *giving* financially. The two are not unrelated.) Misfits, the unattractive, the aberrant can be regarded as waste products of the Devil's world, not as fellow sufferers.

The final smash had not come, as predicted, in 1914.

In 1890, there were, according to the Witnesses' estimates, 400 "Bible Students." By 1914, according to an estimate of the *National Cyclopaedia of American Biography,* there were 50,000 Russellites. In 1976, according to the Witnesses' *Yearbook*, there were 2,248,390 Witnesses in 210 countries. In 1976 alone, 196,656 new Witnesses symbolized their dedication by water baptism. [*Yearbook,* 1977, pp. 30–31] In addition to growing in number, the Witnesses have managed, in the intervening years, to amass millions of dollars' worth of real estate.

Russell's early world tours served to convince him that there was no market for his message in the "Papal countries." He expressed most hope for Nordic and/or WASP countries like Norway, Switzerland, England, Ireland, Scotland. Perhaps he was seeing with the eye of the tourist who is drawn to the "clean," non-exotic lands. As it happens, there are now, by latest count, 102,044 active Witnesses in West Germany and over 114,029 in Nigeria. [*Yearbook,* 1977, pp. 26, 28: Figures for 1976 Peak Publishers]

The Watchtower Society, in November, 1975, had thirty-seven printeries—in Australia, Brazil, Canada, England, Finland, France, Germany, Ghana, Japan, Nigeria, the Philippines, South Africa, Sweden, Switzerland, the United States.

Every two weeks, an average printing of 8,700,000 copies of *The Watchtower* magazine (in 79 languages) rolls off the 64 rotary presses contained in all those factories—an abundance that Russell, whose first edition of *Zion's Watch Tower* had a printing of 6,000 copies, could hardly have foreseen. From these factories comes the book the Watchtower Society claims has outsold all other books written in the 20th century. *The Truth That Leads to Everlasting Life* (1968), a 190-page hardbound book that sells for 25 cents a copy, has sold 74,000,000 copies in 91 languages. [*Yearbook,* 1975, p. 240] In Brooklyn alone, where the bulk of Watchtower property is located, 100,000 books and 800,000 magazines are printed daily. From these presses also comes *Awake!* (a kind of spiritually flavoured *Reader's Digest*), a 32-page semi-monthly published in 39 languages, with an average printing of 7,500,000. Until very recently, the publishers of *Awake!* blurbed it as a magazine with "no fetters . . . It features penetrating articles on social conditions. . . . *Awake!* pledges itself to . . . exposing hidden foes and subtle dangers." Featured articles in 1973 issues of the magazine that "recognizes facts, faces facts, is free to publish facts" were "Snail Fever—Slow Death for Millions"; "My Life as a Gypsy"; "Bamboo—Asia's Towering Grass"; "Twilight Years Can Be Useful Years".

In the United States, in addition to an office building in Pittsburgh, Pennsylvania, the Society owns factory buildings, interconnected by bridges spanning the streets, covering four city blocks in Brooklyn, at the foot of the Brooklyn Bridge—close to 1,265,000 square feet of highly desirable urban property.

The spanking-clean, beige-and-green Watchtower factories dominate the urban landscape at the foot of the Brooklyn and Manhattan bridges. The flashing electric signs that used to advertise Squibb pharmaceutical products now ask us to READ THE BIBLE GOD'S HOLY WORD DAILY. READ THE WATCHTOWER ANNOUNCING GOD'S KINGDOM.

Many factory operations are technologically sophisticated; many others, which in commercial plants might be mechanized or computerized, are designed to require manual labour. This makes economic sense, because Witness labour is so cheap. All members of the Bethel headquarters "family"—editorial and administrative staff as well as factory workers—receive the same small monthly stipend.

The Watchtower Society operates a small fruit farm in Washington, New Jersey, and a grain farm in South Lansing, New York.

A 1,698-acre farm near Newburgh, new York, provides food for the 1,400 headquarters workers.

Wheat, sweetcorn, oats, lettuce, tomatoes, squash, potatoes, onions, turnips, spinach, beets, kale, beans, carrots, apples, peaches, pears, strawberries, blackberries grow on this mini-conglomerate. And there are herds of beef cattle—about 800 head of Hereford, Angus, and Charolais—and dairy cattle; and pigs, and thousands of chickens bred for eating and thousands of Leghorns that lay close on 3,000 eggs a day. Beef is dressed here, bacon smoked, pig jowls are steamed in enormous kettles to be used as liverwurst. Fruit is frozen, canned, preserved; relishes, sauerkraut and horseradish are prepared; from the 420 gallons of milk produced each day, the Watchtower Society manufactures butter, ice cream, cheese—Swiss, Cheddar, Monterey, and Limburger. Everything the self-sustaining headquarters workers consume comes from Watchtower Farm, according to George Couch, the manager—with the exception of fish, condiments, spices, and some flour. The farm, one observer commented, "Exemplifies communal agriculture refined by technological sophistication . . . with the aid of machines, 92 cows are milked in two hours, but pears are still peeled by hand." [*The New York Times,* Jan. 2, 1973]

It takes, Couch told a *Times* reporter, 1,000 pounds of beef for a rib-roast meal, 60 pigs for a pork-chop meal. The meals are hearty, nutritionally balanced, and, on the whole, better than one would expect institutional food to be.

Five hundred workers live in dormitory residences on Watchtower Farm, which also accommodates two factories that provide 400,000 square feet of floor space.

These are the arterial properties. The heart of the religious body is in Brooklyn Heights—a lovely residential area. The Watchtower Society's headquarters staff has grown from 355 men and women in 1950, to 607 in 1960, to 1,449 (approximately 200 of whom are women) in 1970, and its property holdings have grown commensurately. The Society has bought and built to provide offices and residences for factory workers and editorial and administrative staff and to accommodate the missionary school of Gilead, which, as part of a thrust toward centralization, was shifted, in the 1960s, from South Lansing, New York. The Watchtower community (or commune) in Brooklyn Heights is served by its own carpentry shop, laundry, tailor shop, and bakery (approximately 25 chefs and assistants labour to prepare three meals a day for headquarters workers).

Since the "miracle wheat" scandal, the Watchtower Society has maintained a discreetly low financial profile. Federal courts have ruled that the Watchtower Bible and Tract Society, Inc. (New York corporation), and the Watch Tower Bible and Tract Society (Pennsylvania corporation) are entitled to exemption from the filing of income-tax returns under the Federal Internal Revenue Act because the Societies are charitable corporations engaged in religious activity. Similar rulings have been made in Britain and in Canada. The Watchtower Society has not, however, succeeded in silencing speculation about its method of acquiring properties and about the extent of its holdings. Financial reports are never published. Calls from reporters, researchers, state senators inquiring into the finances of the Society go unanswered. Outsiders would need a guided tour through the property holdings of the Society, and the Society provides no tour guides. The Society's attorneys—Koozman and Hartman of New York City—refuse to answer requests for information. The Society's bank of record, Chase Manhattan, likewise gives away no secrets. Rank-and-file Witnesses believe absolutely that the Society's stewardship is beyond reproach; they ask no questions. To question the Lord's "governing body," they are told, is to doubt the Lord Himself.

In order to arrive at some idea of the financial base of the Society's publishing operation, Cooper [Z&L, p. 717] made some calculations from a Society statistical report for November, 1968.

In November, 1968 (according to *Kingdom Ministry*, the Watchtower Society's monthly newsletter), 817,776 copies of *The Truth That Leads to Everlasting Life* were sold at 25 cents per copy. This "would amount," Cooper calculates, "to over two hundred thousand dollars ($204,444). Added to this would be the income from six million *weekly* copies of the bi-monthly magazines *Awake!* and *The Watchtower*, a monthly sum approximating one million two hundred thousand dollars, an equal amount resting in the hands of the 338,663 'publishers' who had 'placed' the magazines for ten cents a copy. On these two published items alone, the Society would well have grossed one million four hundred thousand dollars in one month."

Cooper was working with 1968 statistics for the United States alone. If we look at worldwide statistics for 1974, the suggested gross is larger: in 1974, according to the 1975 *Yearbook*, 27,581,852 bound books were distributed, and 273,238,018 magazines, in addition to 12,409,287 booklets.

Most of these publications were sold for a nominal amount; some were distributed free. The Society gives a 10- to 20-per-cent rebate on all literature sold by local congregations; Witnesses buy the literature they distribute for less than the "contribution" they solicit. They keep, on the average, 10 cents out of every $1 contribution they receive.

No money is ever solicited at meetings of Jehovah's Witnesses. There is, however, a "Contribution Box" in every Kingdom Hall. Local congregations buy, rent, renovate, or erect their meeting places, "Kingdom Halls," with their own funds; often free labour is provided by the Witnesses, who are proud that they do not have to borrow from worldly commercial organizations, but are able to use the funds set aside for the benefit of the chosen of Jehovah.

An idea of the magnitude of Watchtower operations is suggested by the fact that in 1971, according to the 1972 *Yearbook* (p. 255), $7,042,020.01 was contributed toward "expansion" and toward the care and feeding of foreign missionaries.

The public financial facts have not been sufficient to still conjectures in Brooklyn Heights, where the bulk of Watchtower property holdings is concentrated. The Society has been tangling with Heights residents since 1913.

In that year, angry residents of Brooklyn Heights hired a lawyer and brought Russell's financial officers before the City's Board of Tax Commissioners, demanding to know why properties held by the People's Pulpit Association and the Watch Tower Society should be tax-exempt. Treasurer Van Amburgh steered a course through the labyrinth of interlocking corporations and private individuals who held mortgages on property used by the Watch Tower Society, arguing that the properties were used solely and wholly for religious purposes. The Heights residents contended that all Watch Tower premises were used and occupied solely for business purposes and that the Watch Tower Society should be obliged to pay taxes on the property at 122–124 Columbia Heights (assessed, then, at $100,000) and on the Tabernacle at Hicks Street (assessed, in 1912, for $20,000). The ruling went against Russell (who was vacationing in Bermuda) and against the Watch Tower Society. The ruling, however, was overturned by the New York Supreme Court; and tax exemption was again affirmed in a 1915 ruling of the Appellate Division of the Supreme Court.

In 1971, real estate held in the name of the Watch Tower Bible and Tract Society in New York City was valued by the City Tax Commission at $14 million. The city ended the tax exemption the Society had enjoyed for most of its history under a 1971 law that permitted taxation of non-profit organizations that were "not organized or conducted exclusively for religious purposes." The State Legislature had permitted cities to restore to tax rolls all property except that "used exclusively for religious, charitable, hospital, educational, moral or mental improvement of men, women and children." Under protest, the Society paid $2 million to the city.

On July 11, 1974, in a unanimous opinion written by Associate Judge Hugh Jones, the Court of Appeals ruled that the Witnesses were "organized and conducted exclusively for religious purposes within the meaning of the statute." Tax exemption was ordered restored. "Administration of the religious organization of Jehovah's Witnesses," the Court ruled, "stems from the governing body at the international headquarters in Brooklyn, New York. The doctrines and beliefs of Jehovah's Witnesses are first promulgated by this governing body and then published either in *The Watchtower* or some of the other official publications of the society."

Early on the morning of Monday, November 18, 1974, a pipe-bomb explosion ripped open an iron gate and shattered windows in the Watchtower Society's printing complex. The police could suggest no motive for the crime. No one was willing to believe the bombing was a reaction to the Court's ruling; but the Heights' usually civic-minded residents, while deploring the violent act, exhibited no surge of neighbourly goodwill. A community leader expressed the majority sentiment:

"While they're smiling and peddling sweet salvation, they're acting like Godzilla, gobbling up property, evicting people as if we were squatters on land which will eventually belong to them anyhow—when Jehovah gets rid of us. They don't mug anybody, they maintain their property well . . . but they don't pay taxes, and they don't contribute to communal life. How can you preach everlasting life and at the same time not care about people who have lived here all their lives? There are 1500 Witnesses living among us in their headquarters buildings, but they might as well be surrounded by a moat. It's as if we were living with a mediaeval commune in our midst."

In the aftermath of the explosion, Jerry Molohan, the Society's public relations officer, said that the Witnesses did not work with community groups because "Witnesses stay out of political affairs. . . . They don't get involved in our activities, and we don't get involved in theirs." [*New York Post,* No. 19, 1974]

In 1969, according to deeds and tax-exemption records, the Watchtower Society owned, in addition to its printing complex, three prime residential blocks, from Orange Street to Clark Street, on Columbia Heights. According to a *Daily News* reporter, Sylvia Carter, "Residents suspect . . . that the Society has, in fact, bought up adjoining property in private names. [Max] Larson [overseer in charge of printing operations] says individual names are listed on property records so officials have someone to contact about a building. All buildings are legal Witnesses property, they insist. Property questioned by tenants could not be traced, through deeds and tax-exemption records, to the Watchtower Society. But several owner corporations for buildings in the area could not be located at addresses listed on city records." [*Daily News*, March 9, 1969]

Heights merchant and realtor Bernard Atkins, who papers the windows of his florist shop on Montague Street, the main shopping artery for Brooklyn Heights, with magic marker manifestoes about the state of the nation and of the world, said, in one of his weekly position papers, "The Jehovah's Witnesses . . . embark upon a programme of using their tax-free millions to swallow up building after building until they own a major portion of the Heights, a portion on which they pay almost no taxes and contribute nothing to the life of the community except for destroying lovely old brownstone houses and erecting ugly, modern structures." His wife, Charlotte Atkins, well known in the Heights for her support of community causes, was less formal and considerably more bitter. She suggests that the Watchtower Society "hits people with offers of cold cash . . . they're blockbusting, buying buildings for more than they're worth, making offers that can't be refused. They're eating us up in a silent, deathly way." Her wrath is compounded by the fact that a Watchtower proselytizer once told her husband, Bernard, "I see only death in your eyes." Charlotte Atkins, the kind of noisy busybody no neighbourhood can survive without, says, "Next to the Witnesses, Burger King and McDonald's and Kentucky Fried are aesthetic geniuses and angels of light." Charlotte's charge of blockbusting pressure tactics cannot be supported by the known facts, but her bitterness is shared by many merchants.

In recent years, most of the community's animosity has focused on the Watchtower Society's ownership of two properties: a rent-controlled apartment house at One Clark Street and the once-fashionable Towers Hotel at 25 Clark Street.

The Society bought One Clark Street in 1967. Proceeding under the 1969 rent regulations which permitted landlords to evict tenants when apartments were required for the landlord's use, the Society served eviction notices on the building's 42 middle-class families, many of whom were paying a monthly rent of only $150. The Society offered to pay relocation expenses required under law; but the tenants' response was "Where are we going to move *to*?" Many of the tenants—some of whom had children enrolled in local schools—felt that they were being pushed out of reasonable city housing into the suburbs by a vast, impersonal force. They grouped together to form the One Clark Street Tenants' Association.. At one point, three hundred residents of the Heights, most of them elderly women, staged a "flower promenade" protest against the evictions.

They carried daffodils.

Flower power proved unavailing. By 1971 only 12 of the original tenants remained—the rest had departed because of constant harassment, according to the testimony of one resident before the Brooklyn Supreme Court. Dr. Harlow Fischman, a biologist, testified that he had complained to city agencies and the Watchtower Society about loud noises, filth, and lack of services.

As tenants moved out, young male headquarters workers moved in, converting apartments into dorms. Doors of apartments undergoing conversion remained open, according to the tenants; the halls were liberally coated with plaster dust. From time to time there were electricity blackouts, the tenants alleged, and no heat or hot water. One young mother remarked, as she departed for the suburbs, "These are the people who are going to transform the earth into a paradise, right? So far they've succeeded in turning a lot of people—some of them old and sick—out of their apartments. They've transformed city families into suburban families."

To such charges, the Watchtower spokesmen replied that the Witnesses too were really one large family. "How many families," retorted one householder, "do you find who don't have the gas turned on or use a stove, who take ten baths at once so the ceiling leaks, who have their beds made and laundry done each day by a sort of central housekeeping service, or who conduct wrestling matches at midnight?" Most tenants of One Clark Street recited a ritualistic liberal litany: "The Witnesses are good people, they're dedicated to their faith, we don't oppose their religious views. We just don't think they're considering the moral rights of the tenants of the buildings they buy."

The remaining tenants won what community leaders regard as a pyrrhic victory: they secured in the courts the right to stay in their apartments until they chose to move of their own accord. Nothing in law obliged the Watchtower Society to keep the building on the rental market. "I feel as if I'm living on a movie set in my own apartment," one tenant said. "All these earnest young men with briefcases and crew cuts and white socks marching in and out of the halls. . . . My son said to me, 'Daddy, when are we going to live in a real house again?'"

Still smarting from what one tenant called "an invasion of people who think *we're* aliens," the residents of the Heights began again to organize when, in 1974—five years after a Watchtower spokesman assured the press that further expansion plans were not under "current consideration"—rumours began to circulate that the Witnesses were about to buy the sixteen-storey Towers Hotel. On August 10, 1974, 100 tenants of the 480-room hotel at 25 Clark Street, most of them middle-aged and elderly working people, were served eviction notices so that the owner-operator of the residential hotel could rent five additional floors to the Watchtower Society, which already occupied five floors of the shabby but still elegant hotel. Some of the tenants uneasily speculated that the management of the hotel wanted them out so that the property could be sold to the Watchtower Society. The Society's spokesman, Jerry Molohan, denied that the Witnesses were planning to buy the Towers. On November 19, 1974, he said, "I know of no plans to do so. What the future holds I don't know. At the moment it's the hotel's problem, not ours."

Early in 1975, the Watchtower Society bought the Towers Hotel.

It is a sign of the frightened times that contrapuntal voices are now being raised against the chorus of bitterness in Brooklyn Heights. It is still safe to say that most Heights residents deplore the Watchtower Society's tactics. Preservationists for whom the architectural integrity of the Heights is a passion react with snobbish venom to the Witnesses' version of architecture. Small merchants are resentful of a financially self-contained community in their midst. Workers deplore the Witnesses' use of non-union labour. People who are concerned with the flight of the middle class from the city—and those who are concerned with the old, sick and socially dislocated—are enraged. However, there are those who are now inclined to tolerate their massive presence. The Witnesses may wake them up on Sunday mornings with their less-than-glad tidings; but they are safe neighbours. The Witnesses are now seen, among many Heights residents, as "a buffer against decay."

The Witnesses are a bastion of law and order in Brooklyn Heights; they irritate people, but they are beginning less and less to frighten them. They commend themselves to the bewildered, terrified elderly residents of the Heights, and to large segments of the middle class, which is convinced of its impotence.

Under Russell's presidency each $10 contribution to the Watch Tower Bible and Tract Society of Pennsylvania (parent organization of New York's Watchtower Bible and Tract Society and the International Bible Students Association) represented one voting share. In 1917, the Society's second president, J. F. Rutherford, moved to democratize the organization—or at least to provide the "Bible Students" with some feeling that they had a voice in corporate proceedings. He wished, inasmuch as "many of the Lord's dear children are poor in . . . worldly goods," to avoid the suggestion that "lucre" was "speaking for the Lord"; he proposed that every ecclesia (congregation) hold a general meeting to "vote upon their choice for members of the Board of Directors and Officers of the Society." The vote would not constitute a legal election, but would be "advisory, or in the nature of instructions to the Shareholders as to what is the will of the church at large." [*The Watch Tower*, Nov. 1, 1917, pp. 330–32]

During the 1920s and '30s, it became apparent to Rutherford that organizational survival and expansion depended on centralization of all powers in the governing body. In 1932, "elective elders" were replaced in the congregations "by a group of mature brothers called a 'service committee,' who were elected by the congregation to assist the local service director appointed by the Society." [*Yearbook*, 1975, p. 165] Elections, however, led to divisiveness at a time when it was crucial, in view of external pressures, for the Society to maintain a united front. In 1938 voting powers were removed from local congregations; the power to appoint overseers and their assistants was delivered to the Society. This was an arrangement, according to A. H. Macmillan, that would "continue into the new world and for a thousand years of Christ's reign." [*Faith*, p. 159]

The Witnesses reckon that their organization began to be "strengthened in 1918." It took Solomon twenty years to build his empire, and it took them twenty years to build theirs: The "'twentieth year' ends with the beginning of the spring of 1938, and hence corresponds with the (lunar) year 1937 which ends in the spring of 1938. . . ." [*JWDP*, pp. 127–49] Some Witnesses were unable to swallow the analogy; in 1932 and in 1938 there were mass defections: "Those who opposed or resisted the theocratic arrangement," it was explained, "were not opposing or resisting men; they were striving against the spirit of God." [*Faith*, p. 157; see also *Yearbook*, 1975, pp. 164–249]

Under the leadership of Nathan H. Knorr, the organization was further "theocratized"—which is to say, centralized in a self-perpetuating rule.

There are no longer any stockholders in the Watch Tower Bible and Tract Society. In 1944, the Charter of the Society was amended; fixed membership was no longer contingent upon monetary contributions. Membership was limited to 500 men, "all chosen on the basis of their active service to God." Each corporation has a Board of Directors. In addition to these men, there is a central 18-man religious "governing body." The governing body, which meets weekly in Brooklyn, makes secular and religious decisions (the Witnesses, of course, would not recognize the distinction—the work of the governing body is, to them, by nature all spiritual), which are then implemented by the Boards of Directors. Membership in these bodies frequently overlaps.

In 1976, a further change was made in the structure of the governing body: "To facilitate its work, six committees of the Governing Body have been formed. Each will have its Chairman, who will serve for a period of one year. These Committees are supervisory in nature and it is not intended that they will handle all the details and routine work. The various corporations that have been serving the Kingdom interests so well until now will, of course, continue to fulfil their important role as legal agencies of Jehovah's Witnesses, their Governing Body and its committees.

"These six committees, which began functioning on January 1, 1976, are as follows: Service Committee; Writing Committee; Publishing Committee; Teaching Committee; Personnel Committee; Chairman's Committee." [*TW*, Feb. 1, 1976]

This splintering of responsibility gave rise to the conjecture that Knorr—who was then 71 and reputed to be in failing health—had lost his grip on the Society's affairs.

Nathan Homer Knorr, who was born in Bethlehem, Pennsylvania, on April 23, 1905, died of a cancerous tumour on June 8, 1977. He was 72; he had been president of the Watchtower Bible and Tract Society since January 13, 1942. Upon his death, Frederick W. Franz, who was 83 years old, became president of the Watchtower Society by unanimous vote of the Board of Directors.

Franz was born in Covington, Kentucky, in 1893 and terminated his studies at the University of Cincinnati to become a full-time preacher in 1914. A member of the headquarters staff since June 2, 1920, he became a director of the Pennsylvania corporation in 1943 and vice-president of the Watch Tower Bible and Tract Society of Pennsylvania in 1945; he became a director of the New York corporation in 1949.

Franz is a bachelor. He has taught himself several languages, including Hebrew and Greek, and is regarded by the Witnesses as their foremost Bible scholar.

I remember Franz as an ascetic, kindly man, with an engaging sense of humour and a gift for self-mockery. Much loved by the Witnesses, he is as unworldly as Knorr was businesslike. When I knew him, he was adorably sweet-spirited (though, from my point of view, maddeningly earnest when it came to dogma). A flamboyant orator, he was personally reticent, though not inaccessible. He seemed to have scant regard for his personal appearance; still slim and handsome in his 60s, he was as likely as not to be found shuffling around headquarters in bedroom slippers and mismatched socks. His minor, unselfconscious eccentricities of dress and demeanour, and a nature that was by turns reclusive and gregarious, endeared him to all of the headquarters staff.

Franz's great age has necessitated further changes in the Society's structure: each corporation now has not one but, for the first time in Watchtower history, two vice-presidents.

On the next rung of the hierarchical ladder, beneath the Society's officers, are supervisory officials known as district- and circuit-overseers. These men, frequently accompanied by their wives, visit each congregation twice a year, instructing congregational elders and accompanying Witnesses from door to door to help perfect their proselytizing techniques. They inspect and audit local finances, and they file with headquarters confidential progress reports on each congregation as well as a "Personal Qualifications Report" on elders and potential leaders.

Each congregation has a self-perpetuating, non-elected committee that makes recommendations to the Society for appointing overseers and "ministerial servants." All baptized men over 20 are considered for these positions. Meetings of the committee are characterized by a kind of Maoist self-criticism. Each year congregational elders rotate positions; no one enjoys the position of presiding overseer for an entire year.

The question of whether anyone is amassing personal wealth does not arise at the congregational level, where elders and overseers may be full-time preachers or have full- or part-time secular work, but receive no remuneration from the Society.

It doesn't arise at the circuit- or district-overseer level either. These men are given modest monthly allowances by the Society, which barely cover transportation costs. Within the Watchtower hierarchy, they come closest to being *servi servorum Dei*—servants of the servants of God. (The Witnesses refuse to apply the word *hierarchy* to themselves, reserving it as a pejorative term for the Catholic Church. They are all *brothers*.) The peripatetic life of these circuit and district emissaries is sometimes gruelling, and almost always destructive of marital privacy. They have no homes of their own; they are transients, living out of suitcases in homes of the local congregations they serve. Depending on the affluence of the territory assigned them, their accommodations may vary from a poolside villa in Southern California to a curtained-off alcove in an Appalachian shack with no plumbing. They are honoured guests wherever they stay; but in their role as spiritual exemplars, their public lives and their private lives meld, their private lives subsumed into their public lives.

Knorr lived, as do a handful of other high officials (and their wives), in a suite of rooms overlooking the East River. Other Bethelites—including married couples—live two to a pleasant room and share communal toilets and baths. Knorr, in a self-contained apartment, had a valet and ate meals prepared for him in his own kitchen. Certainly no more than one would expect from the leader of a 2-million-member sect, this was remarkable only in the face of his protestations that he enjoyed no extraordinary privileges, and the fact that the Witnesses chose to take him at his word.

We at Bethel used to point with pride to the fact that while missionaries of "false religion" travelled in first-class comfort to their assignments, our missionaries were sent third class and, like a religious Peace Corps, lived like the people among whom they served. It never occurred to us to worry that Knorr travelled first class. We were an adaptive group.

Time speaks softly of the dead. In the case of the Witnesses, it is often mute. During the 1940s and early '50s, when I was a Witness and a member of the headquarters staff, it was as if Charles Taze Russell had never existed. Any discussion of him was likely to be aborted with the phrase "We are not followers of any man." It was not until the mid and late '50s that edited accounts of Russell's life and activities began to appear in Watchtower histories. Merciful time (with help from revisionist historians) has blurred Russell's difficulties.

Though I became a Witness in 1944, two years after the death of Judge Joseph F. Rutherford, Russell's successor, I never heard of the scandal that had attached to him. When I was at Bethel, I heard murmurings, from those who had known him, that Rutherford had been a stern and intimidating man. But there was a general silence and lack of specificity. I never learned what longtime residents meant when they alluded to Rutherford's abrasiveness—or to traitors in their midst who had made devilish capital of it. What they had in mind, I now know, was the Moyle case—which has not yet been cosmeticized like the "miracle wheat" and the Jellyfish episodes. The Moyle Case has no place in the Society's official histories.

In 1943, Olin R. Moyle, who had been general counsel under Rutherford, brought a $100,000 libel suit against eleven leaders of the Society and against the Watchtower corporations. The Appellate Division upheld the verdict of the Brooklyn Supreme Court, modifying it to reduce damages from $30,000 to $15,000.

In 1934, Moyle had divested himself of his material possessions and given up a lucrative law practice to live at Bethel with his wife and son and to serve as the Society's general counsel, receiving, like all his fellow volunteers then, $10 a month for his services. Five years later, he wrote a private letter (dated July 21, 1939) to Judge Rutherford in which he charged Rutherford with encouraging lewdness and drunkenness; with being extraordinarily harsh to members of the Bethel staff who incurred his displeasure; and with living like a man of wealth:

"Shortly after coming to Bethel," Moyle wrote, "we were shocked to witness the spectacle of our brethren receiving a trimming from you. C. J. Woodworth got a tongue lashing and was humiliated and called a jackass for saying that it served the devil to continue the present-day calendar. Knorr and others were similarly treated.

Unfair reproaches have been given and your action violated freedom of speech. [You] called the . . . ushers who were at the Madison Square Garden convention sissies."

Earlier in 1939, rowdies who were presumed to be followers of Father Charles Coughlin, a dissident and anti-Semitic Catholic priest who was subsequently silenced, disrupted a rally in Madison Square Garden; Witnesses acting as ushers, armed with canes for the purpose of quelling interference, were arrested and charged with assault. Moyle defended the ushers, who were subsequently acquitted, in court.

> We publish that all in the Lord's organization are alike [Moyle wrote]. You know that this is not the case. Take for instance the difference between the accommodations furnished to you and your personal attendants compared to those furnished to some of the brethren. You have many homes—Bethel, Staten Island, California—and even at Kingdom Farm. I am informed one house has been kept for your sole use during the short periods you spend there. And what do the brethren at the farm receive? Small rooms, unheated through the bitter cold Winter; they live in their trunks, like campers.
>
> On the question of marriage of those who live at Bethel there is unequal and discriminatory treatment. One brother who left Bethel to get married was refused the privilege of pioneering [preaching full time] in New York as disapproval of his leaving Bethel. On the other hand, when Bonnie Boyd [J.F.R.'s confidential secretary] married she didn't leave Bethel and was permitted to bring in her husband in spite of the rule. . . .

With the letter of July 21, which he signed "Your brother in the King's service," Moyle tendered his resignation, to take effect September 1. Rutherford read the letter to the Bethel Family; he denounced Moyle when the 100-member staff was assembled for a meal in the Bethel dining room and ordered the Moyles to leave Bethel immediately. Moyle moved to Wisconsin. Following hard on his heels was one of Rutherford's "troubleshooters," Malcolm A. Howlett, a director of the Society. Howlett organized meetings for the purpose of telling Wisconsin Witnesses that Moyle had been excommunicated for "unfaithfulness to the organization." As a result, Moyle's attorney argued in court, Moyle was shunned by friends and clients and fellow Witnesses, and obliged to forsake his law practice. Subsequently, two articles in *The Watchtower* described Moyle as a "manpleaser," a "murmurer and complainer"; *Watchtower* articles accused him of not properly defending ushers who had been charged with assault at Madison Square Garden, and called him "a servant of the Evil One," a "Judas."

Moyle's attorney, Walter Bruchhausen, told Supreme Court Justice Henry L. Ughetta and a jury that Moyle had been "hounded, . . . libelled and pursued because he dared to disagree with the ruthless Rutherford."

One of the witnesses for the defence was William J. Heath, a director of the Society and the husband of Bonnie Boyd, a man who travelled extensively with Rutherford and was on close personal terms with him. Heath, who had been punched in the eye in the Madison Square Garden fracas, testified that he had been surprised when Moyle, acting as his attorney, fraternized amiably with the lawyer who was representing his assailant. Later, he said, he complained to Rutherford of Moyle's "strange conduct," and Rutherford put Heath's case in the hands of another lawyer. Rutherford, Heath said, was "always gracious and kindly."

Two witnesses for the defence, G. Paulos and C. Hilton Ellison, testified that they had turned against Moyle, their longtime friend, because of having read in *The Watchtower* that Moyle was unfaithful, "unscriptural." That their faith in *The Watchtower* was total was demonstrated when Moyle's attorney called Paulos' attention to two of its past issues. One, in 1938, had expounded the dogma that Christ died to save all mankind, and the second, in 1941, had declared that Christ had died to save "the obedient ones"—Jehovah's Witnesses. Paulos said he believed that Jehovah's Witnesses were the only earthly organization carrying on God's work, and that Rutherford was "God's representative": "I first learned in *The Watchtower* that certain people will not be benefited by Christ's sacrifice. I accepted the modern version." Paulos, who evidently regarded *The Watchtower* as incapable of error, said he had chosen not to investigate the truth of Moyle's charges. Ellison, whose testimony was crucial because he was taken to be representative of all of the Witnesses, testified that he accepted *The Watchtower* articles and Howlett's statements as undeniable truth. He testified that "evil servants" were those who, like Moyle, "with knowledge of the Truth leave the Society."

Hayden C. Covington, chief defence counsel, replied:

> This libel suit is brought against a religious group which covenanted to wholeheartedly serve God and go from house to house and preach the gospel, as Jesus Christ did. Judge Rutherford was not ruthless. He was a kindly man. . . . Mr. Moyle agreed, as do all others, to abide in Bethel forever or until death or the Lord removed him.
>
> He made vicious, scurrilous charges as a cover for his resignation, but there is no voluntary resignation in our organization. A resolution was properly adopted dismissing him. He criticized the family of God at Bethel, and it is true, as we have stated in *The Watchtower*, that he became a servant of the Evil One. He acted as Judas, and this $100,000 lawsuit is worth 30 pieces of silver. He has already been well paid by the Evil One.

Judge Ughetta, less metaphysically inclined than Covington,

awarded Moyle $30,000 in damages.

(Covington, an indisputably brilliant Constitutional lawyer who took First and Fourteenth Amendment cases to the United States Supreme Court for the Witnesses and won, and thus immeasurably protected us all, was later to leave Bethel himself. During the 1960s he acted, for a time, as Muhammad Ali's defence attorney in the fighter's draft case. Covington based his defence of Ali on the fact that Ali was a minister and therefore not subject to the draft—the same defence he had used successfully for thousands of draft-aged Witnesses. A spokesman in the Legal Department of the Watchtower Society, for whom he laboured for so many years as a "volunteer," answered me evasively when I asked for information about Covington. I conjecture that Covington chose, for a time at least, not to employ his talents for the organization he had defended with so much passion and energy and brilliance.)

V
God Can't Kill Arnold

I asked to be disfellowshipped July 19, 1974. When the new ruling for disfellowshipping smoking-offenders came in, two dear women friends got the axe. I took up smoking again purposely to get the axe, and smoked in front of any Witness who came into my home. I was interested to see who in their elaborate spy system would turn me in. It took about four weeks until the committee called me informing me that they knew. In a letter to headquarters, I told them I wanted to be disfellowshipped:

"I no longer consider you my brothers. I have lost respect for a society of people who want to sit in judgment on my conduct—who want to take the splinter out of my eye when their own has a rafter in it. I have lost respect for a society of people who do not understand that it's not what goes into a man's mouth that defiles him, but what comes out.

"Why have you never answered my letters? . . . Hypocritical Phariseeism is rampant. Love of the brothers has become a meaningless word. Meeting attendance has taken precedence over a brother in need.

"Where will it stop? Will overeating be a disfellowshipping offence next? The Watchtower *and* Awake! *tell us it is 'a sin' to worry. Is worrying a disfellowshipping offence?*

"The Witnesses have lost their joy; they are their own Armageddon, and their own great tribulation."—From a letter sent to me by an ex-communicated Witness.

"Disfellowshipping" is the Watchtower Society's term for excommunication.

The Society's governing body appoints, through its branch offices, "judicial committees" which act on behalf of the entire congregation in hearing cases of "sinful conduct" (such as fornication, adultery, apostasy, smoking) and render decisions that are known as resolutions of explusion. Trial proceedings are confidential; members of the congregation are not permitted to question the decision of the committee and must comply with the committee's judgment. If they act in contravention of the committee's ruling, they become candidates for disfellowshipping on the ground of "rebelliousness." Yet congregation members are often ignorant of the charges that have been brought against a disfellowshipped member and are not allowed to share the testimony that formed the basis of the committee's decision, are not told who it was that instigated the accusations, and have no information as to the accused's defence.

It appears now that many Witnesses are disaffected or at least greatly agitated by the Society's procedures for "disfellowshipping." From Manitoba, Canada, thousands of circulars have been sent to Witnesses in Britain, Europe, the Americas, Australia, and New Zealand complaining of alleged injustices of the governing body.

Until 1974, [*TW*, Aug. 1, 1974] Witnesses were not permitted to exchange a word of greeting with disfellowshipped persons. Obliged to present hard, unyielding faces to sinners, they could not smile at "anti-Christs." A mother whose daughter was disfellowshipped and did not live under her roof could not, under pain of expulsion, speak to her child, unless dire emergency made it necessary. She might be permitted, for example, to inform her daughter of a death in the family, but not share her grief. Perhaps because the Society has been publicly charged with "spiritual murders" for cutting these people off so brutally, it has softened its policy. Witnesses are now permitted to speak with those disfellowshipped, but not, unless they are elders, on "spiritual matters."

While *The Watchtower* [March 15, 1959] admits that occasional injustices have been perpetrated as a result of envy or dislike of the accused, it does not permit open discussion of disfellowshipping. Nor has it ever publicly apologized to people so victimized. The committee's decision must remain unchallenged; and the disfellowshipped person may not be given any spiritual comfort. Tens of thousands of Witnesses have been disfellowshipped since 1959. A disfellowshipped person must confess publicly, and announce and demonstrate to the satisfaction of the elders his intention to change his ways. In the majority of cases the severity of treatment militates against confession and repentance, and the humiliated disfellowshipped Witness enters despair—or, if he is lucky, freedom.

Indeed, despair is often the mirror image of the Witnesses' certainty.

I have often thought that many Witnesses were ambulatory schizophrenics, that their religion provided them with a vehicle for their craziness, a way to accommodate their fear and loathing of the menacing world. A study published in the *British Journal of Psychiatry* [June, 1975] tends to confirm this view: John Spencer, writing on "The Mental Health of Jehovah's Witnesses," reports that a study of Witnesses admitted to the Mental Health Services facilities of Western Australia "suggests that members of this section of the community are more likely to be admitted to a psychiatric hospital than the general population."

Spencer says that the principal problem for a researcher "seems to be to decide whether extreme religiosity such as is seen in the so-called 'neurotic sects' is a symptom of an overt psychiatric disorder, or whether it is a complex defence mechanism against an underlying disorder." His study does not resolve the issue.

Religiosity, as Jung said, is an extremely varied phenomenon about which it is impossible to generalize. It may, as Jung believed, be a creative expression of man's natural urge to worship; it may be, as Erich Fromm writes, a means of self-preservation, a way of silencing anxiety, a symbolic means of communication.

What happens when a person whose psychological needs have been met by Jehovah's Witnesses is deemed unworthy of association with them and is expelled from the congregation? My own observations tell me that the "survival rate" among ex-Witnesses (both those who are disfellowshipped and those who leave of their own accord) is relatively low.

The Witnesses' explanation for deviant behaviour after leaving the community is that "the demons have taken over the minds" of the defectors. It might be closer to the mark to say that the need for certainty and community that led certain people to become Witnesses in the first place drives them to find community and certainty and surcease from pain elsewhere. Ex-Witnesses who are functioning in the world still express anxiety, distress, and at best a lingering sadness.

There is no voluntary resignation in our organization, Covington told a jury in the Moyle case.

For years after I left Bethel, I dreamed that I was back in the antiseptic halls of the Watchtower residence, fighting to find a way out. At each NO EXIT sign a Witness stood, smiling, barring my way: "There is no way out." The dream was trite; my fear was fresh and vivid and palpable.

Since my departure, I have had a series of strange encounters with Watchtower elders, each one puzzling, each one a walking version of the stale nightmare.

On Christmas Day, 1968, a member of the Watchtower headquarters staff rang my doorbell and asked, "Are you Connie Grizzuti's daughter who used to be associated with the Lord's sheep?" I leaped at once to the conclusion that something had happened to my mother. I had thought that I was "killing" my mother by leaving her religion; the appearance of that man at Christmas triggered the guilt I had never been able to expiate. My mother is dead, I thought; I really have killed her.

The reality, less awful, was quite odd enough: "It has come to our attention," the man said, "that in 1963 you were observed making obeisance in the Shiva temple in Warangal, India. You are also known to have made the sign of the cross while passing a Roman Catholic Church in Guatemala City. These are grounds for disfellowshipping. If you can prove, before a group of elders, that you are innocent of the charges, disfellowshipping charges will be halted. If we remain convinced of your guilt, you may be reinstated in the Lord's organization if you beg forgiveness. If we judge you guilty and you do not confess, you will be disfellowshipped. If you refuse to appear before the elders, you will be automatically disfellowshipped."

Odd indeed. There was this silly, but somehow sinister, man underneath my Christmas tree, and there was I, feeling menaced, understanding the absurdity of such feelings, but nonetheless frightened.

It was not until 1974 that I was paid another official visit.

Years before, I had converted a young Brooklyn girl who had later married a Bethelite. They had been assigned to circuit-overseer work in Alabama. Lee and Donald, having returned from their assignment, came to pay me a "friendly visit." I had fond memories of them both. I remembered Lee as a spunky, sweet, feisty kid, not over serious, given to easy laughter. Donald, twenty years her senior, had had impressive reserve and movie-star-perfect good looks. He was serious about everything. We'd had, before he met Lee, a couple of dates. He was courteous, contained, formal. We went roller-skating; he was austere even in a roller-skating rink. He did nothing casually; I should not have been surprised when he said, in firm, measured tones—spacing each word to give it weight—"I'd like this relationship to deepen beyond friendship." But I was taken aback by what seemed, even for a repressed Bethelite, to be an over-calculated approach to romance. I made one of those hopelessly inadequate, awkward speeches that begins, "I like you too much to encourage you. . . ." Still, I had been flattered, and I could not but regard him with affection.

I had not seen either of them for close on twenty years. The years had added dignity to Donald's almost-too-regular features; he was, if anything, more handsome than ever. Tomboy Lee had taken on some of her husband's colouration; she too now spoke in firm, measured tones, and I missed her careless spontaneity. She was dressed in what is called a matron's "ensemble," everything matching. She took in my cluttered living room with a swift, practised glance and said, "It looks like a writer's house." (I took that as a reproach.) There was perfunctory conversation.

The first thing Donald said was that he hadn't come to "blackmail" or to "spank" me. He spoke of the "rife immortality" in the world today and requested my 11-year-old daughter, who was finding all this fascinating, to leave the room so that he could discuss rife immorality. I replied that there was not much that could surprise my daughter (who had meanwhile kicked me in the shins to signal her unwillingness to depart) and that I felt perfectly free to speak in front of her.

Donald: "Do you consider yourself one of Jehovah's Witnesses?"

B.H.: "Of course not."

Donald: "What would you like the congregations to think of you?"

B.H.: "What they think of me is up to them, surely."

Donald: "When you were baptized into the New World Society you took out citizenship in a new order. Are you renouncing your citizenship?"

To that question I had no ready answer; it seemed preposterous that anyone should ask it.

Donald: "There are several reasons for leaving The Truth. One, you reject doctrine. Two, you have had personal conflicts with individual Witnesses or with the organization. Three, you have committed immoral acts, and your shame keeps you away. Which of these reasons applies to you?"

I shrank from the inquisition. I had looked forward to seeing Lee and Donald—partly out of curiosity; partly out of a notion that, once friends, we could find common ground; and partly, I guess, out of arrogance: Perhaps if I explained myself, I might be able to dent their certainty. I *did* want to explain myself. My tentative efforts were impatiently received by Donald. He parried everything I said with Scripture.

"Did you know what you were doing when you were baptized?"

"But I was nine years old!"

"But did you *know* what you were doing?"

Donald grew clearly weary (my answers tended to be long). "Let's concentrate on immorality," he said.

My daughter settled herself in with a pleased anticipatory sigh. She had spent much of the previous week airing her opinions on abortion (pro) and open marriage (con), and she was eager, I could see, to engage herself in what she assumed would be a free-wheeling discussion of morality and mores.

Donald said to his wife, the tone of his voice straightening Anna's spine, "Lee, I'd like you and Anna to leave the room. I'm sure Anna would like to show you her bedroom."

Anna, a dutiful hostess, departed as gracefully as thwarted curiosity would allow.

"I have asked the girls to leave so that if you wish to confide your immorality to me, you can do so privately. I will pray over you, if you like, so that the Lord's spirit may return to you."

When Anna returned, having stayed away for what she judged a decent interval, Donald was still discussing "rife immorality." Anna, grabbing her chance, offered, "Well, I kind of agree with you about immorality. I don't think anybody should fuck unless they really love each other."

Donald and Lee stood up to leave. Donald advised me that if I persisted in my course of action, I stood the risk of being disfellowshipped—like my friend Walter—"And then none of the Lord's people will ever be able to speak to you again."

Anna demanded, "You don't talk to *Walter*? But he's a good person. He's *nice*. That's not religion!"

Later she said, "They act pleasant. But they're not nice."

Three days later, Donald phoned. He proposed to visit with a committee of elders from the congregation to administer "spiritual discipline." I acquiesced almost hungrily. I had found my anger. And I wanted to know, What next?

I was convinced that this time they would inaugurate disfellowshipping procedures against me. I also felt that I needed protection, though I didn't know quite from what. I asked my brother if he would be with me when they came. Donald came not with a committee of three, but with a single member of the headquarters staff. The agenda had been changed: no spiritual discipline, he said, just a talk.

Donald offered a repeat of his previous performance. There were veiled hints of dire consequences if I did not "turn around and confess"; there was explicit spiritual blackmail: I would die at Armageddon. But Donald and his friend seemed to run out of energy; they began to talk about me in the third person, as if I weren't there. They started to preach to my brother. He said, "Hey. You can't get my sister. So now you're hitting on me? Have some respect. You're in my sister's house."

They left. My brother and I looked at each other. "What was that all about?" he said. I said I had no idea.

J. F. Rutherford, according to the records of the testimony in the Moyle case, thundered. Nathan H. Knorr's voice was rather thin, but pleasantly modulated, with an affecting timbre. He spoke with the practised and prim voice of the headmaster who metes out reward and punishment dispassionately. It was a voice I learned, at Bethel, to dread, full of warm if fuzzy paternal concern one day, cold and razor-sharp the next, always rectitudinous. His rebukes were scathing. They came, as had Rutherford's, at mealtimes.

The morning bells woke us at 6:30. At 6:55, showered and dressed, we ran downstairs to the basement dining hall. We sat at tables of ten. Our day began with tension and bustle. Breakfast, served briskly and efficiently by white-coated waiters, lasted ten minutes and was preceded by a discussion of the Bible text for the day. Knorr or, in his absence, a director of the Society called upon members of the "family" for comments on the text. Being late was a Bad Thing: four hundred sets of eyes turned upon you if you attempted to slide invisibly into your place. Absenting oneself from breakfast altogether was a Very Bad Thing. If you were not there when Knorr called upon you, it was a Terrible Thing. (I can remember "sleeping over"—a rare self-indulgence—no more than five times in three and a half years. On those occasions, I had breakfast at a cheap drugstore counter in the Heights; no other meals ever tasted as good. I drank coffee and ate sugary, doughy apple turnovers and looked around and thought wonderingly that this was the way other people lived all the time. I savoured those few moments of anonymity.)

Sometimes, in addition to the discussion of the text there was a harangue. (I remember the aroma of coffee brewing in the kitchen, the effort to look alert and intelligent when one was dopey with sleep and to arrange one's face muscles into an unrevealing mask.) We never, afterward, discussed among ourselves the justice of Knorr's attack; we avoided each other's eyes; there was no redress for the victim, no acquittal in a court of popular opinion.

The attack that stands out most vividly in my mind was one that was wrapped in an anti-Semitism that has infected the Watchtower Society since its beginning. In the Watchtower printery, and at the Bethel residence, we worked eight hours and forty minutes a day, five and a half days a week. We filled out time sheets daily at the factory, and there was no time allotted for coffee or rest breaks. An elderly Bethelite on my floor of the factory kept a small supply of chocolates and candies, which he sold to hungry workers at candy-store cost on an honour system; we dropped our nickels and dimes into a box while he was busy at his menial work. I suppose he made a few pennies' profit each day; and I suppose also that he was one of those who received no financial help from outside, so that those pennies were important. I can't remember ever having heard him speak.

Knorr heard about the little enterprise and read the old man out, at great length, in public. He tied his attack to the fact that the man was a Jew. The Jews, Knorr asserted, had always been wilful, penny-grubbing ingrates. Jehovah had chosen them precisely to show that such unappetizing raw material could be redeemed if they adhered to His laws. The candy seller was, Knorr said, demonstrating all the abysmal qualities that had led the Jews to kill Christ. And so on, for an hour, while I cringed. Part of the horror was in knowing that there was no one I could share it with, no one to whom I would or could protest; part of the horror was my guilt. My silence was complicitous.

We see the beginnings of the return of divine favour to fleshly Israel already manifested in the beginning of a turning away of their blindness and their prejudice against Christ Jesus, in the opening up of the land of promise and their expulsion from other lands, and also in the returning fruitfulness of Palestine itself. . . . Fleshly Israel, recovered from blindness, shall be used as a medium through whom the streams of salvation, issuing from the glorified, spiritual Israel, shall flow to all the families of the earth.—SS, Vol. III (1891), pp. 293, 307

Nothing in the return of the Jews to Palestine and the setting up of the Israeli republic corresponds with Bible prophecies concerning the restoration of Jehovah's name-people to his favour and organization. —*LGBT*, rev. ed., 1952, pp. 213–18

In 1911, Charles Taze Russell returned from a trip around the world to a great ovation in the New York Hippodrome, where he was acclaimed by thousands of New York Jews. Russell supported the Jews' return to Palestine. He saw the Jews as God's instruments. But even as he proclaimed that Israel would be the medium of salvation, he commented on the "unchanged physiognomy of Jews," their hooked noses, and talked with scarcely concealed contempt of their supposed predilections: "Among the relics of antiquity that have come down to our day, there is no other object of so great interest as the Jewish people. . . . The national characteristics of many centuries ago are still prominent, even to their fondness for the leeks and onions and garlic of Egypt, and their stiff-necked obstinacy." [*SS* III, pp. 243–44]

Russell had proclaimed that "the deliverance of fleshy Israel" was due to take place before 1914: "The re-establishment of Israel in the land of Palestine is one of the events to be expected in this day of the Lord." [*Ibid.*, p. 244] The year 1881, he believed, marked the time for "the turning back of special light upon the long-blinded Jews." [p. 278] "Restitution," he wrote, would begin in Palestine: "Abraham, Isaac, and Jacob, with Daniel and all the holy prophets, will be made perfect—awakened from death to perfect manhood, after the Gospel Church has been glorified; and they will constitute the 'princes in all the earth,' the earthly and visible representatives of the Christ." [p. 265] He claimed to have it on the authority of missionaries that since 1878, unprecedented "showers and dews in summer" had blessed the Holy Land, preparing it for the influx of

Jews, who were "buying land, planting and building, and getting possession of the trade of the city . . . many of them . . . rising to distinction far beyond their Gentile neighbours." [pp. 265–66] Jews had been propelled to Palestine by persecution in Russia and Germany, which had been "permitted" by God: "God has permitted . . . afflictions and persecutions to come as a penalty for their national crime of rejection of the gospel and crucifixion of the Redeemer. He will . . . in due time reward the constancy of their faith in his promises. . . . God foreknew their pride and hardness of heart. . . . Within the present century a sifting and separating process is manifest among them, dividing them into two classes, the Orthodox and the Non-orthodox Jews." The Non-orthodox Jews, Russell declaimed, were "losing faith in a personal God . . . drifting toward liberalism, rationalism, infidelity. The Orthodox include most of the poor, oppressed Jews, as well as some of the wealthy and learned, and are vastly more numerous than the Non-orthodox; though the latter are by far the more influential and respected, often bankers, merchants, editors, etc." [p. 248]

Horrified equally by rich Jews and the spectres of socialism and anarchism, that triple threat, as he saw it, could be eradicated by a simple expedient: "Not until further persecutions shall have driven more of the poorer Jews to Palestine, and modern civilization shall be still further advanced there, will the wealthier classes of Jews be attracted thither; and then it will be in great measure from selfish motives—when the general and great time of trouble shall render property less secure in other lands than it is now. Then Palestine, far away from socialism and anarchism, will appear to be a haven of safety to the wealthy Jews." A singularly nasty vision, nor did it come to pass quite as Russell foretold.

It's an old and wicked story. The oppressed are blamed for their oppression: "To this day the natural circumcised Jews are suffering the sad consequences from the works of darkness that were done within their nation nineteen hundred years ago." [*TW*, Nov. 1, 1975, p. 654]

I had grown up in the gross and painful experience of casual anti-Semitism. By the time I was 15, I could no longer countenance it. I fell in love with a Jew. If, before I met and loved Arnold, I felt that life was a tightrope, I felt afterward that my life was lived perpetually on a high wire with no safety net. I was obliged, by every tenet, to despise him. To be "yoked with an unbeliever," an atheist, and an intellectual . . . the pain was exquisite.

Arnold became interested in me because I was smart; he loved me because he thought I was good. He nourished and nurtured me. He paid me the irresistible compliment of totally comprehending me. He hated my religion, but he loved *me*. I had never before been loved unconditionally. He came, unbidden, to sit with me at every school assembly and hold my hand while everyone else stood to salute the flag. We were highly visible, and I was very much comforted. And this was during the McCarthy era. Arnold had a great deal to lose, and he risked it for me. Nobody had ever risked anything for me before. How could I believe he was wicked?

We drank malteds on his porch and read T. S. Eliot and listened to Mozart. We walked for hours, talking of God and goodness and happiness and death. We met surreptitiously. Arnold treated me with infinite tenderness; he was the least alarming man I had ever known. His fierce concentration on me, his solicitous care uncoupled with sexual aggression, was the gentlest and most thrilling love I had ever known. He made me feel what I had never felt before—valuable and good.

It was very hard. All my dreams centred around Arnold, who was becoming more important, certainly more real, to me than God. All my dreams were blood-coloured. I fantasized that Arnold was converted and survived Armageddon to love forever with me in the New World, or that I would die with Arnold, in fire and flames, at Armageddon. I would try to make bargains with God—my life for his. When I entered Bethel, I confessed my terrors to Nathan H. Knorr. I said that I knew I could not rejoice in the destruction of "the wicked" at Armageddon (Arnold would be among them). I was told that being a woman, and therefore weak and sentimental, I would have to go against my sinful nature and obey God's superior wisdom—which meant never seeing Arnold again.

I did see him again. I had no choice. We never exchanged more than a chaste and solemn kiss; but he claimed me.

When I left religion, Arnold alone wept.

When I walked out of the door of Bethel for the last time, one of my fellow workers said, "But *why*?"

"Because God can't kill Arnold," I said.

VI
In Transition

> Some day this man Russell will die, his corruption will be discovered, and his followers will be without a church, without a leader; they will have confidence in no man, and in the end will be a thousand times worse off than had they never heard the name Russell.—Sermon, Rev. J. J. Ross, Hamilton, Toronto, Canada, April 7, 1917.

> "Your dying and this work going on. Why, when you die we will all complacently fold our arms and wait to go to heaven with you. We will quit then."—A. H. Macmillan to C. T. Russell [*Faith*, p. 69].

On October 31, 1916, Charles Taze Russell died in a railway car outside Pampa, Texas. He was 64. Almost nothing he had foreseen had come to pass.

It is doubtful that the Witnesses could have survived the debacle of their dreams had not World War I come along to deliver them. The Great War, which saw the imprisonment of their leaders, and which temporarily put a halt to their work, was the instrument of their salvation. It allowed them to reinterpret Bible prophecy and to reassemble their chronological complexities; and it provided them with an external focus at a time when internal dissension threatened to decimate their ranks.

In 1912, the Watch Tower Society launched what was to have been a final effort to get people out of the established churches. Debates were frequently held with rival Protestant churches. Travelling ministers called "colporteurs" were equipped with "Eureka Drama" outfits (recorded lectures and music); and special representatives rented halls and theatres to show a four-part "Photo-Drama Creation": stereopticon slides and primitive motion pictures, prepared at a cost of $300,000, were synchronized with recorded lectures and music to provide potential converts with a panoramic view of human history, past and future, starting with Creation and ending with the 1,000-year reign of Christ.

The Watchtower Society is now highly bureaucratized, but "C. T. Russell," according to A. H. Macmillan, "had no idea of building a strongly knit organization. . . . We saw no need for it. We expected

1914 would mark the end of this system of things on earth. Our big concern . . . was to preach as effectively and extensively as possible before that date arrived.

The hysteria induced by these expectations was released at "love feasts" at the conventions for which railway cars were hired to transport the Bible Students. Leaders lined up in front of the speakers' platform as Russellites filed along, shaking hands, partaking of diced communion bread, singing "Blest Be the Tie That Binds Our Hearts in Christian Love." They wept tears of joy. Such minor raptures no longer take place among the disciplined and regimented Witnesses, but they were commonplace then. They expected, then, to be united in a perpetual love feast in heaven; and they thought their reward was imminent.

On September 30, 1914, Elder Macmillan told an ecstatic convention audience in California: "This is probably the last public address I shall ever deliver, because we shall be going home soon." *[Ibid.*, p. 47]

On October 2, 1914, Charles Taze Russell entered the Bethel dining room. "The Gentile Times have ended, their kings have had their day," he rumbled. "Anyone disappointed? I'm not. Everything is moving right on schedule." [*Yearbook*, 1975, p. 73]

Thirty-six years previously, in 1878, a small band of Russellites had had to explain why they had not *then* been taken to heaven, since 1874 had marked the beginning of Christ's invisible presence in the spiritual "Temple of Jerusalem" and the economic panic of 1873 had been the first death spasm of a dying world. Once again, in 1914, they found themselves having to account for failure. In 1879, Russell had predicted that an international nihilist-Communist-anarchist uprising would begin early in 1914 and that this period of turbulence would be followed, on October 2, 1914, by the establishment of God's kingdom on earth and the calling of the "living saints" to glory.

When this did not happen, many of Russell's followers, according to his apologists, "grew sour" and left the organization. Those who remained explained: "The mistake C. T. Russell had made . . . was not as to the time, 1914, but his error was only as to *where* the Kingdom had been established—in heaven instead of on earth." [*Faith*, p. 60] World War I was the sign of the Devil's displeasure, and his death throes. He had been booted out of the heavens, where hitherto he had had free access to the angels in the courts of the Lord, and he was now stalking the earth.

That the final collapse, and the final glory, had not occurred in 1914 was proof of God's beneficence: "Had Jehovah's great warrior, the Lord Jesus, continued the assault against Satan and his angels after that first skirmish which dusted those rebels from heaven, . . . no flesh would have been saved. So, for the sake of God's own people, and to fulfil his purpose, Jehovah 'cut short' those days of tribulation against the invisible rebel spirits by stopping his war for a period before . . . Armageddon." [*Ibid.*, pp. 59–60]

This new interpretation paved the way for an intensive proselytizing campaign, which obliged the Witnesses to begin work on a new theology: Before 1914, they had been concerned only with their heavenly destiny, the "harvesting of the saints." Now there began the evolution of a new idea, determined by altered circumstances. A handful of living saints would be called to heaven immediately upon their death; but a great number of as-yet-unredeemed worldlings would be given the opportunity to live forever on a cleansed and perfect earth.

And they scourged themselves for "independent thinking and private interpretation": "While we were looking forward to 1914 and the end of wickedness and sorrow on the earth, many of us were thinking more of our own personal, individual 'change' than anything else." [*Ibid.*, pp. 47–48] But this did not preclude their complaining about non-believers. "As 1914 passed, then 1915 and 1916, the reproach heaped upon us increased. In our effort to discern the meaning of Bible prophecy before the expected events had actually occurred . . . some partially inaccurate public expressions were made. When these minor details did not develop, the more important major fulfilment that actually did occur was entirely overlooked by those lacking full faith in God's word." "Instead of viewing the increasing number of facts, actual events, piling up world-wide from day to day since 1914 as undeniable proof of the correctness of the marked date publicized by the Watch Tower from 1879, scoffers seized upon some minor point of Russell's writings to ridicule and mock." [*Ibid.*, pp. 55–56]

Governments were reproached for not "surrendering their power" to the invisible Kingdom of God and for vesting their hopes instead in "the beast with seven heads"—the League of Nations.

In November, 1914, a month after the Russellites' dreams of glory had been dashed:

> Just how long after the Gentile Times close will be the revealment in "flaming fire" we do not know. . . . How long would this period be, in which present institutions will be ousted, and the present order of things be condemned and done away with, to make way for the Reign of Righteousness? We answer that . . . we might expect a transition to run on a good many years. [*TWT,* 1914, p. 327]

He left the time of "transition" open-ended; and this gave his followers the out they so desperately required. (And the war came along fortuitously, so that the Witnesses are able to point to 1914 as a marked date and to attach their prophecies to it, never mind that they were wrong in all particulars.)

In December, 1914, Russell wrote, with a mixture of pathos and bravado: "Even if the time of our change should not come within ten years, what more should we ask? Are we not a blessed, happy people? Is not our God faithful? If anyone knows anything better, let him take it. If any of you ever find anything better, we hope you will tell us." [*Ibid.*, p. 377]

If anyone knows better, let him take it. That, of course, is one of the keys to the survival of the organization. The Witnesses had nowhere else to go. Their investment in their religion was total; it was their life. To leave it would be a death.

There is some evidence to suggest that Russell's control of his organization was eroding during the last three years of his life. Up to 1913, as majority shareholder of the Watch Tower Bible and Tract Society of Pennsylvania, he was able to control elections, having bought, by varied estimates, $250,000 to $300,000 of voting shares at $10 apiece. After 1913, the number of votes smaller shareholders had bought outnumbered Russell's. [Cole, pp. 60–69; *JWDP*, p. 64] Russell, by the time of his death, had less than one-fifth of the voting shares. The work of the Society, A. H. Macmillan told the *Brooklyn Eagle* [Nov. 28, 1916], had been for several years "largely in the hands of his lieutenants."

Russell's will bequeathed "merely love and Christian good wishes" to his flock and $200 to Maria Russell. He had made no provision for a successor, and the Society's vice-president, A. I. Ritchie, did not automatically succeed to the presidency, although Macmillan told *Eagle* reporters that he had little doubt Ritchie would be elected; Macmillan denied that J. F. Rutherford, then the Society's legal counsel, had a shot at the presidency. Under the provisions of the Society's charter, the board of directors was to handle its affairs until the next election, which was scheduled to be held in Pittsburgh on January 6, 1917. From October 31, 1916, to January 6, 1917, a board-appointed executive committee (composed of Rutherford, secretary-treasurer Van Amburgh, and Ritchie) directed the affairs of the Society; Macmillan, who was not a member of the Pennsylvania board, served as administrative aide.

It was a time of intense politicking, electioneering, manoeuvring, manipulation, conspiracies, and dissension.

One of the bones of contention in the power struggle was A. H. Macmillan. Macmillan claims that shortly before Russell left on his final tour, he "wrote letters to . . . the heads of different departments, . . . informing them that 'A. H. Macmillan is to be in full charge of the office and the Bethel Home during my absence.

Anything he says for you to do you must do; it doesn't make any difference whether you agree or not. If he tells you incorrectly, I'll attend to him when I get home.'" [*Faith*, p. 70]

Russell never got home. A majority of the members of the board was opposed to Macmillan's stewardship, and they were left to fight it out among themselves. Macmillan lost no time exercising his prerogatives. His story is that "a few ambitious ones at headquarters were holding caucuses here and there, doing a little electioneering to get their men in. However, Van Amburgh and I held a large number of votes. Many shareholders, knowing of our long association with Russell, sent their proxies to us to be cast for the one whom we thought best fitted for office"—J. F. Rutherford. [*op. cit.*, p. 68] Four members of the seven-man board of directors vigorously opposed Rutherford's presidency.

In this they were supported by P. S. L. Johnson, a travelling minister whom Russell had sent to England to preach to the troops. Johnson, who arrived in England in November, 1916, and immediately contrived to seize control of the Society's London bank account, is described as "a Jew who had forsaken Judaism to become a Lutheran minister before he came to a knowledge of the truth" and as a man whose "brilliance led to his downfall." [*JWDP*, p. 69] He is clearly seen as a kind of Lucifer. After his dismissal from headquarters, Johnson attempted unsuccessfully to form a sect of his own. He believed until his death he was the world's high priest and Russell's legitimate successor.

On January 6, 1917, Joseph Franklin Rutherford was elected second president of the Watch Tower Bible and Tract Society. The Lord, it was said, had chosen the right man for the job, though many of the headquarters staff evinced an intense antipathy for Rutherford, a wintry-bleak man whose personality could not have been more unlike that of the passionate Pastor, whose fires burned hot, and warmed when they did not scald.

In the spring of 1917, simmering opposition to Rutherford erupted when four directors of the Pennsylvania Society, at an extended session of the annual meeting, attempted to present a resolution amending the bylaws to place administrative powers in the hands of the board. Rutherford won his skirmish effortlessly—he simply ruled the motion out of order. Opposition stiffened, but did not prevail. The four dissenting directors were disposed of handily: as they were attempting to gather a five-man quorum in the Society's Brooklyn Hicks Street office, Macmillan called the cops to evict them. According to his folksy account, "an old Irishman, a typical old fellow . . . came in twirling a long nightstick around in his hand. 'Gentlemen,' he said to the four directors, 'It's after being serious for you now. Faith, and I know . . . Macmillan, but you fellows I don't know. Now you better be after going for fear there'll be trouble.'" After the friendly policeman's performance, the men thus warned, Macmillan says, grabbed their hats, tripped down the stairs, and fled to Borough Hall to get a lawyer. [*Faith,* pp. 79–80]

They could have saved themselves the bother. Through no fault of their own, they were not legally members of the board of directors. Russell had appointed them directors for life; but the law stipulated that they had to be elected by vote of the shareholders each year. Rutherford, having been elected to office, was by law a director, as were his two allies on the board, who had been elected vice-president and secretary-treasurer. Rutherford simply booted his enemies out, and took it upon himself to appoint sympathetic directors to fill the vacancies until the next corporation election in 1918.

Russell's autocratic heedlessness of the law had paid off handsomely for his successor. A legal lapse had altered the history of the Watch Tower Society.

Members of the headquarters staff who supported the dissident directors were more difficult to subdue. Their simmering resentment of Rutherford's and Macmillan's highhandedness erupted in the summer of 1917, when Rutherford, at a midday Bethel meal, presented each member of "the family" with a book called *The Finished Mystery.* This seventh volume of *Studies in the Scriptures*, which consisted of commentaries on Revelation, the Song of Solomon, and Ezekiel, was termed "the posthumous work of Pastor Russell." Headquarters workers fiercely challenged Rutherford's assertion that the volume had been assembled from notes prepared by Russell. For four or five hours they rioted in the dining hall, loudly denouncing Rutherford.

The dissidents were eventually forced out of Bethel; some of them embarked on extensive speaking and letter-writing campaigns throughout the United States, Canada, and Europe. As a result, congregations of Bible Students were split into opposing factions, those loyal to Rutherford and those who thought he had desecrated the memory of their beloved Pastor and refused to accept his authority.

It is estimated by Watchtower sources that one-fifth of the Bible Students defected from the Society between 1917 and 1919. [*Yearbook,* 1975, pp. 93–94]

When I was a young member, Witnesses who had lived through their civil war still spoke of these turncoats with horror and fascination. They scratched away at their sores with a passion that bespoke animal fear.

The Watchtower Society is, in its strength, not loath now to publicize the internal problems that beset it during the World War. The

Society is able, after all, to point to its continued existence; it has prospered, while opposition has foundered. To an unbelieving eye, it might seem apparent that craftiness and wheeling-dealing had won the day, and that legal loopholes and disappointed hopes determined the course of the Watch Tower Society from 1914 to 1918. As far as the Witnesses are concerned, however, this chapter in their history is, once more, a fulfilment of Bible prophecy: Christ had come to the Temple to judge his people in 1918. This was, they say, "a weeding out, a time of judgment, a cleansing of the entire organization" [*Faith*], a "sifting" that was inevitable in view of Jesus' having told his disciples that he would cast the "evil servant" out, and in view of Malachi's having said that God would "purify the sons of Levi."

Rutherford—six feet tall, hazel-eyed, portly and senatorial in appearance—permitted himself affectations in dress and demeanour. In the 1940s, he wore old-fashioned stand-up collars and a little black antebellum string tie, he sported a long black ribbon from which dangled a monocle, and he frequently carried a cane. But under his leadership, the organization became monolithic, and proselytizing techniques became uniform and highly structured. The days of fiery individualism were over. (Russell was fire; Rutherford was acid and ice; Knorr was rock and grey.)

Joseph Franklin Rutherford was born on November 8, 1869, to James and Lenore Strickland Rutherford on their farm in Morgan County, Missouri. Little is known of his early life; Watchtower historians, in an effort to explain away what they call his "blunt" manner—his tattered humanity and his notorious insensitivity to other people's feelings—say that "his father was a strict disciplinarian, which deprived young Rutherford of any emotional life." [*Ibid.*, p. 73] When he was 20, he became official reporter for the courts of the Fourteenth Judicial District in Missouri; at 22, he was admitted to the bar. He practised trial law in Boonville, Missouri, for fifteen years, campaigning briefly for William Jennings Bryan. His enemies, among them Father Coughlin, frequently ridiculed him for appropriating the title "Judge" to himself. His followers, leaping to his defence, protested that he had sat as a substitute judge in Missouri's Fourteenth Judicial District "on more than one occasion." It is probably safe to assume that the title was one of those Southern honorifics conferred upon anyone of any distinction at all (in Boonville, a very small pond, it cannot have been too hard to be a big fish).

The "judge" was introduced to the teachings of the Bible Students when a travelling colporteur brought him a copy of *Millennial Dawn*. Thereafter he and his wife, Mary, began to hold Bible classes in their own home. He was baptized in 1906. In 1907, he became the Watch Tower Society's legal counsel in Pittsburgh; in 1909, he moved to the Society's new headquarters in Brooklyn and was admitted to the New York Bar; on May 24, 1909, he was admitted to practise before the U.S. Supreme Court.

Rutherford is said to have been sceptical of his ability to preach until one day he chanced upon a group of "coloured men" in a field and, exercising Southern *droit de seigneur*, proceeded to lecture the field hands on Life, Death, and the Hereafter. His captive audience gratified him with choruses of "Praise the Lord, Judge!" A Missouri epiphany: From that moment, Rutherford never looked back.

Little is known of Rutherford's wife, Mary, and his son Malcolm. The Judge seems to have lived a compartmentalized life, the private person and the public person never merging, as they did so spectacularly in the person of Charles Taze Russell.

Rutherford was 48 when he was elected president of the Watch Tower Society. a position he was to hold for twenty-four years, until his death in 1942.

In June, 1917, six months after Rutherford became Watch Tower president, Congress passed the Espionage Act, laying heavy penalties on all persons who interfered with mobilization forces. The Sedition Act of 1918 was an even more severe measure to suppress war criticism. Dissenters were often arrested without warrants, hauled off to jail, and held incommunicado without bail. Prejudiced courts sentenced war critics to extraordinarily long prison terms: one adolescent girl was given twenty years. There were government listeners and informers everywhere. Intelligence agencies of the departments of War, Navy, and State employed amateur as well as professional detectives to collect information on citizens.

The Witnesses' accounts of their travails during World War I reflect a parochialism. They view Rutherford's conviction on the charge of espionage and his nine-month imprisonment in the Atlanta penitentiary as proof of a special relationship with God; they ignore the fact that clergymen of all denominations were sent to prison—sometimes for doing nothing more than reading the Sermon on the Mount.

Although Watchtower publications now lambast the rest of the clergy for their chauvinism during the Great War, Bible Students were themselves divided on the question of neutrality. Russell's personal representative delivered words of comfort to troops before they went off to the trenches. Many Bible Students, in the absence of a clear directive from the Society, fought at the front; others served in the Army Medical Corps.

Rutherford disclaimed any responsibility for those of his followers who resisted conscription; defending himself against the charge of sedition, he said that his advice had been simply to suggest that if they could not, in conscience, take part in war, the Draft Act allowed them to apply for exemption. He insisted that he had always advised the Bible Students to conform with the law of the State provided it did not conflict with a higher law.

Passage of the Espionage Act was a disastrous blow to civil liberties, and the Watch Tower Society was caught, as were so many others, in its net. Intelligence agents were disabused of the idea that dismantled radio equipment found in the Society's Brooklyn headquarters had been used to transmit broadcasts to the enemy; nevertheless, warrants for the arrest of Rutherford, Secretary-Treasurer Van Amburgh, A. H. Macmillan, and five members of the *Watch Tower* editorial committee were issued by the U.S. District Court for the Eastern District of New York on May 7, 1918. They were arraigned in Federal Court. A grand jury returned an indictment charging them with "unlawfully, feloniously and wilfully causing and attempting to cause insubordination, disloyalty and refusal of military duty in the military and naval forces of the United States of America, in, through and by personal solicitations, letters, public speeches, distribution and public circulation throughout the United States of America of a certain book called 'Volume Seven—*Scripture Studies—The Finished Mystery*'; and . . . obstructing the recruiting and enlistment service of the United States when the United States was at war." Rutherford, Van Amburgh, Macmillan, and R. J. Martin (one of the compilers of *The Finished Mystery*) were also charged with trading with the enemy. (Funds deposited in the Society's Zurich bank account were alleged to have been earmarked for Germany.) The defendants were released on bail; on May 15, 1918, appearing before Judge Harland B. Howe, they pleaded not guilty to all charges. [*Yearbook*, 1975, pp. 104–05]

The trial lasted fifteen days. Outside, soldiers marched and clergymen stood on corners reading the Lord's Prayer. The defendants testified that they had never conspired to affect the draft or to interfere with the Government's prosecution of the war; that they had never had any intention of interfering in any manner with the war; that their work was wholly religious and not political; that they had never advised or encouraged anyone to resist the draft, but merely offered advice to conscientious objectors; that they were not opposed to the nation's going to war but that, as dedicated Christians, they could not themselves engage in mortal combat.

On June 20, 1918, after deliberating for four and a half hours, a jury returned a verdict of guilty. Seven defendants were sentenced to eighty years in the penitentiary (twenty years each on four counts, to run concurrently), and one defendant, Giovanni

DeCecca, was sentenced to forty years (ten years on each of the same four counts). Friends and families of the convicted men sang "Blessed Be the Tie That Binds" in the Marshal's Office of the Brooklyn Federal Court. Rutherford proclaimed, "This is the happiest day of my life. To serve earthly punishment for the sake of one's religious belief is one of the greatest privileges a man could have." [*Ibid.*, p. 108. Reported in New York *Tribune*, June 22, 1918]

He had, however, gone to great lengths to avoid the "privileges" of earthly punishment. The Society had seriously compromised itself. The Bible Students wished to receive accolades for their neutrality as they also declared their unswerving loyalty to the United States Government: "We are not against the Government in any sense of the word. We recognize the Government of the United States as the best government on earth. We recognize that governments, being political and economic institutions, have the power and authority, under the fundamental law, to declare war and to draft their citizens." [*TWT*, 1917, p. 6221] Watch Tower leaders had conferred with government authorities and agreed to delete objectionable portions of *The Finished Mystery*. They took the further step of advising colporteurs to halt distribution of the volume.

When none of this served to keep their leaders out of prison, the Bible Students, at a convention in Pittsburgh on January 2–5, 1919, unanimously passed a resolution attesting to "their loyalty to the government and people of these United States."

The Watch Tower instructed its readers to honour President Wilson's designation of May 30, 1918, as a day of national prayer and supplication for the success of the American war effort. [*TWT*, June 1, 1918] The Bible Students did not then, nor do the Witnesses now, call themselves pacifists.

About one thing, however, the Bible Students were unequivocal and absolutely certain: "Without a doubt, the prosecution . . . had been initiated by some nominal ecclesiastical adherents. The Bible's terrible arraignment of the Papacy . . . is quite probably the cause of . . . action against them." They saw themselves as victims of a conspiracy of clergymen. [*TWT*, 1917]

Without question some of the orthodox clergy were glad of an excuse to be rid of the Bible Students. But with the end of the war, and a change in the national temper, opposition to the Bible Students ebbed. In February, 1919, liberal newspapers began to agitate for the release of the Society's president and his associates. More than 700,000 names were secured on a petition for their release. On March 2, 1919, the judge who had convicted them recommended "immediate commutation" of their sentences.

On March 25, federal authorities, acting on the instruction of

Supreme Court Justice Louis Brandeis, released the Society's leaders from the penitentiary on bail of $10,000 each, pending further trial. On April 14, 1919, in a hearing before the Federal Second Circuit Court of Appeals in New York, their convictions were reversed, and they were remanded for retrial. The indictments were later dismissed, the government entering a motion of *nolle prosequi*. [See *JWDP*, p. 86]

Jehovah's Witnesses now acknowledge that they "did not," during World War I, "display the proper neutrality of the Christian." [*JWDP*, p. 92] This admission does not prevent them from railing against the clergy for behaving as they did. That the clergy were not pure means that they were the instrument of the Devil; the fact that the *Witnesses* were not pure is, they say, proof that God was using them to fulfil the prophecy of Revelation 11:2, 7: "And I will give power unto my two witnesses, and they shall prophesy a thousand two hundred and threescore days, clothed in sackclock. And when they shall have finished their testimony, the beast that ascendeth out of the bottomless pit shall make war against them, and shall overcome them, and kill them."

The Witnesses claim on the one hand that they were victims of a devilish religious-political conspiracy and, on the other, that they were exiled from God's favour during the War, their own period of "spiritual bondage" having been "typified" by the Jews' languishment in captivity in Babylon.

Their spiritual error, as they later saw it, was to misread Romans 13:1: "Let every soul be subject unto the higher powers. For there is no power but of God: the powers that be are ordained of God." They, like the orthodox churches, had understood the Apostle Paul's words to apply to governmental authorities. Their error, they say, was in not recognizing that the "higher powers" were in fact Jehovah God and Christ Jesus (a construction difficult to make in the context of Paul's injunction to the Romans).

From 1929, up until the politically volatile '60s, the "higher powers," in contradistinction to the World War I interpretation, were stated to be God, Jesus, and the "theocratic organization" through which the Father and Son worked: "When [Paul] says, 'The Powers that be are ordained of God,' does he have any reference whatsoever to the Gentile nations of the earth? Is it not more reasonable that he directs his words exclusively to the powers possessed and exercised in God's organization, and not to those that are exercised in Satan's organization?" [*TWT*, 1929, p. 164] This reading of Paul's words prepared the way for their principled stand of absolute neutrality during World War II—by which time the organization, free of internal problems, had grown so strong it could withstand external pressures, indeed thrive on them. The

Witnesses remained faithful to this interpretation until the early '60s, when it became necessary to differentiate themselves from war protestors and civil-rights agitators and to be regarded as bastions of "normality" in a world that trembled on the brink of massive social change.

As the Witnesses became less and less a threat to the established order and the status quo in America, they performed another 180-degree turn: in the 1960s, without apology or embarrassment and with their customary aplomb, they once again reversed themselves and pronounced human governmental authorities as the "higher powers."

And so they readopted the reading of Romans 13—the reading for which they had once calumnized the clergy.

It is no accident that during the '60s, when war protestors sprang up like dandelions and law-and-order was a rallying cry for the middle class, the expansion-minded Witnesses, who were perceived by the establishment as less of a threat than "hippies" or political radicals, received preferential treatment from draft boards. (See Chapter VII.) They are an example of social Darwinism: they have evolved; and they have survived.

In the calm that followed the storms of war, the Bible Students—the release of their leaders had acted on them like a shot of adrenalin—were mobilized by Rutherford to form an army of "Kingdom advertisers." Canvassers fanned out across the nation; sound trucks jarred the Sunday peace in towns and in the country, blasting Rutherford's denunciations of the churches. The "pastoral work" Russell had initiated was unorganized and low-keyed in comparison with the highly organized proselytizing techniques perfected during the 1920s and '30s. Cities were divided into territorial districts; female Bible Students went from door to door distributing tracts, delivering memorized "testimonies" issued from headquarters, and inviting householders to public lectures delivered by male Bible Students.

The Bible Students were less concerned now with "harvesting the saints" than with aggressive attacks on the clergy: Watchtower publications ran full-page pictures of a preacher walking down the aisle of a church with a gun in one hand and a collection plate in the other. The Roman Catholic Church was branded with "the number of the beast"—666—and was pictured as a semiclad harlot reeling drunkenly into fire and brimstone.

However harsh Pastor Russell's public messages might have been, there was a kind of starry-eyed gentleness, a sweet dreaminess about the Bible Students when they gathered together in his time. Rutherford put an end to that. There were no more "prayer, praise, and testimony" meetings, no more convention "love feasts." Now congregation meetings centred around readings of *The Watch Tower*, and Bible Students were required to answer catechistic questions by summarizing each paragraph of that journal. Their conventions, which had been other-worldly, self-congratulatory affairs of men and women who thought they were soon to reconvene in heaven, became occasions for scathing denunciations of the clergy. At a postwar convention, Rutherford, casting the first stone, "exposed the clergy's disloyalty by participating in the war" [*JWDP*, p. 105] (though the Pope, appalled by the carnage of the war, had called for a negotiated peace after the second battle of the Somme, at a time when the Bible Students were saying their prayers for the success of the American war effort).

The Watch Tower Society was, in fact, pursuing a vigorous course of isolationism: London was branded "the seat of the beast"; "Let Britain withdraw from [the League—the seven-headed beast] tomorrow," Rutherford said in 1926, "and it will go down immediately." [*Ibid.*, p. 111]

During the Depression years Russell's notion that the great war of Armageddon was to be essentially a fight between capital and labour, with Jehovah expropriating the spoils for the unpropertied meek, was dispensed with: Armageddon was now seen as God's fight against "Satan's organization," represented on earth by Religion, Politics, and Commerce; and the function of Jehovah's people was to warn of its arrival and, in the meantime, to abstain from taking any part in the political system.

Underneath was a bedrock of conservatism: the Bible Students talked about the destruction of the status quo but abhorred attempts to change it. The failure of the clergy to fall prostrate before the invisible Christ, and its acceptance of the League, was seen as a major factor in "the rise of radical, revolutionary elements, pictured by the restless 'sea' of Revelation." [*Yearbook*, 1975, p. 136]

As they expanded, the Bible Students became more and more centralized, more and more uniform. The right to appoint congregational overseers was taken away from individual congregations and placed in the hands of the Society. Rutherford, unlike Russell—who had allowed a certain amount of latitude among his travelling representatives and derived some pleasure from the eccentricities and foibles of others, when they did not threaten to eclipse his own—insisted that each public speaker conform absolutely to headquarters material.

By 1927, the pressure for all Bible Students to become door-to-door preachers and to turn in weekly activity reports to headquarters had become so intense that many of Rutherford's followers dropped away. (There is a very high turnover among the Witnesses. One sees disproportionately few elderly people at Watchtower conventions.) The departure of many Bible Students in 1927 was no doubt hastened by the fact that Rutherford, who was as mathematically adroit as his predecessor, had led the Bible Students to believe that 1925 marked the time for Christ's anointed followers to go to heaven and for "the faithful men of old" to be resurrected to rule as princes on the earth. Some Bible Students made preparations for the resurrection of their loved ones in that year—getting spare rooms ready, airing out old clothes from attic trunks.

I wonder about those imaginations: Did they *visualize* the ancient prophets rising from their graves? Were they brushed by a dream, or set on fire by an imagined reality? When I was a child Witness, I used to ask, What will the prophets wear when they're resurrected? Will they take planes from Palestine to Brooklyn? Will they speak English? I wondered if we'd have David and Jonathan to dinner, and whether they'd like Italian food. I tried to imagine Noah riding a subway. My elders, I soon learned, were greatly disquieted by my questions and my conjectures; I learned rapidly to quash my curiosity.

In 1928 Rutherford had dazzled the Bible Students with further proof of their singularity by "revealing" to them the pagan origins of Christmas and birthday celebrations and abjuring them from celebrating those holidays. By 1931, having already framed eight resolutions "indicting ecclesiastics," he had run out of suitably impressive material with which to energize his followers. According to Macmillan, "he began to think about" what he would say to Bible Students that was new and of any consequence at an international convention scheduled for July 24–31 in Cleveland, Ohio. "Isaiah 43 came to his mind": "But now thus saith the Lord that created thee, O Jacob, and he that formed thee, O Israel, Fear not: for I have redeemed thee, I have called thee by thy name; thou art mine. . . . Ye are my witnesses, saith the Lord, and my servant whom I have chosen."—Isaiah 43:1, 10, King James Version. (The American Standard Version, which the Witnesses preferred—at least until they produced their own New World Translation of the Bible—uses *Jehovah* in place of *the Lord*.) Rutherford "got up at two o'clock in the morning . . . and the Lord guided him." [*Yearbook*, 1975, p. 151] What Rutherford had come up with at 2 o'clock in the morning was a new name for Bible Students: Jehovah's witnesses. It was forever after a proof that Jehovah had chosen the Witnesses to be His people: who else was called by His name?

Conventions of Witnesses are like catered weddings: you have to come home with party favours. The illusion that something new and fresh has come down from headquarters is essential to the on-going work of the Society. This was something new; their batteries recharged, the newly christened Jehovah's Witnesses applied greater energy to the search for "the other sheep"—the "great multitude," who, they now saw clearly, would inherit the earth.

They began to de-emphasize the glories of heaven and to focus on those "people of goodwill" who would ally themselves with the "heavenly class" and to whom, as a result, God's Kingdom-Blessings would come on earth. (The new emphasis proceeded in part, perhaps, from their failure to be gathered to heaven in 1925, and also from having to justify amassing property and accelerating their proselytizing in the face of the imminent destruction of the world.) Their God, who before was going to revivify and shower beneficence upon all the disinherited of the earth, had become more discriminating: the "other sheep" would live forever on earth; the "goats" of Jesus' parable would be destroyed. Those who did not heed the Witnesses' message were "goats."

There are 144,000 places reserved in heaven, and most of these, it is assumed, have been taken up by first-century Christians and Russellites and Rutherfordites. The call is now to earthly life. (Vacancies may occur when one of the heavenly class sins against the Holy Spirit.) Attendance at the yearly memorial of Christ's death—when those who expect to go to heaven to serve as Christ's co-regents partake of bread and wine—reflect the changing expectations of the majority of Witnesses. In 1935, 35,000 Witnesses celebrated "the Lord's evening meal" in the United States; 71 per cent of these partook of the Memorial emblems. In 1955, U.S. Memorial attendance was 878,303, and 1.9 per cent ate the bread and drank the wine.

The commission to separate the sheep from the goats took some extravagant forms. In 1938, in London, a thousand-man, six-mile-long parade of Witnesses bore signs reading RELIGION IS A SNARE AND A RACKET. When they were heckled—observers took them for Communists—Rutherford neutralized the signs by adding SERVE GOD AND CHRIST THE KING. It must have been confusing to anyone who didn't know the Witnesses' definition of *religion*, which was that it came from the Latin, *to bind back*, and that it applied to all "false systems" of worship.

The Witnesses no longer carry signs or banners, and the hand of God is seen in this, as it is seen in everything else: Grant Suiter, the Society's current secretary, has said that in view of the many public demonstrations of protest taking place, it must be clearly understood that the Witnesses have no part in these and that this form of their activity has come to an end, showing Jehovah's direction for them.

They are always having to prove themselves, set themselves tests, always investing events with enormous significance; they are naked and afraid in the face of ordinary life and must substitute for the excitement of an inner life the scent of danger—Daniel in the lions' den. The more trouble the outside world gave them, the more they made themselves the butt of opposition, the more secure they became in their beliefs. What was important was that something should always be happening. As we shall see, during the 1930s and '40s, a great deal did happen. There is reason to believe that they were complicit in their own victimization—manipulating national fears, milking national traumas to invite opposition, in order to enhance their self-esteem. In their persecution, they found a kind of peace.

Joseph Franklin Rutherford died on January 8, 1942, in San Diego, California. He was 72 years old. His lieutenants, squabbling with local authorities who refused permission to bury Rutherford in a crypt at Beth-Saarim, did not disclose his death to his followers. The news was released by a local mortician. [*The New York Times*, Jan. 10, 1942] He was buried, three months after his death, on April 26, in Woodrow Cemetery, next to what was then the Watchtower radio station, WBBR.

I worked, the summer of 1953, at the Watchtower cannery in Woodrow, and I never knew Rutherford's grave was there. For all his public exposure, the private man remained mysterious, remote, inaccessible. His grave is unvisited.

VII

Catholics, Mob Violence, Civil Liberties, and the Draft

> The psychological nub of their appeal, I believe, is their conviction that all members of the sect must constantly and fully participate in spreading the gospel of the sect, thus supplying to drab and common-place lives a wonderfully consoling unity of action and purpose. . . . We constantly forget how deep the appeal of a communal life lived for a high purpose and involving sacrifice and even martyrdom is. And this appeal operates impartially whether the common purpose be good or bad, rational or unreasoned. Especially is it strong when it combines with its own intrinsic purpose a sanction for rebellion against constituted authority, moral and civil. . . . When we fail to realize this, when we subject the Witnesses to mob violence or to prison, we play directly into their hands and cease ourselves to be Christian.—Harry Lorin Binsse, *Commonweal*, Jan. 10, 1947, p. 318.

During the 1930s and '40s, hundreds of Jehovah's Witnesses were arrested for selling without a licence, disturbing the peace, violating Sunday Sabbath laws, refusing to salute the flag; 4,500 were jailed during World War II for violation of the Selective Service Act. Their houses were stoned and raided; their meeting halls were sacked; they were struck off relief rolls.

The Witnesses were seen as a threat to national security and to interfaith harmony; they were despised by conservative elements of the Roman Catholic Church, which they had insistently and aggressively calumnized. Both their message and the media they employed to promulgate it aroused ire. The Witnesses defied logic, made public nuisances of themselves, engaged in Know-Nothing Catholic-baiting, refused to participate in a war that was generally perceived to be a good and righteous war, and offended the sensibilities of people of every class. In the opinion of the American Civil Liberties Union's Leon Friedman, they "deliberately, calculatedly tested the law"—and we must all be pleased that they did: they won 150 State Supreme Court cases and more than 30 precedent-setting Supreme Court cases, forcing the Court to broaden the meaning of the First and Fourteenth Amendments. It is impossible to speak of the history of civil liberties in the United States without speaking of them. Whatever their motives, we are very much in their debt.

In the early part of the century, most of the opposition to the Witnesses originated with the Protestant churches, who saw them as wayward children. The Catholic Church, unthreatened, maintained a calm and silent dignity. As the Society expanded, and its fulminations against the Vatican grew louder and more abrasive, it became locked in bitter antagonism with the Catholic Church. With exceptions—all on the side of the Church—nobody behaved scrupulously or well.

Our hatred for the Church was an invigorating elixir. It drove us to heights of inspired lunacy.

I had been baptized Catholic; I had never been confirmed or taken the Sacrament of the Eucharist. Shortly before my conversion, I went with a friend to Sunday Mass. In my working-class neighbourhood, everybody was Catholic or Jewish except our family; we were No Religion. And I didn't much like being No Religion, feeling disinherited and rootless. A priest made some astringent remarks about the anti-religious pests who went from door to door badgering people with lies about the Church, and he told his parishioners to slam their doors when Jehovah's Witnesses called. There was something oily and hateful in his voice from which I recoiled; I felt a surge of sympathy for those poor people—who were obliged to go from door to slammed door. The Church was magnificent, I thought, and magnificence ought not to condescend to abuse insignificant pests. Later I wallowed in the Witnesses' vilification of the Church.

I found the Witnesses, when they came, congenial. At first shocked, I slipped easily into listening without being offended to off-colour jokes about the virginity of Mary; I began to be as derisive as my elders about "dog-collared" priests; I believed absolutely that nuns were forcibly imprisoned (or, alternatively, holding wild orgies within their cloisters); I crossed the street, afraid of contamination, when I passed the local convent; I knew that young girls were corrupted in confessionals—and I censored wicked fantasies of fat-priest hands slipping up my legs. The wickedness of the Church was tangible; it was evidenced in its idols, its purple trappings.

During World War II, the Witnesses—who were themselves being arrested as Fifth Columnists—gave voice to the idea, shared by many non-Catholics, that the Church was an elaborate political organization whose piety was a cloak for Machiavellian schemes of world power; they charged the Church with being the American Fifth Column. Rutherford had made himself highly unpopular by declaring that "religion has always been the chief instrument employed by the Devil to reproach the name of Almighty God." Not content with impugning the Church's relationship to the Almighty, Rutherford also attributed the growth of Communism and Nazism to the Church: "Communism has been encouraged by the Jesuits, the secret order of the Roman Catholic Hierarchy. . . . In this manner, the Nazis of Germany were organized."

I believed, as did all Witnesses, that guns and ammunition were stored in the cellars and crypts of Catholic churches. We believed that the Vatican had a standing army waiting for a command to take over America. (Inasmuch as America was at that time five-sixths Protestant, it is wonderful how the Church managed to horrify and fascinate us so.) Another picturesque conceit of Rutherford's was that when Armageddon came, all priests and nuns would disguise themselves in overalls in a futile attempt to hide their clerical robes from the Lord.

It is the Witnesses' contention that the Church initiated and engineered attacks against the Witnesses. The Witnesses' verbal abuse of the Church did elicit retaliatory attacks; ruffians and hoodlums often interpreted their priests' indictments of the Witnesses as a mandate to abuse the Witnesses physically.

Class prejudice and fear of foreigners and immigrants played a part in this two-way thrashing. The Witnesses, not troubling to substantiate their claim, said that the Ku Klux Klan was a Catholic terrorist organization, and Watchtower Society representatives railed against Catholic mine workers of "foreign extraction" who objected to the Witnesses' blasting the peace with sound-car invectives against the Church. Catholics, calling Jehovah's Witnesses "a wart on the spirit of national advancement," said contrapuntally that the Witnesses were direct spiritual descendants of the American (Know-Nothing) Party of 1835 and spiritual siblings of the KKK, and that the Watchtower Society secured its attention from "the poorer classes of the South's farm tenants; from the hill-billies of the Southwest; from the Okies who, dejected and rejected, wander about hopelessly; from the ignorant, superstitious, and illiterate of large city slums." The Jesuit magazine *America*, while full of ripe invective, showed flashes of insight and pity: "'Pastor' Russell answered their anguish"—the anguish of the chronically unemployed and the victims of social injustice—"by organizing the Russellites," who "continued to rant against and hate everyone and everything not of themselves." [H. C. McGinnis, *America*, Feb. 8, 15, 1941; March 22, 1941]

The Witnesses retorted that the doctrines of the Trinity and the immortality of the soul were "devilish" and that the Church was politically and spiritually corrupt; but the threat they posed to the religious establishment was probably not the determining factor in their persecution during the 1930s and '40s. It is more likely that the threat they posed to secular authorities was what landed them in jail. The American Legion and the Ku Klux Klan vociferated against the Witnesses because they were not patriotic at a time when national security was in jeopardy. What was really at issue was the American flag.

On October 6, 1935, Judge Rutherford spoke on a coast-to-coast chain radio broadcast on "Saluting the Flag." In his scratchy, thin, wobbly but impassioned tenor, he told his listeners that Scriptural obligations and their relationship to God made it impossible for Jehovah's Witnesses to salute any "image or representation," including the American flag; Rutherford interpreted the second of the Ten Commandments—"Thou shalt not make unto thee any graven image, or any likeness . . . Thou shalt not bow down thyself to them, nor serve them"—to mean that saluting the flag constituted "idolatry." His lecture was published in a booklet called *Loyalty*, and the Witnesses distributed millions of copies of what appeared to be an inflammatory attack on a cherished institution.

The Witnesses accepted Rutherford's premises, though inconsistent with the rest of their beliefs—according to them, Christians are under no obligation to obey the letter of the Mosaic Law—with a fanaticism that was generally felt to be unlovely. Their meetings, like their lives, were dull and oppressive. They had to look elsewhere, outside themselves, for the mark of God. He had chosen them, but how could they prove it? Not with magnificent edifices, not with a rich and varied history. They were young, comparatively weak, foolish and insignificant in the eyes of the world; they had no glorious music, no poetry, no formal ritual, no liturgy, and no martyrs. Their first leader had been a haberdasher and, by common view, a scoundrel; their second leader was an intemperate lawyer with a reputation for slick business transactions. However much they suspended disbelief, that must have rankled. Power and glory and all the world and the kingdoms of the world were soon to be theirs, but their leaders were not kings or shepherds or poets or sages. They were wilier, certainly, than most men, and vain, but they were not, by any standards, glorious. Ordinariness was the stale bread of the world from which the Witnesses had fled. To sustain their image of themselves, perhaps they needed to have something immense and extraordinary occur, something that would raise them above themselves, justify and exalt them. Rutherford had one weapon, the law. He used it. He made things happen.

A year and a month after Rutherford's broadcast about flag saluting, something that was to prove to be immense did happen.

On November 6, 1935, two elementary-school children in the coal-mining district of Pennsylvania refused to salute the flag. Their father, Walter Gobitas, was arrested, and the children were expelled from school. Gobitas initiated a suit against the Board of Education, Minersville School District. In 1936, 1,149 Witnesses were arrested for refusal to salute the flag and for violating a variety of state and municipal ordinances. [*Yearbook*, 1975, pp. 169–72]

The Supreme Court, having declined several times to review the expulsion of the Gobitas children for not participating in the flag-saluting ceremony, accepted jurisdiction in 1940. With one dissenting voice, that of Justice Harlan Fiske Stone, the Court ruled to uphold the Gobitas children's expulsion and decided that school boards had the right to choose to require children to salute the American flag. The Court's majority decision, written by Justice Felix Frankfurter, was based on its opinion that religiously motivated refusal to salute the flag represented a threat to nationalism and security.

The Court handed down its decision on June 3, 1940. Between June 12 and June 20, hundreds of physical attacks upon Witnesses were reported to the United States Department of Justice.

The nation was threatened by war. An editorial in *The Saturday Evening Post* said:

> It seems likely that the United States harbours no other out-of-step and out-of-sympathy minority of anything like [the Witnesses'] size and militancy. In the event of war, they are sure to furnish the largest quota of conscientious objectors, and, perhaps, the most troublesome. In this near-war period, no other group so boldly condemns not only the current patriotic trend but patriotism, specifically and in general. No other, for good measure, condemns so many other things by which Americans lay store.

The government did not sanction the fury of the mob. On June 16, 1940, U.S. Solicitor General Francis Biddle told an NBC radio audience: "Jehovah's Witnesses have been repeatedly set upon and beaten. . . . The Attorney General has ordered an immediate investigation of these charges. The people must be alert and watchful, and above all cool and sane. Since mob violence will make the government's task infinitely more difficult, it will not be tolerated. We shall not defeat the Nazi evil by emulating its methods."

In 1940, the ACLU defended 1,300 Witnesses in 200 legal cases.

Nor were the churches monolithically arrayed against the Witnesses; after the first wave of war hysteria had passed, liberal voices were raised in their defence and in reaction against mob terror. An editorial in the October 7, 1942, issue of *Christian Century,* which calls reports of mob violence in Springfield, Illinois, Klamath Falls, Oregon, and Little Rock, Arkansas, "physically nauseating," reflects the growing revulsion against mob violence among civil libertarians who were beginning to understand that their own First and Fourteenth Amendment rights were put in jeopardy when those of Jehovah's Witnesses were threatened.

The Witnesses fought their legal battles with skill. Hayden C. Covington earned a reputation for arguing brilliantly before the Court; but all Witnesses learned to equip themselves to deal with police and judges. At weekly "service meetings" during the war years, they received paralegal training. They held mock trials, some of them lasting for weeks, with overseers role-playing the parts of prosecution and defence attorneys. They were coached in how to respond to arresting officers, and how to behave procedurally in order to establish the basis for appellate review of convictions.

For eight years, the Witnesses maintained their own "Kingdom Schools" for children who had been expelled. The schools were communes. The children were, for the most part, boarders, since petrol rationing made it impossible for them to return more than once or twice a month to their homes. Instructed by Witness teachers, they began each day with a discussion of a Bible text; one half-hour of Bible study daily was part of the curriculum. They performed kitchen chores and, regardless of age, spent most of Saturday and Sunday mornings proselytizing. It cannot be said to have been a carefree childhood.

In 1943, the Witness children went back to their classrooms. Mob violence had abated; America had changed. It had become silly to regard these children as a clear and present danger to the national security; and in fact, most Americans, obsessed with the idea that Japanese-Americans threatened their security, had transferred their fear and hatred to the "slant-eyed devils" in their midst. In 1943, the Supreme Court reversed the Gobitas decision by a vote of 6 to 3.

The way had been prepared for the Court's historic reversal in *West Virginia v. Barnette*:

In an earlier decision, the Court had voted 5 to 4 to uphold the validity of an ordinance requiring the licensing of colporteurs (proselytizers) in cities of Alabama, Arkansas, and Arizona (*Jones v. Opelika,* 316, U.S. 584, 1942). In a vigorous dissenting opinion, Chief Justice Stone declared that in the decision a way had been found "for the effective suppression of speech and religion despite Constitutional guarantees." The liberal trio, Justices Black, Murphy, and Douglas, in their own dissenting opinion, took the unprecedented step of acknowledging that they had been wrong on the Gobitas flag-salute case.

Jones v. Opelika had aroused part of the press to the threat to its own freedom. "As a result," according to an editorial in *Christian Century* (Jan. 13, 1943, p. 38),

> newspapers which undoubtedly regard Jehovah's witnesses as a collection of religious crackpots are now giving powerful support to the effort to obtain a reversal of the court's decision. By keeping the issue before the public and by providing eminent legal counsel they have done much to reinstate it on the docket of the highest tribunal. It is a pity that church bodies, whose interests are equally at stake, have done nothing to parallel the efforts of the press to obtain a new hearing.
>
> There may be a tendency in some quarters to minimize the importance of these cases because it is the rights of Jehovah's witnesses which are immediately involved. Do not the Witnesses stand for a hodgepodge of peculiar millennial ideas . . .? They do. Then why worry about the means which may be taken to force them to conform to community norms or to keep their provocative tracts out of circulation? Because civil liberty under the Constitution means nothing unless it protects the rights of every citizen.

The Court later re-examined the constitutional issue upon which it had divided in *Jones v. Opelika*. The issue was whether religious liberty is violated by the imposition of a non-discriminatory licence tax on the sale of religious books and tracts. The Court ruled in *Murdock v. Pennsylvania* (319 U.S. 105, 1943) that a tax laid on the free exercise of religion, as protected by the First and Fourteenth Amendments, is unconstitutional. Jehovah's Witnesses were, in the opinion of Justice Douglas, engaged in an exercise of religion, equivalent to that of more conventional churches, and not in a commercial enterprise: "The hand distribution of religious tracts . . . occupies the same high estate under the First Amendment as do worship in the churches and preaching from the pulpits."

Ruling that "an itinerant evangelist, however misguided or intolerant he may be, does not become a mere book agent by selling the Bible or religious tracts to help defray his expenses or to sustain him," the Court thus began to legitimize "marginal" religions and to recognize what has been called the minority concept of religion. Street solicitation was accepted as required religious activity and not as commercial peddling; similarly, the right of the Witnesses to regard flag saluting as idolatry, rather than as a patriotic ceremony, was recognized in the *Barnette* case. The right of minority groups to protection under the Bill of Rights was seen as essential to the preservation of the rights of the majority.

Clearly, their defenders did not find Jehovah's Witnesses acceptable; far from it. They found the threat to their own liberties—civil and religious—more odious and pernicious than the sect they were loath to endorse but obliged to defend.

It is significant that the Witnesses, who filed appeals regularly on the basis of freedom of religion during the mid-1930s, did not get very far until they changed their tactics and grounded their appeals on freedom of the press in 1938. In that year, the Court struck down an ordinance against literature distribution (*Lovell v. Griffin,* 303 U.S. 444). Subsequent cases, based on a broad concept of multiple First Amendment rights of speech and advocacy, established new rights for the use of public places, door-to-door solicitation, and "freedom to promulgate."

The Court edged into the question of religious freedom to act, as opposed to freedom to believe, by way of freedom of the press. In 1940, the Court, overturning a conviction for breach of the peace by a Witness proselytizer, ruled that the First Amendment "embraces two concepts—freedom to believe and freedom to act. The first is absolute, but the second remains subject to regulation for the protection of society." Because the proselytizer "raised no such clear and present menace to public peace and order as to render him liable to conviction," his conviction was set aside. (*Cantwell v. Conn.,* 310 U.S. 296 [1940])

The clear-and-present-danger argument was first advanced by Oliver Wendell Holmes and Louis Brandeis. The ambiguous maxim that freedom of speech or of conscience, or any other freedom, is to be upheld except where the actions constitute "a clear and present danger" to the nation was at issue in the Court's review of the Gobitas flag-salute case.

Justice Robert H. Jackson ruled that First Amendment freedoms "are susceptible of restriction only to prevent clear and immediate danger to interests which the state may lawfully protect." When *West Virginia v. Barnette* came before the Court, Justice James F. Byrnes, a liberal Roosevelt appointee, had replaced Justice Wiley Rutledge, a strict constructionist; three members of the Court had changed their minds since *Gobitas*: and two other members of the Court unexpectedly ruled with Justice Jackson that "to compel conscientiously scrupulous children to salute deprives them of the freedom of religion guaranteed by the Fourteenth Amendment."

The claim, widely asserted, that Jehovah's Witnesses through boundless courage and unending perseverance have won more United States Supreme Court victories for the Bill of Rights than any other single group seems to have ample support.—A. L. Wirin, ACLU, *The Open Forum*, Aug. 21, 1943, p. 1.

By the end of World War II, Jehovah's Witnesses had made 190 appeals to higher courts; they had won over 125 State Supreme Court cases, and most of 40 Supreme Court decisions.

The Witnesses established that distribution of literature "calculated to encourage disloyalty to the state and national governments" could not be made the basis for conviction under a sedition statute forbidding that which "tends to create disloyalty and causes an attitude of stubborn refusal to salute the flag":

If the state cannot constrain one to violate his conscientious religious conviction by saluting the national emblem, then it cannot punish him for imparting his view on the subject to his followers and exhorting them to accept those views. . . . As applied to the appellants it punishes them although what they communicated is not claimed or shown to have been done with an evil or a sinister purpose, to have advocated or incited subversive action against the nation or state, or to have threatened any clear and present danger to our institutions or our government. What these appellants communicated were their beliefs and opinions.—*Taylor v. Miss.*, 319 U.S. 583, 1943.

The Witnesses secured the right to preach in privately-owned or government-owned towns, and in apartments without the permission of landlords; the right to use sound amplifiers "at reasonable volume"; the right of parents to retain custody of children reared in their faith; the right to advertise meetings by placards; the right not to serve on juries.

The Court had ruled, in *Barnette v. West Virginia,* that the Witnesses' "spiritual arbitrariness" would not "disintegrate the social order." Unhappily for me, this enlightened view was not shared by school children. At the time I was converted, the threat of mob violence had receded, and the days of communal suffering were an occasion for nostalgia; there was never any question of my being expelled from school or arrested. But I did spend a lot of time in the offices of principals, assistant principals, and deans explaining why I didn't salute the flag; and the Witnesses' admonition not to "make friends with the world" was, for me, almost entirely gratuitous: very few children wanted to make friends with me.

Teachers frequently singled me out for attention. The nicest regarded me with a mixture of admiration and pity; the coarsest treated me with frank and meddlesome curiosity; they all tried to change me. I was a challenge—intelligent, earnest, serious, aloof, passionate, and perverse, living a mysterious inner life that vexed or titillated them depending on their temperaments. This, while it fed but did not satisfy my hunger for approval, did not endear me to my peers.

I was almost always alone. I always had to be assigned a partner for school activities. In high school, walking down the corridor between classes was an agony repeated every forty-five minutes because nobody ever walked with me. I don't think anyone knew I suffered; I appeared remote and self-contained. But while I had created my isolation, and the other children reacted self-preservatively by scorning my difference and my alien behaviour, I hated it. Everything commonplace enthralled me: girls' linking pinkies with other girls in easy friendship, sharing sodas and cupcakes in the lunchroom; it all seemed remarkable and unattainable. (The trouble was, of course, that while I wanted to be just like everybody else, I also enjoyed being extraordinary and unique—I must have wanted that more.)

During World War II, over 8,000 draft-age Witnesses registered with their draft boards as ministers. Roughly half were granted the ministerial classification, 4-D. Approximately 4,000 were imprisoned. It has been estimated that 60 to 70 per cent of all federal offenders convicted for draft violations during World War II were Witnesses.

When World War II ended, the Witnesses imprisoned for draft violations came home like conquering heroes. Denied the ministerial status they sought, they had spent the war years in federal penitentiaries, while at the local congregations myths grew up around them.

We saw the returning convicts as whole of soul, adorable martyrs. Fellow prisoners had tended to see them as enigmatic nuisances.

Jim Peck and Ralph diGia, pacifists who are on the staff of the War Resisters League, were imprisoned conscientious objectors in Danbury Federal Penitentiary, where the Witnesses represented one-third to one-half the draft violators, from 1942 to 1945. They express no small amazement (and irritation) at the Witnesses' homogeneity and their determined aloofness from other prisoners, their lack of spontaneity, warmth and passion:

PECK: If you were unlucky enough to land at a table with them in the mess hall, either they were silent or they tried to push their religion at you. I never saw them kid around, and I never saw them get worked up about anything; they were monomaniacal. When the rest of us complained—we had a three-month strike against racial segregation, and naturally we griped about the food a lot—they remained completely indifferent and aloof. When some of us pulled "tough time," they unbent to the extent of telling us not to worry because *The Watchtower* said the war would be over on such-and-such a date and we'd be out of jail. The funny thing was, when the date came and went and the war still wasn't over, they never had any rationalization or excuse; they simply never mentioned it again.

DIGIA: You couldn't have a real conversation with them. No hope. I never could understand their language. One of the Witnesses tried to convert me, and I said, "Look, we're all human beings." And he said, "No, only God is a Being; we're human creatures." How can you talk to somebody who makes distinctions like that? What does that even mean? . . . They had their own authoritarian leadership; everyone learned the same thing at the same time. They were all strongly anti-Catholic. The main villain was "the Pope of Rome," the Vatican—not Hitler, not the warden, not the U.S. for putting them in jail.

PECK: I never really got to know any of them. And I tried. All the other COs were really friendly. JWs never made a friend. They were quite distinct—they never saw themselves as a community of resisters. They didn't consider themselves COs; they said they weren't conscientiously opposed to wars because they would fight at Armageddon—the final war of good versus evil—if God required them to. They resented being called COs.

DIGIA: Well, they were always together, constantly reinforcing their belief that they had the truth and that they were superior. They nourished one another. They had a high survival rate in concentration camps, I understand, probably for the same reason. The rest of us—well, our outside lives impinged; not them. They were much more together than the other COs. The COs never acted as a homogeneous unit; they did. They were a *We*, doing it for God. We used to debate what was good, what was bad, what was moral, what was immoral; they had all the answers before they asked any of the questions.

PECK: Their attitude toward us was that of the religious toward the heathen.

DIGIA: The enlightened to the unenlightened, the washed to the unwashed.

PECK: Yes. They had no interest in us, no curiosity about us, no fellow feeling—unless we showed signs of accepting their belief.

DIGIA: I can't think what they were interested in except their theology. I can't remember anything that passed for what you'd call a conversation. You know, I have so little sense of them as individuals, I can't remember one singular thing about one single Witness. There was one guy who seemed awfully nice; I had the feeling that he was trying to reach out to us but that he was also afraid to get to know us, because it would scare him if he discovered we weren't bad people. How could any one who liked us believe God was going to savage us?

PECK: I really don't think of them as resisters. I think of them as capitulators. There are times I actually forget that the Witnesses ever went to jail.

Peck and diGia remark that the Witnesses did not think of themselves, nor did they wish to be thought of, as conscientious objectors. Very few Witnesses applied for CO status; those who did were regarded, by the rest of us, as compromisers. The only honourable course—directed by the Watchtower Society—was to apply for ministerial exemption. Even fewer Witnesses agreed to perform alternative civilian service; those who did were treated like outcasts by the rest of us. During the Vietnam War, the Society issued new imperatives: many Witnesses applied for CO status, and when ordered by the courts, they did perform alternative service.

Under the 1940 Selective Service Act (Sec. 5d, Par. 360), "regular or duly ordained ministers of religion" and divinity students were exempted from the draft (but not from registering for the draft). A "regular minister of religion" was defined as "a man who customarily preaches and teaches the principles of religion of a recognized church, religious cult, or religious organization of which he is a member, without having been formally ordained as a minister of religion; and who is recognized by such church, sect, or organization as a minister." Under the Act, the Witnesses were "considered to constitute a recognized religious sect."

Hayden C. Covington and General Lewis B. Hershey, Deputy Director of Selective Service, arranged for the exemption of "full-time" ministers (called "pioneers") and members of the Bethel Family. (It would have been unthinkable, during the First World War, when leaders of the Society were imprisoned under the Sedition and Espionage Acts, for such an agreement to be made.)

Those who were once persecuted were now privileged. But while "pioneers" appointed by the Society, and members of the Bethel family, had no trouble getting ministerial exemptions, such was not the case for Witnesses who spent most of their time in secular employment.

The local boards were empowered to use their own discretion with respect to those Witnesses who were not clearly granted exemption by the Act. As Major Edward S. Shattuck, Chief of the Legal Division of Selective Service, wrote. "In the last analysis, it is the function of the local selective service board to review the facts in each case and make the proper classification decision." (File Ref. III—Ministers; sec. 5d; Par. 360b; Jan. 25, 1941)

Covington contends that many boards acted in an "arbitrary and capricious" manner by denying Witnesses ministerial status. But it can't be denied that the boards, given wide discretionary powers and with popular sentiment to contend with, had a tough time. "Each of Jehovah's witnesses is a minister. If he is not a preacher he is not one of Jehovah's witnesses," Covington argued. The Witnesses' argument, which is difficult to controvert, is that if they are a recognized religion, they do have the right to establish the criteria as to who is a minister of that religion. [Cole, pp. 201–203]

Congress had made no provision for a judicial review of a registrant's classification. Witnesses who were sentenced in district courts for violation of the Selective Service Act were denied the right to plead their cases. The decision of the local boards made in conformity with regulations were final, even though they may have been erroneous. But, after the war in Europe was over, the Supreme Court, reversing a prior decision (*Falbo v. U.S.*, 320 U.S. 549, Jan. 3, 1944), condemned the practice of denying registrants the right to defend themselves against indictments brought against them. William Murray Estep, one of Jehovah's Witnesses, was classified 1-A and ordered to report for induction; he refused to be inducted, claiming he was exempt from service because he was a minister. He was indicted for violation of the Act. At the trial he sought to attack the classification given him by the local board. The court ruled that no such defence could be tendered; he was sentenced to three and one-half years. The judgment of conviction was affirmed on appeal. (*Estep v. U.S.*, 326, U.S. 114, Feb. 4, 1946)

The Supreme Court ruled that Estep's conviction "reduced criminal trials under the Act to proceedings . . . barren of the customary safeguards which the law has designed for the protection of the accused." Mr. Justice Murphy, concurring with the majority opinion of Mr. Justice Douglas, wrote:

> To sustain the convictions . . . would require adherence to the proposition that a person may be criminally punished without ever being accorded the opportunity to prove that the prosecution is based upon an invalid administrative order. That is a proposition to which I cannot subscribe. [p. 9 (Oct. Term 1945. Nos. 292 and 66 on Writ of Certiorari to U.S. Circuit Court of Appeals for the Third Circuit)]

The *Estep* ruling that courts must allow draft registrants to prove that local boards acted without jurisdiction meant that the boards were no longer the final arbiters of registrants' fate—a significant addition to the literature of civil liberties, because it prevented local boards from the unchecked exercise of local prejudices. The *Estep* case is an important one in the annals of civil liberties. The Court did not rule on the merits of Estep's claim that he was a minister; it simply ruled that the appeals court had acted in violation of due process by not allowing him to make a defence. *Estep* set an important precedent; due process of law could not be eroded, even during a national emergency.

At the beginning of the war, district judges, according to Covington, were almost "totally antagonistic. They were against any defence being made by Jehovah's Witnesses at their trials." [*Faith,* p. 187] They were, he says, greatly prejudiced. "After a large number of cases continued to flow through their courts," Covington says, "many of the judges began to change and mellow. They afterward took a more restrained attitude in presiding at the trial of cases involving Jehovah's Witnesses." [*Ibid.,* p. 186]

The *Estep* case had something to do with their "mellowing," of course, as did victory in the European theatre of war. As the threat to national security diminished, both courts and draft boards exerted less pressure on dissenters. Unorthodox religions were beginning, in a less repressive climate, to enjoy the full protection of the courts.

The Korean war saw a further improvement in the Witnesses' status: convicted draft violators were paroled earlier and, by all accounts, treated better than other COs. And during the war in Vietnam, draft-age Witnesses received discriminatory preferential treatment from boards and courts.

Bureau of Prisons statistics show that 75 per cent of the men serving time in jail for draft violations during the Vietnamese war were Jehovah's Witnesses. As of June, 1968, 574 out of 739 Selective Service violators in federal penitentiaries were Jehovah's Witnesses. The reason the number of total draft violators is surprisingly low is, in addition to the fact that Canada harboured many COs, that there were built-in loopholes in the law which many resisters—or evaders—took advantage of; the New York City Board of Education, for example, received 20,000 more applications for teachers' licences in 1969 than it had in 1968. Jehovah's Witnesses could not, for the most part, have leaped into that draft-exempt profession: most have no college degree. It is generally conceded that the Witnesses were accorded more courtesy of belief and trust than any other class of objector.

It may be conjectured that the Witnesses were considerably less threatening to establish authority than radical longhairs. They were not making whoopee or revolution on college campuses (and they were *clean* and quiet; and they didn't "off the pigs"; it's unlikely that many of them had ever even heard of Ho Chi Minh). In a climate of protest and rage, among 1960s freaks and moral anarchists, the Witnesses seemed like a breath of '40s small-town air.

In any case, it is a matter of record that the Witnesses were given preferential treatment by the courts. According to attorney Leon Friedman,

> a strategy developed throughout the Federal judiciary as judge talked to judge; when a judge refused exemption to a Witness, the case would go to appeals. Although the general rule is that a sentence within the statutory maximum will not be disturbed by an appeal court, courts would in fact frequently vacate or reduce sentences. Appeal courts modified sentences imposed by trial courts, sentences which, in the ordinary way, would not be reviewable. In other words, an extraordinary situation arose in which lower courts were allowed to interpret statutes, in spite of the axiom that "a sentence imposed by a Federal district judge, if within the statutory limits, is generally not subject to review."
>
> And draft lawyers loved it: "If you treat the Witnesses that way," we argued, "you have to treat our clients equally well."

VIII
The Lure of Certainty

The world perceives them as different; and they feel themselves to be different. And that is the magic of a religion that fears magic, mystery, poetry—a religion that treats ecstasy as an aberration and flees from passion with a passion that is thoroughly small and dry.

> How wonderful it is to live a pure and simple life! It's really good to sit around a table and share thoughts with simple folk. . . .
>
> Today in the late afternoon, after a nap, I went to Klaus's house, the tailor, the Witness of Jehovah. I was feeling tired and a little bit shy and nauseated because this morning I bought a dirndl, a pocket-book, and a bakery bun, and as always when I deal with worldly things, it drained me. . . .
>
> I will write to my brother and tell him I have found The Truth.
>
> What a wonderful thing it is to be able to really trust people because you know they're seeking after the truth. How can I describe the atmosphere around these good, honest people? Brother O. spoke so wisely while we were sitting there drinking a bit of schnapps and eating a bit of garlic, bacon, cheese, and bread. He also spoke of his six years in prison under Hitler. Oh, how brave! How I admire that happiness of his, and I know it's good.
>
> —from the diary of Vera Retsoff

Vera was 17 when she wrote this, having been converted by Jehovah's Witnesses in a small village in Germany. Multilingual, from an affluent, achieving family, Vera ran away from college and was a Jesus Freak for two years before she became a Witness. She remained a Witness for three years, until her marriage to her childhood sweetheart; and her growing doubts together with her growing conviction that it was not "selfish" to use her talents effectively divorced her from the Society.

> Yeah, it's hard. It's hard to be a Jehovah's Witness. It's hard . . . like the Witnesses can't . . . you don't supposed to like . . . you gotta be good, you can't party, you gotta go to all the meetings, field service and stuff. And like people on the street are saying, like lots of people think we're crazy, so it's hard to cope with the people. But what else is there? You be out on the streets, man, you be missin' a good thing. 'Cause there's *nothin'* out there. I mean, the majority of teen-agers is bad. I'm gonna keep on tryin'. But it's hard. I mean, it's bad on the street, but we

gotta be out on the street. Now, me, I been president of the Black Knights—there was thousands of us. I'm not talkin' about killin' nobody, you understand; but I wanted to feel big, dig it? I'm tryin' now, though, you know. To be good. 'Cause the Witnesses are right: There's nobody out there gonna do *nothin'* about all the poverty and shit and war and stuff. *Nobody.*
—Booker Smith, a 17-year-old black from Harlem who is an unbaptized Witness.

You get used to the South Bronx; you don't see the suffering anymore. To the people who live there, it's not suffering, it's their life. They are casualties of the Devil's system. And so are you. From Adam all have sinned and all are victimized. You too. Jehovah's Witnesses are not hanging out on street corners or into immorality or dope. We're not violent like the rest of the people. *Our* people in the South Bronx are physically and spiritually clean. . . . As far as all those programmes to feed people and help people with dope problems, and day-care centres and social work . . . some people think that's doing good, but if they're not following the Bible, they're not doing good.
—Thomas Bart, 21-year-old black Witness elder.

All of a sudden there are so many questions and they're so heavy. Jehovah knows I want to serve him. But how can I do so out of a clean heart with no reservations or disagreements? How come there are so many questions when I really know all the answers? What about all the wickedness and suffering God has permitted on the earth? Why, if he has the power . . . why, if he loves? Why? I know the answer from the book: The issue is political—God's rule against Satan's. For the last 6,000 years, man has had the opportunity to rule, and he has proved incapable of doing so. And the suffering of the innocent is the result of man's choosing worldly governments instead of God's heavenly kingdom. The suffering is a result of man's choice, not God's doing. Also, because he hasn't ended the world yet, Jehovah is really merciful: He's giving more people the opportunity to serve him. . . . But way down deep, I don't really believe it. . . . The waiting seems so long. I wish the end would come now. This instant. Now. I'm tired of waiting. . . .
—from the diary of a 23-year-old Witness who left the Society soon after she wrote this.

It's odd; I really don't like anything about being a Witness, but I gave myself to them fully and completely. I held nothing in reserve. I was looking to them for honesty and decency. I couldn't find it. But I couldn't allow myself to be critical. Then I had a nervous breakdown. Maybe that was my way of getting out? The Witnesses felt betrayed by my breakdown. Their faces were so hard. No help. After the breakdown, I couldn't go from door to door any more. I wanted God to tell me directly what to do. I couldn't get Him off my back. . . . I was so conscientious. Wouldn't you think that the more conscientious I was,

the more rewards I should have had? But the more I lent myself to the Witnesses, the more I suffered.
—a former Witness.

They shrink from the intolerable fear that God does not care about men. Perhaps the original impulse was one of love: can a God-hungry soul contemplate the thought of souls damned in hell? Charles Taze Russell gazed into the fires of hell, averted his eyes from that vision of eternal suffering and damnation, and substituted for the God of Passion—the suffering Christ of the gospel—a pragmatic, tribal God.

For some men, the stubborn, painful certainty that God does not exist has (though suffused with nausea and dread) been gorgeously energizing.

For other men, the absence of the sure knowledge of God has been a thrilling and lucid invitation to act absolutely as if He did not exist, to be fully human, to substitute duty and struggle and human love for the impulse to devotion and praise, to adore a flawed and wonderful world.

For Russell and his followers, who had a sense of premonition and foreboding, it was necessary to invent a personal, concrete, and immediate solution to the injustices of life. "The mean and the vulgar flourish, the righteous suffer," said the Psalmist, praising God in radiant despair. The mean and the vulgar flourish, the righteous suffer, said Russell . . . and he made charts and juggled dates and numbers in a frenzied attempt to reduce the beauty and the terror of the world to manageable proportions. In the process —in his fear of the absurd, the unexplained, the incomprehensible, in his flight from mystery, from the desert of God's uncertain grace —he was obliged to renounce both the world and the divinity of Christ.

The Witnesses have modified their ideology through the years, but what has never changed is that in order to accommodate a wholesome hatred for injustice, the Witnesses have had to embrace an unhealthy hatred of the physical, material world. The world is evil, loathsome and abhorrent; man's nature is evil, loathsome, and abhorrent. They have never been able to reconcile love of God with love of the world.

Their religion is neither one of austere penance nor one of sublime contemplation. They move in our midst like disdainful strangers, waiting for Jehovah—a hard and irritable judge, not a living flame—to enter into wrath. They neither tremble at the abyss nor swoon at the altar of a magnificent God. They spit out the world as if it tasted of ashes; they reject the large idea of a mystical union with God, a communion of brothers and saints. Their God is querulous and small; their religion nourishes damaged deserters from the world, offering them a brittle certainty.

Because God will accomplish all things without the collaboration of man, they do not strive to accomplish the Kingdom of Heaven on earth.

Because they believe the world exists only to be despised, because they believe it is rotten, they are content to leave it to rot.

It is alien to their thinking that God and man can work together to perfect and transform the world—and just as alien to their thinking that man, unsupported by God, is made beautiful by struggle and human love. They do not rejoice in the salvation of man by God-made-man, or in the redemption of man by man. They are outside the tradition of the other Christian churches: they do not believe in the Trinity, the Incarnation, the Eucharist, the immortality of the soul. Their linear, eschatological religion is literalist. The consequences of not acting are, of course, as weighty as the consequences of acting. Absenting themselves from the conflicts of the world, they surrender the organization of the world to others.

It would be easy to conclude that they love neither God (if by God we mean the God of the gospel who died for men's sins), nor man; to judge them so lacking in idealism and compassion as to be monstrous in their indifference. Still, their religion allows them to believe that the world is terrible, but that life is not hopeless. Because it rigidly controls all aspects of their behaviour, it gives them the illusion of moral superiority, and of safety. It delivers people who have no tolerance for ambiguity from having to make ethical choices. It allows self-loathers to project their hatred on to the world. It translates the allure of the world into Satanic temptation, so that those who fear its enticements are armed against seduction. Moralistic rather than moral, it rescues its adherents from vice (drug addiction, criminality, dirty dishes) and from the demands of art. Obsession, which characterizes geniuses, children, madmen, saints, and artists, is seen as idolatrous.

Yet in the heart of every Witness is the felt knowledge that should he leave his spiritual home, he will die a social death at the hands of his brothers now, a spiritual death at the hands of his God later. And the messages received by the Witnesses from their leaders remind them always of the first Fall, the dangerous tightrope they walk between omnipotence and disinheritance. Repressing human needs, individual desires, they may seem smug—but never entirely, never joyously, sure.

To understand them, it is necessary to understand their doctrine, and particularly their views on evil and salvation, from which all their hopes and fears and their social attitudes (and their appeal—which seems to outsiders bloodless and legalistic) stem:

Evil; The Fall; Immortality

By revealing an original fall, Christianity provides our intelligence with a reason for the disconcerting excess of sin and suffering. . . . Next, in order to win our love and secure our faith, it unveils to our eyes and hearts the moving and unfathomable reality of the historical Christ in whom the exemplary life of an individual man conceals this mysterious drama.—Pierre Teilhard de Chardin, *The Divine Milieu* (pp. 102–3)

The existence of evil is the central problem for all religions. Jehovah's Witnesses explain it by legalisms:

God, though able to bring an end to bad things, restrains himself for mankind's own benefit.—*TW*, June 1, 1974

[God's] vindication is more important than the salvation of men.—*LGBT* (See pp. 29–36.)

The fundamental issue between God and Satan . . . involves man's integrity to Jehovah as his Sovereign.—*All Scrip* (See pp. 7–8.)

They base their case on Job's great cry of despair, tidying his heart's pain into logic:

Why does God permit evil? . . . From the book of Job we can see that Jehovah has permitted such because of a boast that his adversary, Satan the Devil, made, namely, that he could turn all men away from God . . . if God would let him get at Job, a very righteous man, Satan could cause Job to curse God. God accepted the challenge. . . . But Satan failed to turn Job against God. Job thereby upheld Jehovah as the rightful Sovereign and the One deserving to be feared and worshipped.
—*TW*, April 15, 1976

It began, of course, in Eden 6,000 years ago: perfect Adam and Eve were created "free moral agents"; but Satan, in the form of the Serpent, caused the first human pair to eat of the forbidden fruit (a real tree, a real fruit, in the Witnesses' literal version):

The Devil was originally a spirit son of God and, as such, he was perfect; but he allowed pride and greed for power to be like God to develop in his heart, and this led him to rebel and to get Adam and Even to join him in his rebellion. He wanted to be a god and have creatures worship and serve him. [*This Good*]

Adam and Eve, "although they were perfect in body and mind, . . . were as yet untried, and God gave them the opportunity of proving their obedience to him under the test." [*Ibid.*]

God gave to his human son and daughter the freedom of choice, free moral agency . . . because God cared about them and had feeling for them. He had shown love by bringing them to life and by his preparations for their earthly happiness. If God had created them so that they were automatically obedient and incapable of doing otherwise, then they could never show genuine love in return to their Creator. [*Awake!*, Oct. 8, 1974, p. 12]

Had Adam and Eve not been seduced by the Serpent's invitation to "become like Gods," they would have lived forever on a perfect earth. Instead, they were cast out of the Edenic paradise garden to the "unfinished" part of the earth, there to live out their days in toil and pain.

Thus, Adam and Eve sinned through disobedience to God, and their sin involved all men in death, depriving man of infinite bliss in Eden and of free access to the tree of life.

God has permitted Satan (evil) to exist in order to "raise up his witnesses to declare and publish his fame or name throughout all the earth before all his enemies are destroyed." [*LGBT*]

The absorbing problem of whether God calls men to Him or if, on the other hand, men choose God, the question of where grace and will join to provide redemption and union is not directly addressed by the Witnesses.

The closest approach to the problem of grace and will or whether salvation depends on faith or works, is the distinction between "the heart" and "the mind":

> The mind must of necessity take in and digest information. It is the seat of intellect, the knowledge-processing centre. It assembles information and by process of reason and logic it reaches certain conclusions. . . . The heart has a vital role, for with it are associated the affections and motivation. The heart's direction of one's whole course in life becomes evident to onlookers. They find out eventually what the person really is on the inside. But Jehovah at all times knows the "secret person of the heart." . . . At times the heart may overrule the conclusions of the mind. [*TMSG*, Study 15: "Reaching the Heart of Your Listeners," p. 75]

This evades the question of how God's grace operates to save men. It does allow the Witnesses to explain why men who are held in general to be good or wise reject their message: Their "hearts" are "bad".

THE DIVINITY OF CHRIST; THE TRINITY: THE RANSOM

But truly, Lord, if I wanted to cherish only a man, then I would surely turn to those whom you have given me in the allurement of their present flowering. Are there not, with our mothers, brothers, friends and sisters, enough irresistibly lovable people around us? Why should we turn to Judaea two thousand years ago? No, what I cry out for, like every being, with my whole life and all my earthly passion, is something very different from an equal to cherish: it is a God to adore.—Teilhard, p. 127

I want no pallid humanitarianism—If Christ be not God, I want none of him; I will hack my way through existence alone.—Romano Guardini

> If God gave his life for a man, would that be a corresponding ransom? Could a lion redeem a mouse?—Watchtower Society.

In addition to denying the immortality of the soul, the Witnesses deny the Incarnation.

Dorothy Sayers called the Incarnation and the crucifixion the terrifying drama of which God is the victim and the hero. It is that ecstatic version of God—the version that says that God bore the anguish of being human (by virtue of which, as Teilhard says, "nothing is profane") that permits of the idea that we may be sacramentally joined to Him.

Traditional Christianity teaches us that God became man to die for our sins; and that the godhead is composed of God the Father, God the Son, and God the Holy Spirit; that the Incarnation may be realized, for each individual, through the Eucharist.

The Witnesses, perhaps out of aversion to mystery and a determination to root everything in the concrete, deny the personality and the deity of the Holy Spirit, which they define, instead, as "the active force of God" which moves His servants to do His will. They argue that the Trinity is a pagan doctrine that originated with the Egyptians, Hindus, and Babylonians.

The Witnesses say that Jesus was a perfect human creature, no more, no less; and that God his father required the sacrifice of a perfect human life to "buy back," or ransom, what the perfect Adam had forfeited—life forever (for the faithful) on a perfect earth.

> He was a spirit person, just as "God is a Spirit"; he was a mighty one, although not almighty as Jehovah God is; also he was before all others of God's creatures, for he was the first son that Jehovah God brought forth. . . . He was the first of Jehovah God's creations. . . . The life of the Son of God was transferred from his glorious position with God his father in heaven to the embryo of a human. On the third day of his being dead in the grave his immortal Father Jehovah God raised him from the dead, not as a human Son, but as a mighty immortal spirit Son, with all power in heaven and earth under the Most High God. . . . [*LGBT*, see pp. 31–36, 115–16. See also *Aid*, pp. 917–32.]

So, in the Witness version of Christ, there would seem to be three Christs (none in God); and each is independent of the other. There is the spiritual archangel Michael (called also "the Word," or "Logos"); then there is the perfect human Jesus—who sacrificed his human nature on the stake; and finally there is the resurrected Christ, who enters a higher spiritual plane than the one he enjoyed in his prehuman existence.

The Witnesses say it was not Jesus' earthly body, but a kind of "suit of flesh" that manifested itself to his disciples upon the resurrection on the third day. Rutherford, ever inventive, suggested that God might have preserved Jesus' human body somewhere to exhibit it during the Millennium. [*The Harp of God* (New York: WB&TS, 1928)]

The churches have consistently argued that to deny the divinity of Christ, the agony of God in the garden, is heresy. To deny the divinity of Christ is also to deny oneself the Eucharistic sacrament: When Jehovah's Witnesses "celebrate" the "Memorial" of Christ's death, a small number—those who expect a heavenly, rather than an earthly, reward—share unleavened bread and wine. The bread is merely "symbolic of [Christ's] own fleshly body, head and all"; the wine is "symbolic of his own blood"; and to partake of these emblems is a token that one "imitates Jesus," and "appreciates the sanctification of his blood." The Witnesses believe that human endeavour is, by its nature, devoid of God, and that God is not present in the evil world. Nor is one baptized into the Church as an infant. Adult baptism is a "symbol of one's dedication to do God's will." [*LGBT*, pp. 296–98]

Charles Taze Russell's waspish attitudes toward the Mass, the sacraments, the Eucharist set the tone for future Watchtower writings: "Papacy denies and sets aside the true Continual Sacrifice, and substitutes the 'abomination,' the Mass, in its stead." [*SS*, Vol. III, *Thy Kingdom Come*, p. 102]

How splendid it must be, how exalting, to feel, to know:

> Ah, you know it yourself, Lord, through having borne the anguish of it as man: On certain days the world seems a terrifying thing: huge, blind, and brutal. . . . The things in our life which terrify us, the things that threw you yourself into agony in the garden, are, ultimately, only the species or appearance, the matter of one and the same sacrament. We have only to believe.

"We have only to believe." [Teilhard, pp. 136–37] Irresistible words; there is a tension amounting to glory even in resisting them.

But for Russell, everything not rooted in numbers and dates and legal analyses was anathema. The low churches did not escape the raspings of his sharp tongue, either:

"[The] year 1846 witnessed the organization of Protestant sects into one great system called the Evangelical Alliance . . . many of those . . . cleansed . . . thus became entangled with the yoke of bondage." [*SS*, Vol. III, pp. 119–20] The Papacy and the Protestants were both wiped out by Russell's heavy, whipping, sex-stained hand.

And how do the churches feel about what they are obliged to regard as apostasy?

Father Robert Kennedy (of the Brooklyn diocese) says, most charitably:

> Catholics are indeed dissatisfied with the institutional aspects of the

Church, with its wealth and clericalism. They turn to Jehovah's Witnesses as an alternative. . . . In Latin America, for example, where the Witnesses make great gains, Catholic belief tends to be authoritarian. We have, in the past, represented forces of oppression, and worship revolves around the saints and the Virgin. The Church's Christology—the Christ of the Trinity—is remote. Jehovah's Witnesses offer an immediate, vivid, living Christ—a man, even as other men—who, they think, has relevance to their lives. . . . Intellectual Catholics ask refined questions. Jehovah's Witnesses ask no questions.

The evangelical churches regard Jehovah's Witnesses as "people of the cults . . . unreached by the church." The Witnesses are equated with Reverend Ike, the Mormons, Christian Science, and Sun Myung Moon: "All of them turn away from the central doctrine of the Christian faith." And they are considered as pernicious as the occult—as "witches, Satanism, astrology, and tarot cards." Dr. Walter Martin, of the Christian Research Institute of Melodyland, California, says:

Satan manipulates the church. The Christians have been afraid of the cults. A JW comes to the door . . . a million times a day all over the world this happens. The Christian says, "Well, I belong to such-and-such a church; I'm a Christian." Then the JW zaps him with the Trinity: "Can you prove to me that it's in the Bible?" he asks. The Christian can't prove it; he's frustrated when he can't answer questions. . . .

What we should recognize is that JWs are lost souls for whom Christ has died. . . . The church has failed them for a hundred years: "Let the Lord convert them," we've said; "Don't have them in your homes, whatever you do; just be positive, preach Jesus and everything will work out fine."

Well, it hasn't. The ostrich approach has made things worse. What we have to do is evangelize by presenting them with answers. We need to go to them. . . . We have teams of people all over Southern California being trained to go to JW meeting places and pass out tracts to lead these people back to Christ. . . .

We send out one tract—*100 Years of Divine Direction*—and quote from *The Watchtower*. We show how they predicted Armageddon seventeen times, and were wrong each time. They missed 1874, 1914, 1918, 1925, 1941—and most recently, October, 1975. . . . We have to wake up to the fact that this is a mission field. [Christian Broadcasting Network 700 Club broadcast, June 11, 1976]

To grasp the Witnesses' theology, it must be asked, For whom was Christ's ransom sacrifice made? For whose sins did he atone? Not, according to the Witnesses, for *all* men: Departing again from Christian tradition, the Witnesses say there are two "classes" of people who will benefit from his sacrifice: "a heavenly class," and "an earthly class." For a "great multitude" of "other sheep" the reward for faithful service to God will be everlasting life on an earth soon to be reclaimed from the wicked at Armageddon. A much smaller number, "the anointed," 144,000 spiritual brothers of Christ, will be "co-rulers" and "associate kings" with Christ in heaven.

Charles Taze Russell distinguished between two classes of "spiritual-begotten" people—a higher class, which (with his passion for numbers and dates and concrete emblems which extend even to the alphabet) he called Class *n*, who would sit with the resurrected Lord in heavenly glory; and Class *m*, mortals who "shrank from the death of the human will" and as a consequence would not reign with Christ in glory, but would become spirit beings of a lower order within the divine nature. [*SS*, Vol. I, *The Divine Plan of the Ages*] As the Witnesses had to accommodate more and more converts, however, a new scenario was invented. *M* and *n* are no longer operative.

THE SCENARIO:

> At Har-Magedon, . . . the kings and their armies and those having the marks of the "wild beast" will all be "killed off" in execution of the death sentence that proceeds out of the mouth of the victorious King of kings like a "long sword." Their corpses will not be buried with religious, military, or civil honours. All the scavenger birds will feast upon their dead bodies, and the eyes of God's protected remnant and their "great crowd" of godly companions will also feast. These will be satisfied at seeing this glorious vindication of the universal sovereignty of the Most High God, Jehovah. . . . They will be glad afterward to bury any bones remaining of the wicked ones and so cleanse the earth. . . . This will also serve as a health measure, to rid the earth of the foul smell of putrefying human corpses and to prevent water and air pollution and the spreading of diseases to the survivors of this war at "Har-Magedon." [*Babylon;* see p. 630]

Before Armageddon, this is what the Witnesses say will happen: "A scarlet-coloured wild beast with seven heads and ten horns" will turn against "the international religious harlot, Babylon the Great" [*TW*, Jan. 15, 1976], who has been "riding the beast," and will destroy the "symbolical woman that, figuratively speaking, has had immoral sexual relations with the world."

Less vividly, all worldly rulers, acting through the United Nations, will turn against organized religion and destroy all religions:

> They will make her appear shameful like a naked woman in public. [Like the] dogs that ate up . . . Jezebel . . . they will devour her body with which they once had liked to unite. They will destroy all her beauty of form and her religious capacity to give soothing pleasure to ungodly, worldly men. [*Ibid.;* see pp. 599–604.]

The seven-headed scarlet-coloured dragon spoken of in the 17th chapter of Revelation is the eighth (and final) world power of

Satan's organization set up to rival God's: it is the United Nations, which God bends to His will to destroy "false religion." In the Old Testament book of Daniel, seven wild beasts are spoken of; for reasons impervious to logic, these beasts represent, to the Witnesses, seven successive world powers. The first six are Egypt, Assyria, Babylonia, Medo-Persia, Greece, and Rome, all of whom have ranged themselves against God. The seventh beast represents "the dual world power of Great Britain and the United States." (Other great civilizations, such as the Mayans and the Indus Valley, to say nothing of the Axis powers and China and the Communist countries, have no place in this collage.) Now, it follows that the eighth world power is necessarily the United Nations—because it springs from the previous seven world powers.

"Since these religious organizations claim to represent the true God, the desolator [the beast, or the UN] will act also in hatred against the One whom they pretend to serve. This vicious, beastly attitude against God [is] blaspheming his name." [*TW*, Dec. 15, 1975, p. 744] God is obliged to destroy the UN.

Meanwhile, what about the Witnesses? One can hardly expect them not to assign themselves a leading role in this theatre of the absurd:

> Should the [Watchtower] Society survive that violent destruction of Babylon . . . the Society will absolutely refuse to unite itself [with the UN]. Such a refusal would certainly move the [UN] to take drastic action against the Society and the Christian witnesses of Jehovah whom the Society represents and serves. . . . International action against these announcers of Jehovah's Kingdom . . . would be the way in which the UN "wild beast" fights against the "lamb," the Lord of Lords and King of Kings. . . . Anti-religious political authorities of the earth will be able to dissolve religious corporations . . . but never will they be able to dissolve the worldwide brotherhood of Jehovah's Christian witnesses. [*TW*, Jan. 15, 1976]

> Jehovah's witnesses, sheltered within his Theocratic organization, will be under siege and will seem threatened with destruction by the overwhelming hosts of . . . Satan. . . . Yet be not anxious . . . Jehovah will fight the battle for his remnant and their companions. He will perform his "strange act" at Armageddon. [*TW*, April 1, 1945, pp. 108–9]

There will then follow, so the scenario goes, a period of anarchy. As Charles Taze Russell wrote, "The closing in of this night will evidently put a stop to any further labour to disseminate the truth, which, misunderstood by the public generally, will probably be accused of being the cause of much of the anarchy and confusion then prevailing."

After all the survivors of Armageddon pile up dead bones and watch birds feast on the eyes of dead enemies, they will begin, under the direction of God, to prepare the earth for Paradise. The 1,000-year reign of Christ will have begun.

Satan, for the duration of the reign of Christ and his "144,000 royal associates," is "abyssed" before his ultimate annihilation. For a thousand years, a series of "resurrections" will take place: Brought forth to "a resurrection of life" will be "the other sheep" who died before Armageddon and "the faithful men of old"—pre-Christian "Witnesses." Brought forth to "a resurrection of judgment" will be people "whose hearts may have been wanting to do right, but who died without ever having had an opportunity to hear of God's purposes or to learn what he expects of men." [*FPL*, p. 229]

Other, less literal, religions might simply trust in God and hope for the good. But the Witnesses have worked it all out in advance, down to the closest half-acre:

> A very liberal estimate of the number of persons that have ever lived on earth is twenty billion. . . . Not *all* of these . . . will receive a resurrection, but even assuming that they did, there would be no problem as to living space and food for them. The land surface of the earth at present is about 57,000,000 square miles . . . or more than 36,000,000,000 acres. . . . Even allowing half of that to be set aside for other uses, there would be more than half an acre . . . for each person . . One-half acre . . . will actually provide much more than enough food for one person. . . .
>
> Let us assume that those who compose the "great crowd" of righteous persons who "come out of the great tribulation" on this system of things alive . . . number one million (about . . . one thirty-five hundredth of earth's present population). Then if, after allowing, say, one hundred years spent in their training and "subduing" a portion of the earth . . . God purposes to bring back three per cent of this number, this would mean that each newly arrived person would be looked after by thirty-three trained ones. Since a yearly increase of three per cent, compounded, doubles the number about every twenty-four years, the entire twenty billion could be resurrected before five hundred years of Christ's thousand-year reign had elapsed. [*Paradise Restored to Mankind by Theocracy!*]

Not all, after these resurrections, is yet perfect: After the Millennium (during which man will have achieved physical and mental perfection), God will schedule another test of man's integrity. Satan is "let loose out of his prison," and he and "his demons come again into the vicinity of the earth, where they can exert an invisible control over those of mankind who succumb to them." For reasons that are unclear, "Satan the Devil will be confident of himself, in spite of the mental, moral, spiritual, physical perfection of mankind." He will again "challenge God's sovereignty"; the issue will at last be settled in God's favour. [*God's Kingdom of 1000 Years Has Approached* (New York: WB & TS, 1973), p. 149] Anyone seduced by the Devil will be consigned to "the second death." (All of this, for anyone who's interested, is an odd reading of Ezekiel and Revelation.) With God's name "sanctified forever," Christ will be able to hand over to his Father a forever-perfect kingdom; and all shall be well, world without end.

He hath made everything beautiful in his time.—Ecclesiastes 3:11, KJV.

Everything he has made pretty in its time.—Ecclesiastes 3:11, NWT.

The Witnesses' translation of the Old and New Testaments (which they prefer to call the Hebrew and Greek Scriptures) both diminishes emotions and—by clever manipulation of words and punctuation unsupported by unbiased scholars—furthers their own doctrine. (For example, "Cross" is translated "torturestake"; by a replacement of a comma, the meaning of Luke 23:43 is changed to destroy the idea that Jesus was offering the malefactor who died with him immortality: "Verily I say unto thee, Today shalt thou be with me in paradise."—KJV. "Truly I tell you today, You will be with me in Paradise."—NWT.)

The Watchtower Society published its translation of the New Testament (the "Greek Scriptures") in 1950—to something short of critical acclaim. The Old Testament (the "Hebrew Scriptures") was published in five volumes from 1953 to 1960, and the entire New World Translation of the Bible was published in 1961.

This New World Translation was intended to bring the Bible as close to present-day readers as were the original Scriptures to their audience. An announcement was made on September 3, 1949, at the Society's Brooklyn headquarters that a committee had completed such a translation and was presenting it to the Society for publication. The gift also gave the Society complete possession and control of the property, in recognition of its work in spreading knowledge of the Scriptures. The translation was accepted by the directors of the Society, who then proceeded to have it published.

This bland account implies that Knorr had stumbled upon a work by disinterested (anonymous) translators. The New World Translation of the Bible was, of course, an in-house version. The "Committee" laboured with Knorr peering over their shoulders. All of us who worked at Watchtower headquarters knew it was in the works; Fred Franz, then the Society's vice-president and Knorr's confidant, was known to be the chief translator; I proofread portions of it when I worked at headquarters.

The New World Translation places ("restores" according to the

Watchtower Society) the name *Jehovah* 6,962 times in the Old Testament and 237 times in the New Testament.

One of the aims of the translators was to achieve a high "degree of literalness":

> Many Bible translators have abandoned literalness for what they contend to be elegance of language and form. They argue that literal renderings are wooden, stiff and confining. However, their abandonment of literal translation has brought about many departures from the accurate, original statements of truth. They have in fact watered down the very thoughts of God. [*All Scrip*, p. 325]

This presupposes, of course, that the Watchtower Society alone knows what "the very thoughts of God" are. How well its translators succeeded in achieving "a high degree of literalness" may be seen from the following comparative readings:

> The Lord reigneth; let the people tremble; he sitteth between the cherubims; let the earth be moved.—Psalm 99:1, KJV
> Jehovah himself has become King. Let the peoples be agitated. He is sitting upon the cherubs.—Psalm 99:1, NWT

> But who may abide the day of his coming? and who shall stand when he appeareth? for he is like a refiner's fire.—Malachi 3:2, KJV
> Who will be the one standing when he appears? For he will be like the lye of laundrymen.—Malachi 3:2, NWT [Try setting that to Handel.]

> The Lord is my shepherd; I shall not want.—Psalm 23:1, KJV
> Jehovah is my shepherd, I shall lack nothing.—Psalm 23:1, NWT

> Lo, I am with you alway, even unto the end of the world. Amen.—Matthew 28:20, KJV
> Look, I am with you all the days until the conclusion of the system of things.—Matthew 28:20, NWT

The New World Translation is inelegant, not to say tin-eared, lacking "the perfect order of speech, and the beauty of incantation." What the Committee says is "Ideas, once cloaked in archaic English, now shine out with meaningful brilliance. Its everyday language helps you to grasp information vital for eternal life." [*All Scrip*. See pp. 327–28]

In fact, the Watchtower Society despises "ideas." The Committee says:

> Since the Bible has been written in these down-to-earth, easily understandable terms, it is possible to translate its symbols and actions clearly and accurately into most modern-day images. The original power and force of truth are preserved. . . . Simple everyday words, such as "horse," "war," "crown," "throne," "husband," "wife," and "children" communicate accurate thought clearly in every language. This is in contrast to human philosophical writings, which do not lend themselves

to accurate translation. Their complicated expressions and up-in-the-air terminology often cannot be conveyed precisely in another tongue. [*Ibid.*, p. 9]

Well, it is easier to translate *horse* than it is to translate *existential,* as it's easier to translate *war* than *goodness*. Still, is the Book of Revelation any more accessible than "human philosophical writings"? One gets the feeling that when the Watchtower Society talks about "human philosophical writings" it means anything other than common nouns; the Society cherishes the facts and it alone determines what the facts "mean." [*Ibid.*]

The point about the New World Translation is not just that it is inelegant and uncharming; it is hardly worth labouring the point that God ought to be praised (or, for that matter, damned) in language that attempts to approximate His magnificence (or His awfulness). Nor is it profitable to point up a pious Philistinism of the Witnesses. What the New World Translation reveals about the Watchtower Society is its fear of the terror, beauty and wonder of the world, its fierce desire to make all that is awful pallid, its determination to reduce the world to small, manageable proportions. Its lust for literalness is a desperation for certainty.

But one of the odd things about the Society (some people have experienced this as terrible) is that while it has provided its followers with a narrow certainty, there is something niggling about its dogma, something thin-voiced about its imperatives, that denies its followers the rapture of abandon. It is dogmatic rather than Absolute. The lure of certainty attracts different kinds of people. Some (most) of Jehovah's Witnesses choose their belief in order to be enhanced: It confers upon them a status, a feeling of being accepted, that they would otherwise never enjoy. Others choose the Witnesses out of a need to be reduced; some of these—particularly those who suffer from the guilt of affluence, combined with idealistic temperaments—wish to be delivered from the fullness of their personalities; they have a need to throw in their lot with the oppressed. Whatever the reason for the choice, however, many ultimately feel cheated—because the dry certitude they are given is not a substitute for Absolution.

Jesus please let there be much less of me . . . And Jesus, please, much more of you.—Vera Retsoff.

Vera went looking for a large ecstasy, and found a shrivelling pain instead. She found herself, as she was later to say, not "reduced to an atom of praise," but "diminished to a speck of suffering."

Vera was born to a large, rich, aristocratic White Russian family of artistic and cultivated exemplars. Her mother was a socialite.

Multilingual, Vera spent part of her childhood in boarding schools in England and Switzerland. She was a stern and an ardent adolescent. Her early journals and diaries are full of sincere, albeit self-conscious, ennui, rage, self-loathing, self-adoration, necessity to fix the blame and seesawing between narcissism and masochism. She disliked her mother, whom she regarded as narrow-minded and intolerant.

Vera spoke to me as she was on the verge of leaving the Witnesses. During the whole of our conversation she spoke of the Witnesses as "They" (not "We"). I think she was really out already, but didn't know it. It was one of the hungriest conversations I've ever been involved in. Vera's need to explain herself was so immense it was almost as if she wanted to be exposed and eaten and every part of her found good; she wanted my life (which was, while in some disarray, clearly a chosen life) to prove to her that one could leave "The Truth" and not only survive, but live with some grace and hope of joy. She searched my children's faces and found (to her mild astonishment, I think) that there was nothing to despise in them. She gazed and gazed at me, wondering, I think, if some visible stain could be found on me, some brand of the wickedness she had been told to expect. She even attempted to extract messages from tangible objects; I remember her running her fingers over the smooth surfaces of waxed tables, tentatively touching plants and *objets*, and taking surprised delight in each thing that was whole and fresh and thriving and clean and beautiful.

When Vera was 16, she had written in her diary, "I'm so rotten that the only person who could love me is God and He's not there—and I'm mad at Him; why doesn't He *make* me believe in Him?"

Because she didn't want to go to college, she ran away to Mexico.

> I couldn't imagine what good art and poetry were. Everybody in my family was successful. But still, life is terrible: people get old and they're thrown out like garbage. I felt there had to be an answer to all the suffering . . . and a community of people who had the answer. And I felt that if I had any talent—like languages, or acting—I should use my talents to help humanity. What good was it to write a book? So many other people had—practically everybody in my family had. I wanted my cause to be *the* cause.
>
> When I was in Mexico I met some Jesus Freaks. What I really wanted was to relate to people on a deep level—a deep intellectual level and a deep emotional level, and no artsy bullshit. I accepted Jesus. I thought I found what I'd wanted—a community; but there was no real sharing. I couldn't talk about my inner life. Praying and speaking in tongues seemed to me a good substitute for acid and protests, but it was all so simplistic. And I had this terrible feeling that it was too easy. Why would Jesus suddenly allow me to find Him? I wanted an intellectual exploration of religion, and that wasn't happening; so I lulled myself

into thinking that I had at least found enthusiasm, love, and security.

I came back home to Long Island, and then I went off to a small mountain village in Germany. I had my Bible. I imagined I'd be ascetic, I would fast, I'd get involved with simple crafts—and leave all my selfish, ugly ambitions behind. . . . I'd hitchhike, and preach in my primitive way.

I wanted fellowship. My landlady introduced me to the people down the road. They were Jehovah's Witnesses. The first question they asked me was Do you read the Bible? I wanted to embrace them! *They* loved God too! I felt as if I were starving and they were offering me food. They tried to turn me on to the name *Jehovah*, which I saw as a denial of my personal attachment to Christ. I wanted to believe that Jesus was God, and they were taking that away from me. But I allowed myself to be convinced by their arguments.

When Vera was very young, she had written in her diary: "Is thinking bad? Is feeling bad? Or both? Or neither? How can I just *be*?" What impressed her about O-Ma, the grandmotherly woman who converted her, was her apparent homely simplicity:

She never had to ask herself whether she had to forfeit her intelligence or her instincts. She just was. All she wanted out of life was to live in the New World on a little farm and raise pigs. That's all she asked of God.

But the idyll was wormy. It was not so simple and good after all. Vera says:

I loved feeling like a real woman, not an intellectual machine. I gardened and cooked and sewed—all the things I'd never done. In my aristocratic family, those were things servants had done. But pretty soon I understood that some of the Witnesses thought I was a prize—they used to point me out to people as an example of an educated, upper-class hippie who'd doped and slept around.

Vera came back to New York, and her parents wanted her to return to college; she wanted to become a missionary. They made a deal: "My father said he'd study the Bible with the Witnesses if I went to college. So I studied Russian at school. I had a fantasy that I'd go to Russia and help all the spiritually thirsty people there. And I fantasized about being thrown into prison camps. I loved the idea of going to prison, suffering for—maybe dying for—Jehovah."

While Vera was enjoying her persecution fantasies, she also derived pleasure from preaching in the poor, black part of town—to people whom she would otherwise never have known.

It really turned me on to go into the black part of town—think what my socialite mother would have said to that! I know there was an element of rebellion in what I was doing; but I did truly love feeling that I could be with different kinds of people and be accepted as an equal. I could go into a black house and feel that we could transcend our differences . . . there was a feeling of community; social reform and protest became irrelevant because you got this feeling that it had all happened already—that we were black and white and together and loved one another.

While Vera was in this heightened state of consciousness, she met André, a French Jehovah's Witness whose Russian mother had been in a concentration camp in Germany. He seemed to be the fulfilment of her fantasies: they would marry, go to Russia together, and preach. But she describes him as a "paper person."

> I wanted a mating of souls. He wanted to quote Scriptures. He told me that all my efforts to "understand" him were "Devilish psychology"—and he told me that all the fairy tales I grew up with and loved (I used to read them to him in Russian) were "demonism." He wanted to quote Scriptures—and he had a huge erection all the while he was talking about "demonism." I started dreaming about David; and I started masturbating. I tried to convince myself that God had provided me with André, a perfect mate. But I'd masturbate and think of David and love David and know that God would take His spirit away from me because I was masturbating. . . .

Out of all this conflict came Vera's decision to go back to the simplicity of the people who had converted her in Germany. She thought they would put her right, but:

> That whole congregation—the congregation I had thought was so pure and simple and sweet and wise—had split apart over the issue of whether women should wear pants or not!

Vera came back to America. David agreed to study the Bible with the Witnesses . . . and the inevitable upshot was that Vera and David went to bed together. Vera had by this time been celibate for three years.

> Once I had sinned against Jehovah by sleeping with David—although in my heart I could never feel that my love for him, and my full expression of it, was a sin—my relationship with Him was broken. I couldn't pray anymore. . . . I felt totally abandoned. By God, by the Society—and of course my terrible fear was that David would abandon me too.
>
> So after David and I got married, which we did almost immediately after we'd made love, I confessed to the elders. I was "put on public reproof." It was announced at the meeting in the Kingdom Hall that I'd committed fornication; and there was fifteen minutes of graphic description of what we'd done and how often we'd done it. I was, of course, humiliated. But relieved, too. I thought God's spirit would return to me.

What happened instead was that Vera's doubts about the Witnesses increased; and the Witnesses' coldness towards her increased. At the time I spoke with her, she still hadn't figured out which was cause and which was effect.

Several months after I met Vera, I got this letter from her:

Dear Barbara,

I went to an assembly at Ozone Park to test my feelings. There was this black woman there with a little baby on her back and her babypack was slipping off and she was having a hard time with it, and I was trying to help her. And she immediately told me she was disfellowshipped, as if she were warning me off her, as if she were a leper, not clean, not good enough to talk to. And I felt, out of all the people there, she was the only one who was really my sister. . . . As you are my sister. . . .

I will never go back again. I am trying to be good and happy. (Are they the same thing?)

Love,
Vera.

Vera is now acting, and working with Soviet dissidents, and researching a biography of one of her ancestors—and living happily with David. She has survived her experiences remarkably unscathed—although, as in the case with many ex-Witnesses, her longing for a "perfect brotherhood," a communion or community, will probably never leave her. Unlike many ex-Witnesses, she is not shopping for a new certainty; her experience has taught her to tolerate ambiguity—and to tolerate herself.

When Vera was a Witness, one of her fantasies was that she would be "persecuted"—die, perhaps, for Jehovah in a Russian prison camp.

I have never known a Witness who did not have a similar notion. (According to a recent Watchtower publication, one of Jehovah's Witnesses in an unspecified country named her baby "Persecution"—and one must believe that that mother thought she was blessing, not cursing, her infant.)

I remember how the hot exploration of evil poisoned my childhood; how Witness women sat around kitchen tables (those kitchens never seemed sunny) and spoke with lust of the evil in men's hearts—of doctors who maimed, teachers who corrupted, public figures whose dishonour was disclosed.

When my mother went shopping or to a restaurant, she handled everything that did not belong to her as if there were some hidden menace in it; she had repulsion and fear for everything she had not appropriated. Her look to all inanimate objects said, Stop; let whatever evil lies in you be obedient to my will. She touched skirts on hangers gingerly, with trepidation and fascination, as if they might leap off and enshroud her. Until she got them home. Then she cared for them so solicitously, as tenderly as if they were frail children who could have no independent existence without her. She fingered rolls in restaurants as if they were malignant objects that might attack or hiss at her or explode in her face. Then she conquered them, ate them up ravenously—and pronounced them good. Everything that was hers was good. Everything that was *other*—that existed apart from her—was bad. In order to love things, she had to make them *her* things.

The Witnesses have to make the world *theirs*. They love only what they appropriate.

One way to control the world is to formalize one's behaviour in it. The Witnesses have the illusion of total control; they are instructed on what to do and how to feel on everything from grief to body odour to baseball statistics (an encyclopaedic knowledge of the latter is criticized as "unbecoming passion") to music to fashion.

The reduction of everything terrible and large in order to make the world manageable and comprehensible (which, because it can never be fully successful, turns back on itself to produce spasms of guilt in all of Jehovah's Witnesses)—characterizes everything the Watchtower Society publishes.

About dreams, for example, the Society, speaking as if Freud or Jung had never existed, says, "Natural dreams may be stimulated by certain thoughts or emotions, sensations or daily activities (anxiety, one's physical condition, his occupation, and so forth). These dreams are of no great significance." [*Aid*, p. 465] "What about gaining insight into one's own personality? No human can provide that through interpretation of dreams, no matter how skilful the analyst." [*Aw*, Jan. 22, 1975] But it isn't enough for the Watchtower Society to say that dreams are "insignificant," thus closing off the most direct path to the believer's inner life. The Society attempts to manipulate the subconscious (implicitly recognizing that dreams are significant) in a way that can lead to the most excruciating guilt: "But what if you are troubled by repetition of the same type of unpleasant dreams, perhaps ones that contain allusions to sexual immorality, egotism, aggression or similar things. Remember the close relationship between recent events and dreams. The cause for your bad dreams may be in the things you practise and dwell on mentally from day to day. The solution to bad dreams may call for an adjustment in your routine of life, especially in what you regularly feed your mind." [*Ibid.*] The Witnesses are cut off from their own feelings, censoring not just data from the outside world, but their own revealing fantasies.

(Psychiatrists have reported that under the Nazis, dissident Germans frequently censored their own dreams—a self-protective device. They automatically awakened whenever anything in their dreams began to signal to them disobedience to, or vengeance toward, Hitler, the SS, or the Gestapo. Sometimes their startled awakening was triggered by the appearance, in their dreams, of a uniformed Nazi hovering over their beds demanding that they cease such "unnatural" dream activity. To what extent this censoring of their own assertiveness and this internalizing of authoritarian imperatives contributed to the national psychosis is an interesting question.)

Of course Jehovah's Witnesses consider psychology and all allied disciplines a threat to their own control over the minds of their followers. As an elder once told me, "Superiority and inferiority complexes are all the same words for self-centredness." Retrospection and introspection are considered evil; and Witnesses are told to abjure the "unprofitable study of philosophy, sociology and similar professions" to get instead "the mind of God." [*Faith*]

No literature that threatens their system of belief may be included in the Witnesses' Kingdom Hall libraries.

One must be constantly on guard. The Devil lurks in all the material zones of the world. One must, for example, abhor even the suggestion of "demonism" or witchcraft; one must even be vigilant about entertaining "strange talk" from fellow workers at one's secular place of employment.

Self-help, and "getting the mind of the Lord" are suggested to ameliorate all problems, from mental illness to muggings.

The suggestion that mental health is a matter of willpower and of reading *The Watchtower* and *Awake!* does not strike the Witnesses as exaggerated.

> Victims themselves often provoke crimes. . . . The self-control that can protect you from such violence is a product of God's spirit, available to those who apply Bible counsel. [*Aw*, Nov. 22, 1975, p. 12, "How Can You Protect Yourself?"]

Blaming the victim leads the Watchtower Society inevitably—though it claims to be apolitical—to a position of social and political conservatism.

An ingrained conservatism which proceeds from the Witnesses' view of evil extends to hunger and food shortages. One reality of life the Watchtower Society finds it convenient to ignore is agribusiness. It perpetuates the myth of the small farmer who has "difficulty in hiring honest and dependable labour. . . . 'Many farmers feel that their occupation brings them close to God.' . . . But they detest the oppressive worldwide system that will work honest men—farmers, packers, sellers, shippers, distributors—day and night, give them minimum returns for their labours and then somehow never get the food to the people that really need it." [*Aw*, June 22, 1975, pp. 10, 13]

The "oppressive worldwide system" is never identified; only one villain needs to be—the Devil. Class analysis has no place in Watchtower rhetoric. Given a choice between what the Watchtower Society terms "international communism" and "capitalistic democracy," the Witnesses choose the latter: "[Communism] is for the regimentation, the complete regulation, of the people in their private and public affairs. . . . The other side ['capitalist democracy'] allows for a measure of liberty in the personal lives and pursuits of the citizens." [*TW*, Nov. 1, 1975, p. 652]

In 1940, after the Great Depression, the Catholic magazine *America*— calling attention to the fact that many Witnesses came from "the poorer classes of Southern farm tenants; . . . from the Okies who, dejected and rejected, wander about hopelessly; from the ignorant, superstitious, and illiterate of the city slums"—remarked astutely that Pastor Russell and "Judge" Rutherford "answered the anguish" of the chronically unemployed and victims of social injustice.

We are again living in a time of social dislocation and distress; it is no accident that blacks are now turning to the Witnesses in enormous numbers.

Think what it must mean to be poor, black, and uneducated and to read and believe that "The wise men of this world are highly intelligent but they cannot understand the good news. . . . Let them know that you are . . . an instrument to bring things to their attention." [*TW*, June 1, 1974]

Fired by the conviction that their status derives not from their "secular work" (a janitor may be a congregational elder) or from their standing in the blind eyes of the world, but from their relationship to God and the Watchtower Society, Witnesses—including former convicts, addicts, and criminals—change their lives in matters big and small. Watchtower publications are full of testimonials, all no doubt true, of formerly "marginal" people who have begun to exercise middle-class virtues. ("The home that had been very dirty and disorderly was now neat and clean. The children were dressed presentably." [*Aw*, Oct. 8, 1975, p. 19, "Proof in the Lives of People"]

Work in the world is viewed not as an inward renewal, but as a means to purchase time in which to serve God in prescribed fashion. Man's secular work enhances neither man nor god; the Witnesses lack what Teilhard called "faith in the heavenly value of human endeavour," "the loveable duty of growth." It does not occur to them that one's natural talents can bear fruit that will praise God and serve man. This enforced separation of the secular from the narrowly "religious"—the failure to see that there is an interrelation between matter (or labour, art) and soul and God—is of a piece with their theology; it comes from the same mind-set that separates the Godhead into three separate entities, Father, lesser son, and (impersonal) Holy Spirit. There is, in the Witnesses, a proclivity to fragment which leads, perhaps, to the lack of integration in their own personalities. And it also follows, from their view of work as an essentially meaningless means to a religious end (rather than as a collaboration with God to perfect the world), that business is much to be preferred to art as a means of making money: Art is a personal (and therefore a suspect) statement. One of Jehovah's Witnesses may be a storm-window-manufacturer millionaire and not be despised by his peers; if, on the other hand, he were to have a painting at the Whitney, he would immediately become the object of derision. Witnesses give up promising careers in the arts, and are given group recognition for so doing. Creative work has one's personal signature; it is far better to labour anonymously, without credit, in entrepreneurial fields. Only God may have a name: *Jehovah*. For an individual to have a "name" is seen as a diminishment of God.

There is a strongly Calvinistic flavour to Watchtower advice, which reinforces middle-class values: Honesty is good because honesty "pays": Jehovah's Witnesses don't steal, and as a consequence they are offered managerial jobs; living in accordance with Bible principles brings material reward.

We don't spearhead anything. We're not reformers. When the door opened for coloured and white brothers to meet together, we took advantage of it. We didn't sit-in, we didn't protest, we didn't march. We didn't push. We don't *push. We practised strict segregation when local law dictated it. We give to Caesar what belongs to him.*— Fountain Van Shriver

Fountain Van Shriver, a 50-year-old New York City subway worker who is a congregational elder in Harlem, spent most of his life in Georgia, under circumstances calculated, one would think, to leave any black man with a bitter residue of anger. At the Watchtower convention at Aqueduct Race Track at which I met Van Shriver, black Witnesses outnumbered white Witnesses by roughly 3 to 1. (It is estimated in the early 1960s [Lee Cooper, Z&L] that 20 to 30 per cent of all Jehovah's Witnesses in the United States were black. If these estimates are correct, there are almost twice as many blacks among Witnesses as among the general population.) At Aqueduct, white and black Witnesses were baptized together and were together generally in a way that seemed genuinely easy and friendly. But it interested me that there were no black administrators managing the Witnesses' affairs at Aqueduct. (It interested the Witnesses not at all.) Every convention official I spoke with was white, male, and middle-aged. Young black men, who might reasonably have been expected to deplore, or at least to question this state of affairs, smilingly assured me that they were "confident Jehovah [had] picked the right men."

"Is everybody in heaven going to be white, then?" I asked.

I was accused of racism: "You're seeing discrimination where none exists. Satan comes in *all* colours and sizes and shapes."

Black liberation?

"We are like Jesus. We remain neutral in the struggles of this world. God will take care of that. All of Jehovah's servants are like flowers in His sight—different colours and shapes, but equal, and beautiful."

Black Witnesses reject strenuously the notion that, their leadership being white, their religion is racist. No voices are heard in protest. So great are the satisfactions they derive from being of the Chosen, it would do little good to remind them of Pastor Russell's implicit racism. In 1904, Russell wrote that

> The interests of the New Creation will, we believe, be generally conserved by the preservation of a measure of separation in the flesh, because the ideals, tastes, appetites, dispositions, etc., of one race necessarily are more or less in conflict with the ideals, etc., of another; hence the several races of humanity will probably find their spiritual interests as New Creatures best conserved by a measure of separateness. [*SS*, Vol. VI]

When I was at Bethel headquarters in the 1950s, there were only, as I recall, two (male) black Witnesses working there—both at menial tasks. The explanation given for this disproportionately low number of black Witnesses was that it might "stumble"—that is, distress, or give a bad impression to—the Witnesses' Brooklyn Heights neighbours, who were presumed not to want Negroes in their moneyed midst. In the late 1960s, when not to be overtly racist became chic (the Heights is a liberal neighbourhood), the Watchtower Society pragmatically admitted many more blacks to its headquarters staff.

In any case, black Witnesses are likely to give offence only to the most obdurate racist. They, as they are fond of pointing out, stay out of trouble. That was clear at the convention at Aqueduct.

When, at that convention, I came upon two black Witnesses who did not fit the standard mould (they were dressed vividly and, not having forgotten street language, they talked vividly, too, and their loose-limbed bodies made the other Witnesses look like stick figures), it became apparent immediately that we were under surveillance. Within minutes, eight or ten standard-product black Witnesses converged upon us and tried to put a wedge between me and "these two young men who are like two immature babies speaking on their own authority. They haven't dedicated their lives. Why are you talking to them? What you should do is tape the speeches at the convention—and then you won't ever have to talk to anyone."

It had, in fact, amazed me (but not the Witnesses, apparently) that at an earlier convention in Yankee Stadium, in the Witnesses' "demonstrations" (skits), white Witnesses role-played middle-class businessmen, while young black Witnesses role-played street kids who smoked what they anachronistically referred to as "reefers."

An account by a black Witness [*TW*, Dec. 1, 1974] illuminates what blacks gain, and also what they lose, by becoming Jehovah's Witnesses.

The young man who writes this (anonymous) account was the child of sharecroppers. His story (up to the time he became a Witness) might, with minor variations, be the story of thousands of angry black men: "Why, I asked myself, did whites want to keep us down? What was wrong with being black?"

Threatened with lynching because he'd held a gun to the head of his landowner for his refusal to take a sick black child to hospital, the young man's father fled to New York, where eventually his son joined him. The North—with the opportunity it provided him to study "singing, ballet, journalism . . . nursing and . . . modelling," and to go to college and become "a recording artist, working at one time with Paul Simon"—seemed, for a time, like heaven. "In time," however, he realized "that I was a victim . . . of self-deception. I was unrealistic to think that perhaps the colour of one's skin did not matter. It was a lie that racism existed only in the South; it was bad, too, in the North, only neatly camouflaged."

His response to this delayed understanding—and to the deaths of Chaney, Schwerner, and Goodman—was to work for CORE and for SNCC. Another illusion crumbled when Martin Luther King was murdered. "I had to ask myself, . . . 'What did the non-violence he advocated accomplish?'" Then a personal tragedy: His father was brutally murdered. "I refused to cry. Instead, in my heart I made a vow. I was going to do something about the injustices I saw my people suffering."

So far, clearly, this young black man has feelings, but no ideology. He is completely unarmoured.

He joins the Panthers. "By then I agreed with their ideology that it was time for blacks to arm themselves." In 1970, he joins a group of "radicals" (he doesn't say which group) to go to Cuba "for advanced training in revolutionary tactics. My goal was to initiate armed insurrection against the American system." By the end of his stay in Cuba, where, he says, he "worked side by side with hard-core Communist fighters from Vietnam, Africa, Korea, and Russia," he is "willing to fight and die to bring about the liberation of black people."

He is asked by "a revolutionary group" to "subvert the military, to use 'any means necessary' to find and bring over to the revolutionary side black military men who had technical skills that could be used."

(So far, what is remarkable, it seems to me, about this story is its studied absence of specificity: no names of individuals or groups or comrades are mentioned, nor is the author's own. What is also remarkable is the kind of unfocused quality of his life: he still has no developed ideology; he has only a history of pain around which to centre. He is ripe for a religious withdrawal from worldly defeat.)

And disillusion piles upon disillusion (in all of which self-loathing plays its wormy part): "Soon . . . I became totally repelled by the way I was using myself. . . . The revolutionaries I knew did not live up to the moral idealism I had come to expect of the liberation movement. They became grossly promiscuous. One night, after a comrade had relations with his woman companion, he turned to me. I saw this . . . as revolting."

It is at this point in his life—when he has made the mistake of confusing the justice of a cause with the behaviour of its adherents—that one of Jehovah's Witnesses knocks at his door. (It is also at this point in his account that it becomes clear that the past no longer has any reality or meaning to him—except to prove a point.)

His immediate capitulation to the simplicities the Witness offers can be explained only in terms of his weariness (how many black militants were *not* weary in 1970?), his ardent desire to achieve an eschatological finality. He is tired of having to renew the struggle every day; he reminds himself that even in socialist countries, people "still get sick, grow old, and die. Human rulers are unable to prevent this."

And so, when the Witness reads rhetorical questions to him from a Watchtower publication—"Do you want to live in peace and happiness? Do you desire good health and long life for yourself and your loved ones? Why is the world so filled with trouble? What does it all mean? Is there any sound reason to believe that things will get better in our lifetime?"—he says, with the innocent rapacity of a dying man who has been offered a quick pill cure for cancer, "I had never seen a book with such thought-provoking questions."

He is won over. He will become part of the elect—and withdraw from the struggle. Everything that was difficult has become simple: The Devil is the source of all oppression; Jehovah will soon destroy the Devil and all worldly governments; Jehovah's Witnesses are His people.

He has found a teleological explanation, and a community, a completely unambiguous solution to everything in his life that oppressed him.

The need to belong to a community, and the appeal, to weary souls, of final solutions, lead otherwise rational people to take leave of their (vexing) senses.

I have a young black friend who, raised as a Witness in the South Bronx, left the Society when she was 22, when the world and its opportunities (and its sorrows) opened up for her. What had catapulted her out of the Society was her work in a drug-rehabilitation centre (work the Society frowned upon), her deep involvement with hard-core addicts, and her feeling that the Watchtower Society was irrelevant to these lives. She could not make herself stop loving and caring for addicts who did not respond to "Scriptural" treatment and Watchtower self-help advice. For several years she led a busy and purposeful, sensual, exploring life. Then she was offered a scholarship to a small Northeastern college. After six months at school—having confronted not just racism, but the reality of class privilege (she was no happier among rich blacks than among rich whites), and having felt herself to be exploited by sexually demanding men, who asked her to violate her own conventional nature in the name of "liberation"—she was ready to become a Witness again. "How can you?" I asked. "You know you don't believe it." "I don't believe it," she said, "but what else is there? I can't stand the way nobody seems to care about anybody else at college, and I can't stand all the screwing around; and I want to be anchored again." "You know the Witnesses are really racist and sexist," I said; "what will you do about that?" "*Everybody's* racist and sexist," she said tearfully. "What I'll do about it is overlook it—and throw myself so hard into Witness activity I'll numb myself to it. . . . I want to be with people who all want the same thing and don't make me feel like a freak." "Do you think you'll be able to blunt your sexuality and numb your intelligence?" "My sexuality and my intelligence haven't got me much." "You won't be able to be my friend any more; you'll have to think of me as evil. That makes me very sad. Doesn't it make you sad?" "Life is terrible," she said; "when I believed in the New World, I could stand it." (Six months later, again involved in a drug-rehabilitation programme, and having found compatible people at school, she put her passing desire to rejoin the Witnesses down to a bout of mono-nucleosis—and guilt over a one-night stand.)

The former revolutionary who chose the simplicities and certainties and the community that my friend (not without a certain amount of sadness) put behind her concludes his account by saying that now "no government official need ever fear trouble at my hand."

He has a point.

I'll never forget the camaraderie that existed among Witnesses travelling to conventions. It was like a frontier spirit we had. I remember in '41 we drove in a caravan to a convention in St. Louis, and as we drove along, more and more cars with Watchtower posters would join us, and we'd sing . . . it really felt like making a joyful noise unto the Lord. . . . You have to remember that we were a small group then, in lots of trouble with the law; and that all-alone-in-the-cold-world feeling intensified our joy. We knew that every time we'd find another Witness, we'd find a brother. . . . Woodstock and the peace marches really knocked me out, because it was like a replay of those convention times—or I wanted it to be. . . . You miss that communal tenderness. I do.—Walter Szykitka, ex-Witness.

I agree with my friend Walter Szykitka that Watchtower conventions have a spirit of "communal tenderness," They are also extraordinarily well run. It's too bad the Witnesses don't organize protests and boycotts; they're good at logistics.

The spirit of communal tenderness Walter speaks of nostalgically is noticeably missing, however, at weekly congregation meetings, which tend, in my experience, to be repetitive, dull, infantilizing, leaden, and oppressive. But they are an important part of Witnesses' lives; and there are built-in rewards for attending them. The Witnesses are "schooled" at these meetings—and for people who lack formal education, they are an important means of acquiring status and self-respect. The Witnesses are continually assured, at these meetings, that they are indeed chosen and special and will receive the reward of eternal life (but only if they're letter-of-the-law good: the meetings inspire as much guilt as confidence); they are trained in public speaking and proselytizing; their behaviour is modified (or, as Lee Cooper more delicately puts it, they receive "moral guidance by an unambiguous code").

All programmes at all meetings are dictated by Watchtower headquarters, which provides a yearly schedule for each congregation.

Meetings are opened and closed with a song. (The Watchtower Society has its own hymnal, *Singing and Accompanying Yourselves with Music in Your Hearts* [1966]. This is a sample lyric: "Hail the good news of the Kingdom rule that Jesus Christ foretold! / This good news of the Kingdom let us preach! And in preaching this good news let's be courageous, firm and bold. / This good news of the Kingdom let us preach! Preach the good news of the Kingdom on the streets, from door to door; / Preach this good news with the printed page all nations o'er. / Preach with skill and preach with kindness, with more zeal than e'er before. / This good news of the Kingdom let us preach!" [pp. 28–29]) There are no meetings devoted exclusively to song or prayer or praise, nor anything that resembles a liturgical year; there is, of course, no litany and no Mass.

On a midweek evening, small clusters of Witnesses from within the local congregation meet in private homes (these "cells" also work as proselytizing teams); they study, paragraph by paragraph, by means of a question-and-answer rote formula, the Society's latest handbook.

At the Kingdom Hall midweek, there is another two-hour meeting, during the course of which Witnesses are given speech training (in the "Theocratic Ministry School") and instructed on proselytizing techniques (at the "Service Meeting"). Just as a lot of *The Watchtower* consists of admonitions to read *The Watchtower*, a lot of the Service Meeting is devoted to the admonition to go to Service Meetings.

The Society exhorts parents not to permit small children to "occupy their time with material that is foreign to the programme." [*TMSG*, p. 27] In typically Skinnerian fashion, it recommends that "As a stimulus to listening, [children] can be given to understand that when they get home they will be asked to repeat something they have learned. And they should be warmly commended if they do remember or make note of something said during the meeting." [*Ibid.*, p. 12] The Witnesses are also told that "concentration comes more easily if we have been careful to avoid eating a heavy meal just prior to meeting time, for this is sleep inducing. . . ."[*Ibid.*] Actually, it's the meetings that are sleep-inducing; but the Witnesses are not permitted to acknowledge, even to themselves, that the meetings are boring. If they are bored, they have only themselves, they are told, to blame. No wonder they operate at a high level of anxiety. Inducing a high level of anxiety is a standard device for authoritarian groups that deal in persuasion.

The first audience-participation event at the Service Meeting I attended was a rehash of an article in *Kingdom Ministry* (a four-page tabloid newsletter received by each congregation but not distributed to outsiders): "How Elders Encourage Brothers to Come [to meetings] on Time." These are some of the questions asked and answered from the printed material:

Q: What questions might one ask about getting to the meeting on time?
A: Am I on time for all meetings? Do I come early enough to greet people warmly?
Q: When we're punctual for meetings, who is it we're really pleasing?
A: Jehovah.
Q: If we come late what do we miss?
A: The song.
Q: If we come even later, who is affected?
A: Brothers who come on time.

This was followed by a ten-minute speech on "Keeping in Touch with the Brothers During Times of Pressure," the theme of which was how, in spite of the fact that the wars and revolutions of worldlings discommoded the brothers and caused them to be "persecuted"—in Ireland, the speaker said, Witnesses had often as a result of the "Catholic-Protestant" war, to wait up to forty-five minutes for a bus to get to a meeting, and in China the Witnesses were required to read Chairman Mao's writings for four hours every day—they should remember that nothing was more important than coming to meetings on time.

Then there was a skit on family problems. Three men discussed how to be "good family heads":

"My wife is a bad cook, she burns things, she isn't thrifty."

"*My* wife is something *else*. She doesn't even *cook!*"

Elder: "Take the lead in loving her. . . . Even if she improves in small ways, compliment her. If a decision isn't important, let *her* make it."

The rest of the Service Meeting was given over to a detailed training course on how to present the Society's latest handbook to householders: ("One might ask: 'Do you think it is possible to establish a completely righteous government that will last for a thousand years?' Pause for reply.")

In the Theocratic Ministry School, which followed the Service Meeting, a fifteen-minute "instruction speech" was given by an elder: "The Bible Views on Sex." A middle-aged man who looked hand-pressed, deodorized, and as if sex and he had been strangers for many years informed us that "nudidity" [sic] was not "upbuilding" and that "all the perverts, pornography, homosexuality, and sex murders are because youth does not have a proper understanding of sex. God approves of sex, but there are limits to everything. Eating is good, but you don't eat for hours and hours. The same with drinking and sleeping and the same with sex: too much is no good. Proper use of your sexual organs will protect your happiness."

After this depressing exercise in guilt-producing obfuscation (how much sex is "too much sex"?) there were two skits.

In one, two women demonstrated how to "preach to our neighbours on our jobs during coffee breaks": "You might illustrate to your fellow worker how Jehovah's Witnesses are blessed through being persecuted. For example, one Witness in Africa compromised his integrity under duress, and he dropped dead six months later."

In the second of the skits, two women demonstrated how "talking to one's fleshly [*i.e.*, natural, not spiritual] sister should be uplifting and encouraging": "During meals, we should talk about *Watchtower* articles and field service, not about movies. Although there is nothing wrong with talking about something humorous or informative, Jehovah really blessed us by providing us with a tongue; we should show our appreciation by talking about spiritual things."

It was hard for me to believe, as I sat through these meetings, that (lacking anything resembling a sense of humour) I hadn't been bored out of my skull all those years I attended them. Then I remembered what had kept me from being bored. In later years, it was the prospect of meeting men, of flirting with unattainable objects—which, in my case, meant trying desperately to prove that I was smart and good (and wondering why nobody loved me, and guessing that it was because I was too smart and not good enough). What had kept me from being bored into somnolence earlier, however, was that at the Theocratic Ministry School my profound ignorance of life (and learning) was papered over with what then seemed to me like exotic knowledge. What other 9-year-old knew about prepositions? Or got instructed on "fluent, conversational, proper pronunciation"?

At some Ministry School meetings the Witnesses are instructed on how to approach "tenants who live in exclusive apartment buildings . . . by means of letters." ("It helps to have a fairly uniform margin. . . . Smudges do not give a good impression." [*TMSG*])

Granted, it sounds not unlike a Dale Carnegie Course, or something offered on the back of a match folder; but think how a high school dropout feels when he is invited to give a talk on—say—The New World Translation of the Bible, using the Society's material to discuss "the genitive and accusative cases in the Greek Scriptures," or "The Important [Hebrew] Verbal Form Called Today the Waw Consecutive." He may never have read *Hamlet*; he may know nothing about the "Catholic-Protestant" war in Ireland; but he feels terrific.

The negative part of all this is that while their training does help some Witnesses to feel good about themselves, it also makes them feel smugly superior to everybody else. True, they may meet many people in their ministry who've read Tolstoy and Blake (which they have not); but how many will have heard of the "waw consecutive"? The Witnesses have the illusion of wisdom, while in fact they have esoteric pieces of knowledge. And they feel good about themselves only in relation to "worldlings"; their relationship to God and to "his organization" is a constant source of guilt and anxiety. It may not be calculated to have this effect, but even the speech counsel the Witnesses receive keeps them off balance: Be confident, but not overconfident. Increase your vocabulary, but don't use multisyllabic words to put on airs. Express warmth, but don't be overemotional. Not only does advice like this encourage extreme and debilitating self-consciousness; it increases the individual's dependence on the Society, which alone can assure him whether he has passed its tests.

The guilt and the anxiety take their toll: One-third of American Witnesses have been members of the Society for less than five years.

[*KM*, April, 1974, p. 1] This figure reflects not only the rapid growth of the movement, but the rapid turnover. The dropout rate, as several former headquarters-staff members will testify, is high; for many, this escape from the hardships and humiliations of life proves only temporary.

For those who remain Witnesses for ten, twenty, or thirty years—preoccupation with Armageddon growing with the passing time—each year provides at least one occasion for refreshment, one source of sweetness: the communal tenderness that is so lacking in dreary local congregational meetings is in evidence at large conventions of Jehovah's Witnesses, and particularly at international conventions.

In 1958, for example, almost a quarter of a million Witnesses from 123 countries gathered at the "Divine Will International Assembly" held at Yankee Stadium, with an overflow filling New York's Polo Grounds, to reaffirm their faith, and to rejoice in the samenesses that transcended their national differences.

In 1955, for a series of thirteen conventions held in the United States and Europe, the Society chartered planes and two ocean liners to carry American Witnesses to European cities in what was referred to as "probably the biggest mass movement of Americans through Europe since the Allied invasion during World War II."

I went to a number of those European conventions (in a chartered converted Flying Tiger prop cargo plane), and my waning faith (soon to die a total death) was briefly, vividly, revived: I don't forget, even now, standing with 100,000 Witnesses at the convention grounds at the Zeppelinwiese in Nuremberg and thinking "Here is where Hitler—who sought to crush us—held his barbaric rallies; and now he is dead, and we survive." It seemed to me a glorious victory of good over evil; and because such transcendental moments are so rare in the ordered life of the Witnesses, they are the more thrilling when they come.

All those smiling faces, smiling because they are together, united in a common cause! I remember how good and sweet it felt to suspend disbelief and feel, however fleetingly, that all around me were my brothers and sisters; and that nothing, oceans or persecution or the Devil's wrath, could separate us. And I remember too, how boring the speeches were: It was context, not content, that mattered.

Even when something is anticlimactic, at a large convention, it was made to feel, at least in retrospect, climactic—as, for example, at Yankee Stadium in August, 1950, where the Witnesses were reminded of the old belief that God's faithful—Abraham, Joseph, David—would rise from the dead before the end of the world. This aroused tremendous expectations, which were heightened by the speaker, F. W. Franz, when he suggested that among those gathered together were the "Princes of the New Earth."

The spectators were roused to tears by the prevailing excitement, expecting to see these biblical figures. Some stood up; others rushed to the entrance near the speakers' stand, where they would have a better view. The speaker quieted the crowd and then compared the new Jehovah's Witnesses to those of old. In effect, he assured them that they were the new princes, those who had turned their backs on a world slated for doom and who must persevere in going forward to build the New Jerusalem.

Forward, indeed. This was, in fact, a denial of a previously cherished and defended belief, couched so as to make conventioneers feel that something had been added unto, not taken away from, them. David didn't pop out of the dugout, and Solomon didn't surface on the speaking stand; but Franz thrilled his audience nonetheless. (I myself was irritated—though I applauded as fervently as anyone else; I had a distinct sense of having been had, and I felt guilt as a consequence. And I wondered how many coronaries Franz had occasioned by his initial provocative remarks. And from some of the mutterings I heard as I left the Stadium that night, I deduced that others were irritated as well, though not, perhaps, as guilt-stricken as I was for allowing myself to feel vexed.)

During the late 1930s and early '40s, when the Witnesses were undergoing legal trials, the conventions were suffused with special joy. The Witnesses huddled together for warmth; infatuated with their pain, they took violent satisfaction in their suffering. The assemblies were a blessed relief from their tribulations. They were like sanctuaries. Today's assemblies have lost that encampment feeling; they are no longer a refuge, a benevolent enclosure. (But they receive a terrifically good press—the Witnesses *behave* so well at conventions; and that, perhaps, is almost as gratifying to the Witnesses as feeling threatened and besieged.)

In any case, whatever the circumstances, Watchtower conventions have been and are well-oiled machines, impressively run by an all-volunteer army of administrators, menial workers, and technicians.

Now that the Witnesses have grown in numbers, they are obliged to have fewer national, and more regional, conventions.

The assembly I attended at Aqueduct Race Track in Queens, in 1974, was one of eighty-five held around the world; in all, almost a million people attended. Each convention delegate—whether in Tahiti or Kansas City—heard the same programme, designed at Brooklyn headquarters.

Over 4,700 volunteers, some as young as 10 years old, worked in the twenty highly organized convention departments set up at Watchtower headquarters.

Volunteer workers erected a California-contemporary simulated-slate-and-brick patio/stage; speakers were sheltered from the sun by a 20-x-70-foot "ornamental" shingled structure flanked by masses of plastic ferns, peonies, and giant mums. A jet-aircraft balancing agent nailed the shingles, and an optician and a refrigerator engineer stained them.

Volunteer cooks and butchers working in Aqueduct's kitchens fed 4,000 to 7,000 people noonday and evening meals in an impromptu cafeteria set up by volunteer carpenters. It was an operation the Salvation Army might well have envied. Substantial meals cost convention delegates only $1 each. Everything had been thought of: Witnesses had bought their meal tickets at local congregations in advance of the assembly. The order and discipline of hungry conventioneers—whose appetite for "spiritual food" had been appeased by a six-hour daily diet of sermons, discussions, and skits—were as impressive as the food was bland.

Volunteer janitors kept Aqueduct so litter-free that a racing fan, had he inadvertently wandered in, would surely have been the victim of culture shock. (There wasn't much to clean up: as an Association sanitation officer remarked to me, glancing balefully at my lit cigarette, "I haven't seen one smoker. The crowd is very interesting and very pleasant and they throw everything in baskets." There weren't any beer cans to clean up, either, because there wasn't any beer.)

Volunteer ushers kept track of attendance.

Volunteer plumbers installed the above-ground plastic pool in which 1,003 new converts were immersed to "symbolize their dedication to do God's will." In this pool, ringed with fuchsia plastic flowers, volunteers immersed the converts—among whom there were no bikinis, an 11-year-old boy with chicken pox, an 86-year-old woman, and a 350-pound woman totally immobilized in a wheelchair—with deft assembly-line dispatch.

According to the Pinkerton guards, and according to New York's 106th Precinct cops assigned to the assembly, and according to the drivers who drove the chartered buses that brought the Witnesses to Aqueduct, and according to the waitresses at the nearby Big A Restaurant on Rockaway Boulevard, the Witnesses were "the most courteous, orderly, law-abiding, decent, sincere, best bunchapeople we ever saw."

It was a young crowd.

Outside the gates of Aqueduct were a handful of ex-Witnesses, who, looking forlorn and exhausted of hope, attempted to distribute mimeographed anti-Witness literature, offering their own speculations about the date of Armageddon—and being pointedly ignored. Their presence was a reminder of the high dropout rate among Jehovah's Witnesses, and of their inability to sever ties with the Watchtower Society completely. They were still drawn to certainty, schismatically.

My mother raised me to believe that there were some very nice people who were not Jehovah's Witnesses and some stinkers who were; so I was prepared to discover that there were nice people who weren't really *nice people . . . but I stuck at their being destroyed at Armageddon.*—Walter Szykitka, ex-Witness.

Some ex-Witnesses do make a final and complete break, though they frequently substitute one form of certainty for another. For those who remain with the Society, the sustaining conviction is that God will destroy their enemies in their time and restore them to a perfect life in the New World; that hope redeems them from the degradations of daily living. "This is good; this is what I want; what I've been looking for": that is what H.M. Macmillan, who was a member of the Society for over fifty years, says, of his conversion by a Watchtower representative, in his autobiography, *Faith on the March*. What he was saying was "This *ought* to be; therefore it is."

For others, it is not enough that it *ought* to be. Some begin to doubt the premises upon which their waiting is based; or they quail, ultimately revulsed, at the idea that their entry into the New World will be paved, as it were, with the bones and carcasses of "nice" (but insufficiently nice) unbelievers; or they doubt the good faith and goodwill of the Society which claims to be God's own.

All these factors were at work in the person of Walter Szykitka, who, having been raised a Witness, left the Society after eight years at Bethel headquarters (where his father, before he married, had also worked). Walter began to doubt the accuracy of the chronology upon which his expectations that Armageddon would come in his lifetime were based; he questioned the arbitrary nature of the decisions he saw made at Bethel and the mischief he saw practised there; and he began to love "worldly people."

There are problems and disaffections common to all religious communities; and Walter used the rationale standardly employed by religious people who see abuse of temporal power at the hands of "sacred" authority: "I figured the Lord's servants were 'imperfect vessels,' and that however harshly or whimsically they behaved, that was nothing compared with the fact that they had The Truth."

That rationale works, however, only as long as one is absolutely convinced that the words of one's leaders spring from The Word; and Walter was beginning to have his doubts.

Even after Walter left Bethel, he could not tear himself away from the organization he had served for all his life. With his wife,

Peggy, whom he'd met at Bethel, he continued to participate in local congregational activities, and to go from door to door, almost as if by reflex (and despairingly: if *he* didn't really believe, how could he convince anybody else?).

And he had an extraordinary correspondence with the Society on the subject of Biblical chronology.

My own instinct tells me that Walter's preoccupation with chronological accuracy had less to do with wanting to be certain that Armageddon would come, as predicted, in this generation than with his metamorphosis from a person who relished the notion of a newly ordered universe to a person who was no longer able to take the required delight and relish in a disaster for which he could find no justification and which could by no effort of his be ameliorated.

Walter still believes in large solutions. During the 1960s, when Buckminster Fuller and Marshall McLuhan were his heroes, he substituted the counterculture for God; and he believes that everything that conduces to individual happiness and fulfilment produces "waves of goodness" that will eventually change society. He sees now "a movement toward an incredible expansion of human consciousness, awareness of our essential social nature. . . . This System is based on competition and evil and greed; but humanity will reach a point in evolution when suddenly it becomes more beneficial for human beings to cooperate with one another because competing for the survival of the fittest has got us nowhere. We're moving in that direction now. What's happening now is different from anything that has happened before."

He believes (as he once believed, but for different reasons) that we are living in a marked time. Whatever one might think of Walter's beliefs—regarding them as naive, or as the mirror image of the fantasies of dread apocalypse he lived with for so long—they spring from a mind that can no longer entertain visions of God-death and destruction; from a soul that joins its struggle with life; and from an ego sufficiently strong to dispense with the false comforts of the no-comforters. Walter's Yes may not suit everyone (it is not, for example, mine); but it is at work, and at play, in a larger world of human beings he had once been taught to despise.

Still, it is interesting that Walter, once obsessed with Biblical chronology, sees human evolution toward goodness as "a kind of *mathematical* progression" (or accumulation); he describes his perspective as "global."

Walter is a lucky survivor, able to integrate his past with his present. Not all ex-Witnesses are so fortunate. And he is also proof that once one has been drawn to certainty, it is almost impossible not to seek it in other places.

IX
The Heroic Opportunity and Adventure: Jehovah's Witnesses Overseas

> All invasive moral states and passionate enthusiasms make one feelingless to evil in some direction. When the passion is extreme, suffering may actually be gloried in; provided it be for the ideal cause, death may lose its sting, the grave its victory. In these states, the ordinary contrast of good and ill seems to be swallowed up in a higher denomination, an omnipotent excitement which engulfs the evil, and which the human being welcomes as the crowning experience of his life. This, he says, is truly to live, and I exult in the heroic opportunity and adventure.
> —William James, *The Varieties of Religious Experience*

In the Witnesses' solipsistic view of human history, World War II was a demon-inspired "global attack on Jehovah's Witnesses" executed by the "Nazi-Fascist-Catholic" coalition, "an international . . . conspiracy to 'get' Jehovah's witnesses." [*Yearbook*, 1974; *Faith*, pp. 171–72; *JWDP*, p. 153] This egocentric view may give rise to justifiable irritation. Nevertheless, the facts demonstrate amply that the Witnesses were persecuted during World War II, that their treatment at the hands of totalitarian or war-threatened governments was barbaric. They suffered, gloried in their suffering, and endured.

More recently, revolutionary governments (such as Dr. Banda's Malawi) have seen in them a threat to national unity; emerging nations have regarded their nonparticipation as a drain on the vital energy necessary to make political and economic policies cohere. In Europe and in Latin America, conservative elements of the Church have been happy to align themselves with conservative governments to paralyze or to place constraints upon the work of the Witnesses.

On the other hand, the Witnesses have sometimes lent support to conservative governments by refusing (as in South Africa) to protest against injustice; by not bearing witness, like many of us, they have helped in some totalitarian countries to maintain the status quo.

As the Nazis overran Europe, the Witnesses were restrained and their work banned in France, Spain, Poland, Belgium, Greece, Bulgaria, Hungary, Italy, the Netherlands, Rumania, Yugoslavia,

Estonia, Denmark and Norway, as well as Northern Rhodesia, Southern Rhodesia, Nigeria, and the Gold Coast.

After 1941, their work was proscribed in Japan, the Philippines, Burma, Malaya, the East Indies, Fiji, New Zealand, and Ceylon.

Bans were imposed throughout the British Empire. There were 12,000 Witnesses living in the British Isles when war broke out. They were able to continue to preach and to gather together in spite of what they now refer to as "Catholic-inspired action."

The witnesses claim to have received three threats from "those maniacs signing themselves as the I.R.A. in the course of four months." [*Yearbook*, 1940, pp. 81–82; *JWDP*, pp. 152–53]

Over 1,500 Witnesses were sentenced to prison in Britain for failure to join the armed services; 334 female Witnesses received prison terms for failure to perform war duties. Witnesses from Poland, Germany, Austria, Belgium, and France who had come to England before the war were interned in a camp on the Isle of Man for the duration. American and Swiss nationals were deported.

The Witnesses regarded their London headquarters as a Luftwaffe target (or a target of "demons"), offering as proof the bombings that took place near the Society's London office. One of the bombs exploded directly across the street from Bethel; another, only seventy yards to its rear. In all, twenty-nine bombs were dropped close to the office within a space of three months. Despite the heavy bombing, the Witnesses continued to preach and push their work forward.

An Australian Order-in-Council banning Jehovah's Witnesses in Australia was declared illegal by the High Court of Australia, which ruled in favour of the Witnesses and against the Commonwealth. The Court held that Jehovah's Witnesses were not a subversive organization prejudicial to the prosecution of the war.

Germany

Nowhere is the record of suffering by Witnesses more awful than in Nazi Germany. And nowhere is one of their paradoxes more marked: They refused to Heil Hitler (regarding the salute as idolatrous), and to bear arms; and they were assigned to death camps. But, on the the other hand, some boast of having received special privileges at the hands of the SS for their docility in the camps; and some consented to work as domestics in the Lebensbornheime, the notorious Nazi breeding farms.

It would be ridiculous to seek to diminish the extent of the Witnesses' suffering, and of their commitment and zeal, but one remarks that they offered both their deaths and their "miraculous escapes from death" as proof that they are chosen by Jehovah;

everything attested to their singularity.

Opposition to the Witnesses in Germany was most virulent during the mid-1930s; pressure on them abated somewhat at the height of the war, when the Reich tended to see them as valuable work units. (Himmler is said to have called them "good-natured lunatics.") Toward the end of the war, when Hitler's armies were everywhere in retreat, Himmler

> expressed admiration for the Witnesses, who, he suggested, once victory had been won, would be a useful group to settle in the vast plains of Russia where they would act as a barrier to Russian ambitions beyond the fringes of the German empire. [Conway, *NPC* pp. 198–99; from Himmler's personal files, quoted in F. Zipfel, *Kirchenkampf in Deutschland* (Berlin, 1965) p. 200.]

At the very last, when the camps were about to be liberated by the Allies, the Witnesses were included in Himmler's directives that everyone within the camps should be exterminated.

Watchtower sources estimate that at any one time, 10,000 Witnesses (known in Germany as Bible Students) were incarcerated, "while equal thousands were free on the outside to maintain underground activity and energetic, though cautious, witness work." [*JWDP*, p. 163] Out of approximately 25,000 Bible Students then active in Germany, 6,019 received prison sentences; 203 of the 253 Witnesses sentenced to death were actually executed —shot or beheaded; and 635 died in prison, most of them of starvation. [*Aw,* Feb. 22, 1975, and *Yearbook*, 1974, p. 212] According to the same sources, 860 Witness children were forcibly taken from their parents by the Reich.

A historian sympathetic to the Witnesses (Conway, *op. cit.*) offers a different set of figures: He says that "a higher proportion (97%) suffered some form of persecution than any other churches" and that "No less that a third of the whole following were to lose their lives as a result of refusal to conform or compromise." (If Conway is correct, over 8,000 Witnesses were killed in the camps; the Witnesses themselves claim only 838 deaths out of their total number, which they give as 25,000)

Opposition to the Witnesses (or Bible Students) began in 1933. The German Witnesses were vociferously anti-communist. That may have been one reason they were not viewed, until the accession of Hitler to full power, as a threat to the Reich. A directive from the Ministry of the Interior, April 19, 1930, circulated among police officers, stated that "The [Watchtower] association at present pursues solely religious objectives and is not politically active . . . in the future the introduction of criminal proceedings, especially as regards violations of the Reich's Peddling Laws, is to be avoided." [*Yearbook*, 1974, p. 105]

By 1933, however, conditions had changed dramatically. The Witnesses were listed first on the List of Proscribed Sects. [*NPC*, p. 371] In June of 1933, according to Watchtower sources, the American-held property of the Watch Tower Society in Magdeburg was seized; public meetings and literature distribution were banned. Following negotiations between the U.S. State Department and the German government, the property was returned to the American Society in October of 1933. In that same year, Hitler issued an edict to confiscate all Watch Tower literature. Bavaria was the first German state to impose a total ban on all gatherings of Witnesses, including singing and praying in private homes. By 1935, the ban had become national. And Gestapo searches of Witnesses' homes had become routine.

In a White Paper (Germany No. 2, Treatment of German Nationals in Germany, issued October 30, 1939) based on a report compiled by Sir Neville Henderson, Britain's ambassador to Berlin until war was declared, it was noted that Bible Students were obliged to wear violet arm badges and that they were allowed no communication with the outside world, but that, on the other hand, their rations were not cut down. Sir Neville remarks that they "professed themselves ready to suffer to the uttermost what they felt God had ordained for them." [*JWDP*, p. 155]

What God had ordained for them they believed the Catholic Church had arranged for them. In American Watchtower publications during the late 1930s and '40s, representatives of the Vatican and the Nazis were pictured in lurid embrace; Fascists and Nazis and the Vatican were depicted as piling money into and out of one another's coffers. The Witnesses had no doubt that the Roman Catholic Hierarchy instigated all atrocities against them. They presume that the Church used Hitler as its instrument to destroy the Witnesses, the Vatican is the archenemy that instigated their persecution in Nazi Germany, and the churches were apostate during the war.

The churches were derelict; but for that matter, the Witnesses did not raise their voices, though they maintained their integrity by refusing to fight.

The evidence is that Hitler conducted a war of attrition against the churches, signing the Concordat with the Vatican in order to lull the Church into a false sense of security and in order not to alienate the large Catholic population.

The facts prove also that Hitler did everything within his power to stir up anticlerical feeling among the Germans; that the Nazis exerted control over all aspects of church life; that his aim was to crush Christianity, and to substitute state religion. From historians like Conway and Guenter Lewy we learn that while the churches were indeed complicit in their own victimization, Hitler always considered both the Evangelical and the Catholic Church to be his rivals; he never considered his aims and theirs identical. The Catholic hierarchy welcomed the signing of the Concordat all too readily in 1933; and it cannot be denied that "By compromising themselves in this way, the Catholic hierarchy was never able to lead the Catholic Church in wholehearted opposition to the Nazis, even after the hostile intentions of the latter were all too plainly revealed." [*NPC*, Introduction, pp. xxii–xxiii]

Guilty of political quietism, the Church, it has been argued, surrendered. And the churches have admitted their guilt and their shame: Meeting in the ruined city of Stuttgart in October, 1945, the German Evangelical church declared:

> . . . we know ourselves to be one with our people in a great company of suffering and in a great solidarity of guilt. With great pain do we say: Through us endless suffering has been brought to many people and countries. . . . We accuse ourselves for not witnessing more courageously, for not praying more faithfully, for not believing more joyously, and for not loving more ardently. [*Ibid.*, p. 332; quoted in S. W. Herman, *The Rebirth of the German Church* (London, 1946), p. 137]

Too late, one might argue, to acknowledge guilt—after the terrible moral damage had been done. And yet, if we are playing a numbers game, more churchmen suffered and died for their Christian beliefs than did Witnesses—and the Witnesses refuse to honour their suffering. Without seeking to denigrate the Witnesses, it is necessary to point out that the churches, too, had their martyrs; and that churchmen praised God by naming the monster:

> As early as 1931, Karl Barth, then Professor of Systematic Theology in Bonn, had attacked what he described as hyphenated Christianity, in which the role of Christ himself was linked with nationalist feelings. [*NPC*, pp. 10–11]

In 1933, Protestant pastor Dietrich Bonhoeffer was arrested; he was hanged in Flossenburg Concentration Camp, April 9, 1945 [*Ibid.*, p. 400]

> In the Catholic Church, a number of clearsighted theologians saw the incompatibility between Christian doctrine and the Nazi ideas of so-called "positive Christianity." In several parts of Germany [in 1930], Catholics were explicitly forbidden to become members of the Nazi party, and Nazi members were forbidden to take part in such Church ceremonies as funerals. The Bishop of Mainz refused to admit Nazi Party members to the sacraments. In his New Year's message on 1 January 1931, the Presiding Bishop in Germany, Cardinal Bertram of Breslau, issued a warning against false prophets and agitators, declaring that extreme nationalism, by overglorifying the Race, could

lead only to a despisal of the revelation and commandments of God: "Away therefore with the vain imaginings of a national religious society, which is to be torn away from the Rock of Peter, and only guided by the racial theories of an Aryan-heathen teaching about salvation. This is no more than the foolish imaginings of false prophets." Despite such warnings, fear of "Marxist heresies" became a standard feature in the declarations of Catholic speakers. [*Ibid.*, pp. 6–7; from Hans Müller, *Katholische Kirche und Nationalsozialismus* (Munich, 1963), p. 17]

But there were other voices:

One was that of Niemöller himself, a pastor of the Evangelical Confessing Church. In his Sermon for the Fourth Sunday before Easter (1934), Niemöller identified Nazism as satanic:

> We have all of us—the whole Church and the whole community—been thrown into the Tempter's sieve, and he is shaking and the wind is blowing, and it must now become manifest whether we are wheat or chaff! Verily, a time of sifting has come upon us, and even the most indolent and peaceful person among us must see that the calm of a meditative Christianity is at an end. [*NPC*, dedication page]

Niemöller was arrested by direct order of Hitler. By November, 1937, over 700 pastors of the Confessing Church had been arrested. [*Ibid.*, p. 209]

The Witnesses admit that "some churchmen [were] persecuted"; but they enter the caveat that the persecution of the churches was a result of "anti-Nazi *political* activity." [*Aw*, Feb. 22, 1975, pp. 20–21] This raises the question of how to divorce the political from the moral. Is it a political act to speak out against genocide? against armed aggression? against euthanasia? This dichotomy between the spiritual and the political is the same one advanced by Goebbels and Goering in order to clamp down on the churches.

It may be argued that the moment a Christian ceases to apply spiritual values to the events of the material world, and to protest against injustice, he ceases to be a Christian and becomes apostate. This is, in fact, exactly what the Barmen Synod declared in 1934: "We reject the false doctrine, as though there were areas of our life in which we would not belong to Jesus Christ, but to other Lords—areas in which we would not need justification and sanctification through him." [*NPC.*, p. 335]

With the outbreak of war, and the necessity to mobilize the German people behind the war effort, Hitler declared that "no further action should be taken against the Evangelical and Catholic Churches for the duration of the war." [*NPC.*, p. 232; quoted in a circular from the Chief of the Race and Settlement Headquarters, Sept. 8, 1939, unpublished Nuremberg Documents NG-1392 and NG-1755] Both the Evangelical and Catholic bishops called upon their followers to support the war—in spite of Nazi atrocities against Catholic priests and laypersons in Poland, details of which were broadcast by the Vatican radio. [*NPC*, p. 235; from Lewry, Guenter, *The Catholic Church and Nazi Germany* (Boston, 1964), p. 229]

However, in 1941, when the Nazis launched a series of new offences against Eastern Europe, new and more stringent measures began to be taken against the churches: Himmler ordered the complete evacuation of all church properties without compensation. Monasteries and convents were emptied. In Luxembourg, 400 priests were evacuated on Hitler's personal orders. All Church hospitals were declared secular institutions. Catholic orphanages and kindergartens and welfare agencies were placed under the control of the state. The Catholic press was suppressed. Tolerating no rivalry, Heydrich ordered that immediate action be taken against all small sects, including Christian Scientists and the Salvation Army.

Hitler was forced to come to some degree of accommodation with the churches by virtue of their vast numbers. But it is manifestly clear from his words, as well as from the actions of the Reich, that he was intent upon a policy of deliberate repression. He loathed what he called the "satanic superstition" of the "hypocritical priests," who, he said, in language reminiscent of that of the Witnesses, were interested "in raking in the money" and "befuddling the minds of the gullible." [*Ibid.*, p. 3; from *Hitler's Table Talk*] Hitler fostered the illusion that he was pious; he never officially left the Church, and he continued to pay compulsory Church taxes. But his determination to avenge himself against the churches is left in no doubt. Hitler's attitude toward the churches was governed by pragmatism; and the churches, in turn, evolved their own ill-conceived pragmatic response.

Events proved the hierarchy wrong in its estimation of Hitler. But it was the threat to the spiritual and physical well-being of twenty million German Catholics that induced Eugenio Cardinal Pacelli (later Pope Pius XII) to sign the Concordat with Hitler. The signing of the Concordat effectively eliminated the Church as a potent political force. Hitler signed the Concordat because a subservient clergy was preferable to a host of noisy martyrs.

Among the Evangelical churches, which were "politically conservative, patriotic and paternalistic," [*NPC*, p. 9] there was a tendency to welcome the Nazi revolution "as a first step towards the reintroduction of government by Christian authorities, affirming with St. Paul (Romans 13) that 'the powers that be are ordained of God.'" [*Ibid.*, p. 10] (That scripture, which the Witnesses too have time and again bent to their necessities, has perhaps created more political confusion—and mischief—than any other in the Bible.)

How the churches must have felt when the Nazis give birth to a new heathenism it is not difficult to imagine. Christian doctrines—the fall of man, redemption, salvation, Judgment—were transformed into an ersatz Nazi theology. [*Ibid.*, p. 145] The Nazis substituted their own liturgy, their own baptism and marriage and burial services for those of the Church. They parodied the Nicene Creed. The blood shed at the time of Hitler's unsuccessful Putsch of November 9, 1923, said Hitler, "is become the altar of baptism for our Reich." [*Ibid.*, p. 140] That blood was celebrated as a sacrament.

The Church, having signed the Concordat and lost its moral authority, was silent. It is even more amazing that while official anti-Nazi pronouncements were rare, and while both the Evangelical churches and the Catholic Church hierarchy maintained, for the most part, an official silence, some individuals did not fail. One such was Franz Jägerstätter. And the Witnesses have claimed him as their own.

Franz Jägerstätter was an Austrian peasant. He lived in St. Radegund, a small village in Upper Austria, where he was the sexton of the parish church. When Hitler's troops moved into Austria in 1938, Jägerstätter was the only man in the village to vote against Anschluss. When he was greeted with the Nazi salute—Heil Hitler!—he replied, "Pfui Hitler!" Acting on his Christian beliefs, he publicly declared that he would not fight in an unjust war. When he was reminded that other Catholics had found it possible to fight for Hitler—with the approval of their bishops—he replied, "They have not been given the grace" to do otherwise; he declared that this was a matter of individual conscience, between him and the God and the living Church he served. He was adamant that he would not serve the government that was persecuting his Church.

Jägerstätter was called to active duty, was imprisoned, and was sentenced to death. After his trial, he wrote his wife: "Only do not forget me in prayer, even as I will not forget you—and remember me especially at Mass. I can also give you the good news that I had a visit yesterday, and from a priest, no less! Next Tuesday he will come with the Holy of Holies. Even here, one is not abandoned by God." He went in the same spirit to his death, knowingly and heroically. He was beheaded after a military trial, on August 9, 1943. It is said that he walked to his death in a calm and composed manner. Before his execution, he had written, "I cannot . . . take an oath in favour of a government that is fighting an unjust war. . . . May God accept my life in reparation not only for my sins but for the sins of others as well." He left his wife and three daughters in the hands of God.

A Mother Superior of an Austrian convent remembers that Father Jochmann, the chaplain of Brandenberg prison, said to an audience of nuns, after Jägerstätter's death: "I can only congratulate you on this countryman of yours who lived as a saint and has now died a hero. I say with certainty that this simple man is the only saint that I have ever met in my lifetime." (The above information is taken from Gordon Zahn, *In Solitary Witness: The Life and Death of Franz Jägerstätter* [New York: Holt, Rinehart & Winston, 1964].)

The Witnesses call attention to the fact that "the courageous stand of [Austrian Bible Students] had some influence on the Catholic Franz Jägerstätter. Gordon Zahn reports that his village pastor noted that 'Franz had often spoken with admiration of their faithfulness,' and villagers who knew him made much of the fact that he 'spent hours discussing religion and studying the Bible' with his *Bibelforscher* cousin, the only non-Catholic in the village." [*Aw*, Feb. 22, 1975, p. 22]

Professor Zahn quite emphatically denies that Jägerstätter's refusal to serve in the army can in any way be attributed to his Bible Student cousin:

> Those closest to Franz at the time make it quite clear that this was not the case. One close friend introduced the surprising note that Franz had never really liked his cousin. Jägerstätter's wife insisted that his cousin had no influence at all upon her husband. Perhaps the most conclusive testimony at this point was provided by Fr. Furthauer and the woman who was married to the cousin at that time. The priest insisted that in all his discussions with Franz he had never brought up the theological position maintained by the sect. Fr. Furthauer was aware of the close relationship between his sexton and the local *Bibelforscher*; it is true, he admitted, that they spent a great deal of time together in religious discussions. The fact of the matter was that Jägerstätter was trying to bring his cousin into the Catholic fold. Moreover, he added, the cousin had already been inducted into the Home Guard before Jägerstätter was called into service in February, 1943. [Zahn, *op. cit.*, pp. 108–109]

The priest's claims might be dismissed as self-serving, but when "the cousin's former wife was interviewed," she reinforced them:

> When she was asked to indicate how much influence her husband and his religious beliefs had had upon Jägerstätter and his stand, she answered promptly and emphatically: "None at all." As she saw it, Jägerstätter had studied the Bible on his own until he became "too one-sided" on the issue of the Fifth Commandment and its application—this led him to the independent conclusion that he could not fight in the war. Franz and her husband had discussed this issue at great length, but as for the question of influence, it was Jägerstätter who was always "working on" her husband. Her husband had taken the position that

> the individual believer should not permit himself to be trapped into a hopeless situation by taking the absolutist stand of refusing all military service; instead, he felt, one should try to get into some limited or noncombatant service. Jägerstätter, on the other hand, always insisted that nothing less than total refusal was required—and even after her husband had left for service—in the Signal Corps, she recalled—Franz continued to insist that his cousin had done the wrong thing. . . .
>
> It is quite clear, then, that Jägerstätter's position cannot be traced to the influence of this fundamentalist sect. However, Pastor Karobath did introduce one reservation. He agreed that the sect's theology had no influence upon Franz's action, but he suggested that the *example* set by the members of that sect in holding fast to their beliefs no matter what sacrifice they were called upon to make might have strengthened his commitment. [*Ibid.*, pp. 108–110]

The Witnesses find it amazing that a man should bear solitary witness; it is essential to their belief that no one can do without a supportive organization (*their* organization). The Witnesses, from their fringe position, totally repudiated the world. Jägerstätter believed in the living Church of martyrs; and he believed that that Church—no matter what the hierarchy said—required open civil dissent when secular values threatened spiritual values. He did not divorce morality or religion from politics. And he believed in the communion of saints, even when his Church leaders urged him on to a different set of actions.

By all accounts, the behaviour of Witnesses held in Buchenwald, Ravensbrück, Sachsenhausen, Dachau, and Belsen was characterized by extraordinary bravery. The vast majority refused to sign a declaration disavowing their faith—a declaration that would have ensured their release from the camps. The Society contends that those Witnesses who succumbed to torture and threats received poisoned meats from God in return. They were, having "placed themselves outside of Jehovah's protection," imprisoned by the Soviets, starved, raped . . . Those who joined the German military, the Society says, for the most part "lost their lives." [*Yearbook*, 1974, p. 178]

So the Witnesses talk about their martyrs (those who died for their faith), and about those who died because their faith weakened —using both sets of circumstances as proof of divine dispensation. They need to see immediate rewards, immediate punishments, direct consequences to every act—as if faith must pay off promptly with tangible rewards.

There were, the Society acknowledges, Witnesses who did sign declarations disavowing their faith; later, before they were actually released from the camps, they had their signatures annulled. And there were others who were released as a result of their disavowal but who, "after the breakdown of Hitler's regime, spontaneously joined the [Witnesses'] ranks." (Commenting on this, the *Yearbook* reports charitably (and correctly): "Many were comforted by the experience of Peter, who had denied his Lord and Master too, but had been taken back into his favour." [*Ibid.*, p. 178] I find this remark from a Watchtower publication refreshing, because it treats tenderly of human frailty and acknowledges that human beings do sometimes act out of human motives and human circumstances—especially since so often what one reads suggests that everything that happens to Jehovah's Witnesses is a result of angelic or demonic intervention. It has the sweet taste of the merciful God of the Gospels: we did not need Christ to teach us ethics—we needed Him to understand mercy.)

The cohesive ideology of the Witnesses—like the cohesive ideology of the Communists—and their communal life and faith in the camps (where they even managed to baptize new converts by total immersion in water) enabled them to survive their ordeals. It is significant that *after* their liberation from the camps many Witnesses fell away from their faith. It is almost as if their persecution had been the jell that united them to one another and to God, the adrenalin that charged and sustained them. They got through tragedy, with its harsh, sharp focus, together; like most of us, they found commonplace muddle harder to deal with.

In general, behaviour of the Witnesses as a whole in the camps seems to be survival behaviour, and Watchtower publications report not only stories of sadistic treatment at the hands of the SS, but the fact that the Witnesses were placed, even in Auschwitz, in "positions of trust".

Both sets of treatment—the torture they received and the special treatment they received—are used as proof of God's providence.

What appears to have happened is that after 1942, when the Nazis were more concerned with winning the war than with eradicating one small dissident sect, many Witnesses were employed in "projects productive to the economy" and were therefore left alone, since all available manpower was being mobilized for production.

Because of this new policy, prisoners, including Witnesses, were better fed. The officials were careful, too, not to force Witnesses to work in armament factories, but placed them in shops where the work was suitable to their abilities. For this, the Witnesses praised God in the belief that He had directed their enemies.

This is a variation of "God works in strange and wondrous ways": the implication is that the Witnesses' integrity aroused the ire of Satan and their docility and industriousness aroused the sympathy of Satan's agents. And, indeed, except when their faith was directly assaulted, the Witnesses appear to have been docile and cooperative in the camps (they have always prided themselves as being model prisoners); they were thus more valuable to the state alive than dead.

In the early 1900s, Pastor Russell pointed out that the Witnesses ought to reap their greatest rewards in Germany, for it was there that the Society had gone to its greatest expense to spread the word. He added the caveat, however, that the large numbers of the "consecrated" might have been diminished by immigration to the United States.

The work Russell started in Germany, a country for which he had a great affinity, has not fared badly. In 1975, there were, in West Germany, over 100,000 Witnesses—or one Witness in every 597 West Germans. [*Yearbook*, 1976]

Africa

Malawi:

They are not Jehovah's Witnesses, they are the Devil's Witnesses. —Dr. H. K. Banda, President of Malawi, 1972 [reported in *Newsweek*, May 10, 1976, p. 106]

The determination of Jehovah's Witnesses to remain aloof from politics has brought them into conflict with African nationalism—particularly in Malawi.

On October 23, Jehovah's Witnesses were officially listed, in *The Times* of Malawi, as an "unlawful society." In 1972, contending that the 30,000 Malawian Witnesses hindered the country's political and economic development, the Malawi Congress Party is reported to have adopted the following resolution:

> . . . Resolved that all the members of these fanatical religious sects employed in commerce and industry should be dismissed forthwith, and that any commercial or industrial concern that does not comply with this resolution should have its licence cancelled.
>
> Resolved that all members of these fanatical religious sects employed by the Government should be dismissed forthwith and that any member of these sects who is self-employed, either in business or farming, have his business or farming activities discouraged.
>
> Resolved that all the members of these sects who live in the villages should be chased away from there, and appealed to the Government [*sic*] to give maximum possible protection to members of the party who deal with the adherents to these sects. [*Aw*, Dec. 8, 1975, p. 6]

Newsweek reported:

> A series of pogrom-style persecutions has apparently decimated the sect [in Malawi]. Newsmen have been banned from Malawi, but numerous eyewitness reports of torture and murder have leaked out of the small southeastern African nation. Jehovah's Witnesses have reportedly been hacked to death, gang-raped and forced to walk with nails through their feet. Thousands of Witnesses have fled to neigh-

bouring Zambia and Mozambique only to be deported back to Malawi. "There are still 12,000 to 15,000 of our members in Malawi," says Jehovah's Witness leader Keath Eaton in Salisbury, Rhodesia. "Most are being persecuted and about a third are in concentration camps." [*Op. cit.*, p. 106]

The Witnesses' offence in Malawi was to refuse to purchase a 25-cent membership card in the Malawi Congress Party.

A massive letter-writing campaign initiated by American Witnesses resulted in statements of concern from Senator Frank Church and from Representatives George Brown, Paul Tsongas, and Tom Hartkin.

Mozambique:

When, in the summer of 1975, Portugal relinquished control of Mozambique to the Front for the Liberation of Mozambique (FRELIMO), the 7,000 Witnesses of that newly independent country became subject to mass arrests and, according to a story in *Awake!* of January 8, 1976, to harassment and torture. FRELIMO propaganda organs denounced them as "agents left behind by Portuguese colonialism," "former 'Pides' [Portuguese secret police] whose aim was to upset the social order." [*Noticias*, Oct. 9, 1975] *A Tribuna* [Oct. 22, 1975] accused them of "a religious fanaticism" that permitted them "not to show respect for the social order and to annihilate the mobilization and organization of the people."

"When we were tied and beaten by Portuguese colonialists, where were these Witnesses of Jehovah?" Mozambique President Samora Machel asked. [*Noticias, op. cit.*]

The Witnesses' response is that they too were imprisoned—by the Pides.

The main charge levelled against the Witnesses by the Portuguese authorities and the secret police had been that they refused to take part in fighting against FRELIMO. But in 1973, when another wave of persecution hit the Witnesses, they were accused of having been *supporters* of FRELIMO. And when FRELIMO took full power, the revolutionary government accused them of "obscurantism." Radio and press dispatches repeated that "Mozambique is not Jehovah's country"; "these fanatical 'Jehovahs' must be reeducated," Beatings, torture, and mass arrests have followed; Witnesses have been separated from their children, and their property has been confiscated.

It is true that African countries that have been colonized, whose fight for independence has been arduous and bitter, interpret the Witnesses' history of political "neutrality" as a kind of passive resistance to progressive change. The Witnesses themselves argue that they have been a "stabilizing element" in the native populations that were oppressed by imperialist regimes. What some newly independent African nations (whose use of force against the Witnesses is not, of course, justifiable, while it may be understandable) feel about Jehovah's Witnesses is not unlike what Jesus said to his erstwhile followers: If "you are not for me, you are against me: if you are neither hot not cold, but lukewarm, I will spit you out of my mouth."

Zambia:

Kenneth Kaunda of Zambia, for example (himself a devout Christian and a believer in Gandhian non-violence), must find it hard to love the Witnesses when he remembers that their role in pre-independent Northern Rhodesia was, in effect, to be "good natives":

> One incident involving the brothers that took place in 1940 shows the good effect the truth was having on them. Mine workers at Rhokana Corporation's Nkana Mine went on strike, but the brothers employed at the mine continued to present themselves for work, since soldiers had been called in to prevent picketing. It began to be realized by employers that Jehovah's witnesses were in fact a stabilizing element in the population. [*Yearbook*, 1972, pp. 238–39]

Another edition of the *Yearbook* says blandly, speaking of a 1940 "riot" in the Copper Belt, that "the ringleaders were all Roman Catholic." [*Yearbook*, 1976, p. 155]

The Witnesses were not officially recognized in Northern Rhodesia until after 1946—although they were generally perceived to be "good natives." There were, in fact, no white Northern Rhodesians who were Witnesses until 1944, though the Society's branch depot and the administration of the local Witnesses were in the hands of a white South African Llewelyn Phillips. During World War II, Phillips was arrested by government authorities for refusing to surrender Watchtower publications and for refusal to join the army. A ban was placed on Watchtower activity by the Solicitor General.

Still, as Watchtower publications point out, the services of black Witnesses were in great demand: "The Society's adherents have the best reputation of any in this [labour] Corps and it is well known that farmers and other employers specify that they specially want them." [*Yearbook*, 1944]

After World War II, when the Witnesses were no longer seen as a threat to national security, they were permitted to go about their work unmolested. They were, in fact, as agitation for independence accelerated, viewed by colonial administrators as a stabilizing influence. The Witnesses cite with pride a pre-independence newspaper editorial that remarked that "those areas in which Jehovah's

Witnesses are strongest among Africans are now . . . more trouble-free than the average. Certainly they have been active against agitators, witchcraft, drunkenness and violence of any kind." [*Yearbook*, 1972] The newspaper also eulogizes their middle-class propriety: "the Witness families [are] easily recognized in their meetings as little clusters of father, mother and children." [*Ibid.*] The political passivity that endeared them to colonialists made them the targets for attack by African political nationalists and activists; just prior to independence, African militants—seeing in their docility and co-operation with the state an implicit threat to independence and national freedom—harassed and persecuted them.

When there is internal stability, the Witnesses are usually unmolested, their work placed under no restraints; according to the 1977 *Yearbook*, this is the case today with the more than 57,000 Witnesses now in Zambia. It is not surprising that a sect that does not practise a social gospel, and that has had white men as its leaders, has given rise, among black Africans who tend to view white missionaries as partners of white imperialists, to fear and suspicion.

Southern Africa:

To be a Christian in South Africa—if one understands Christianity to mean not only obeying the awesomely difficult injunction to "love one another" but performing the equally difficult task of "bearing witness"—is not easy.

The Witnesses have proselytized in the face of enormous difficulties in South Africa and maintained their neutrality in the face of bloody racial conflict; but their construction of "neutrality" precludes the kind of savage/compassionate outrage against racial injustice that men like Father Huddleston and Alan Paton have found it in their duty to express. As the Church hierarchy did not vehemently attack the treatment of the Jews in Hitler's Germany, the Witnesses do not attack and expose the treatment of black South Africans.

They carry no man's cross but their own. If they deplore, say, the massacre at Sharpeville, their modest indignation is no different in tone from their derision of rock music; both, for them, are proofs that the Devil rules the world. Their anger does not burn hot; indeed, they reserve their scathing attacks for members of the clergy who *do* denounce racial atrocities—because, according to them, those churchmen have entered the secular arena, in which they themselves claim to have no part.

They do, however, love one another. When a drought in Lesotho in 1970 created a severe food shortage, South African Witnesses provided relief maize and cash; and acts of charity like this convince black Witnesses that their white brothers love them: "We reached the point where we had nothing in our house, not even ten cents to buy some mealie meal. Then the money for food arrived from our white brothers in South Africa. I could only cry and not say anything."—Report from a black Witness in Lesotho [*Yearbook*, 1976, p. 212]

The Witnesses' own account of their history in South Africa is fascinating, particularly as it reveals the sect's antipathy to social reform and reformers, and its almost rabid wish to disassociate itself from "indigenous" nationalistic Watchtower movements.

The proselytizing work of the Witnesses in South Africa began at the turn of the century. Russellite literature was carried into the Transvaal in 1902 by a Dutch Reform missionary. In 1906, two Scottish Bible Students began to collect subscriptions for *Zion's Watch Tower* in Durban.

It is at this point—when there were forty subscribers to the *Watch Tower* in South Africa—that the man cast by the Witnesses as a villain enters the "simple" life of the country. In 1907, Joseph Booth, an Englishman who had been a sheep farmer in New Zealand and an entrepreneur in Australia before he found his vocation, "appeared on the stage of the Kingdom drama" [p. 70] in Southern Africa. In the last decade of the 19th century, Booth, who had allied himself with various adventist sects at different times, came to Nyasaland (now Malawi) as an independent missionary. He was outspoken in his espousal of African equality; and his slogan—"Africa for the Africans"—put him in bad odour with government authorities, with whom he was soon *persona non grata.*

Knowing nothing of this, Pastor Russell interviewed Booth in 1906, and as a result the Society underwrote his missionary activities for a time, under the impression that he would open up wide new fields for the brethren. Unfortunately for the Society—and for Russell—Booth's activities merely increased its difficulties and brought its name into disrepute.

Booth took off for South Africa, where he acquired a fervent disciple, an African miner named Elliott Kamwana, who had been educated at the Livingstonia Mission on Lake Nyasa. Soon Kamwana was distributing Russellite tracts among Africans in Johannesburg and Pretoria. He claimed to have baptized over 9,000 Africans in Nyasaland in one year, 1909, alone.

But Booth and Kamwana, while they appear to have used Watch Tower literature to some extent, were at least as much interested in social justice and equality on earth as they were in preaching a heavenly reward. The 1976 *Yearbook* reports that while Bible Students in Durban sang "Free from the Law" (referring to the Mosaic Law), Booth stationed himself outside their meeting hall and sang, in protest, "Not free from the law" (meaning South Africa's discriminatory racial laws). [p. 73].

("Actually," says the *Yearbook*, "neither Booth nor Kamwana had really left Babylon the Great, or false religion; they never became Bible Students or Jehovah's Christian witnesses. Their relationship with the Watch Tower Society was short and superficial." [*Ibid.*])

When Kamwana got back to his native Nyasaland—carrying Booth's social gospel with him—he was deported to the Seychelles Islands. He was not permitted to return to his homeland until 1937. Upon his return, he became the leader of an indigenous "Watch Tower movement"—one of many that proliferated in the Rhodesias, the Congo, and South Africa; they sprang, it is likely, from seeds sown in Nyasaland by Booth and Kamwana; and the schismatic Watch Tower movement was carried from Nyasaland by Africans emigrating for work.

Kamwana, who called his sect "The Watchtower Mission," used some of Russell's ideas and more of his own. He regarded the American Watch Tower Bible and Tract Society as a European organization.

Russell was nervous; in 1910, he sent European Bible Students in good standing with the Society to oversee the work in Southern Africa. But the indigenous Watchtower movements continued to flourish—and to cause grave concern to the American Society, which had no wish to be associated, in the public mind, with the indigenous religious/socialist/nationalist groups, many of which refused to pay taxes and engaged in other acts of civil disobedience.

So many groups were going around calling themselves "Watch Tower" people that there was understandable confusion about who was who. In January of 1915, there was an uprising—quickly crushed by African troops under European officers and European volunteers—in Nyasaland. It was led by one John Chilembwe.

"Subsequently," according to the 1976 *Yearbook*,

> accusations were made that the Watch Tower Society had something to do with the revolt. In fact, the official *History of the Great War* refers to Chilembwe as a "religious fanatic . . . of the so-called 'Watch Tower' sect." Careful investigation has since proved that those in Nyasaland who were interested in the truth, and even those of Kamwana's movement, a false 'Watchtower movement,' as such, had no direct connection with or responsibility for the rioting.

The Watchtower Society is determined to imprint on the official mind its separateness from any indigenous African-run movements; the way in which it has done this is to insist, for the public record, that it represents no threat to the status quo.

Their being good natives does not ensure that Witnesses will be treated benevolently in times of national unrest or total mobilization. Before the outbreak of World War II, Watch Tower literature was impounded in Southern Rhodesia. The Supreme Court of South Africa (*The Magistrate, Bulawayo v. Kabungo*, 1938 S.A. Law Reports 304–316) held that Watch Tower publications did not violate the Sedition Act of Southern Rhodesia. The court ordered that the literature seized and retained be returned to the Witnesses. After the war, they were permitted to carry on their work without disturbance in South Africa and in fact were granted exemption from the draft up to 1972. But with increasing racial unrest, after 1972, the Witnesses who refused to undergo military training became subject to arrest. Any Witness who refuses to take military training is now sentenced to detention barracks for one year, after which he is exempt from service.

In looking at the Witnesses in South Africa, we are again confronted with moral ambiguity and anomalies. Here is a small sect, brave, willing to suffer for its beliefs, non-violent—but unwilling to bear witness to the suffering of others, to give powerful voice to that indignation which Simone Weil called "the fiercest form of love."

The Witnesses do not, as does the Catholic Church, actively challenge apartheid; it may be argued that their religion serves as an opiate to keep non-Europeans satisfied with their painful earthly lives. The Witnesses would counter that they do genuinely enjoy fellowship when, within the context of the law, it is possible.

Mass assemblies held in South Africa are, of necessity held in separate auditoriums for Coloureds, Blacks, and Europeans. In stadiums where the government permits mixed groups to meet, each group is obliged to sit separately.

An exception to this arrangement occurred on January 6, 1974, at Rand Stadium in Johannesburg. (Convention delegates from outside the country were in many cases refused visas because the Department of Interior was exercised over the refusal of South African Witnesses to comply with draft laws.)

On that occasion segregation was not practised. Regardless of colour, all worshipped together, and many chose to sit with their brothers of other races. Those who spoke Portuguese could sit where they wished, as could Zulu-, Afrikaans-, Lesotho-, and English-speaking individuals. The group was happily integrated; they were so joyful that applause had to be held down, and for many of the company it was the most joyous occasion in their experience.

Luckily (according to the Witnesses, "under divine guidance and without realizing it"), the Witnesses had convened in the only Johannesburg stadium used for international, interracial meetings for which no permit was necessary for a single gathering.

The Witnesses point out that the European brethren do what is regarded as "native" work in South Africa: housekeeping, janitorial, and laundry duties; while the Africans take care of the office work and do the typing. Working together on a building project in South Africa brought all the races together—white, African, Coloured, Indian—and achieved a unity they regard as unknown in the secular world.

The Witnesses do not pray that the world may achieve it. They long for the day when God will erase all outside noises; they yearn for Armageddon, when, in one bloody swoop, Jehovah will wipe away all the blood and all the anguish. It is an understandable, if ultimately dangerous, withdrawal from worldly defeat.

Communist Countries: China, Vietnam, Soviet Union, East Germany

China:

Zion's Watch Tower magazine was first introduced to China in 1883. In 1898 a Baptist missionary resigned from his church and began to proselytize for the Bible Students in Protestant missions. In 1912, C. T. Russell paid a brief visit to Shanghai. Very brief; in an article headed "'Pastor' Russell's Tour Exposed" in the *Brooklyn Eagle* (Oct. 14, 1912), an interviewer chats with Russell, who, among other things, thought Nippon was a city in Japan; Russell, who had been on what appears to have been a 107-day cruise around the world, seems quite eager to prove that he spent one full day on solid ground in Shanghai, where, by his own admission, he did not meet a single missionary. In any case, in 1939, two years after the Sino-Japanese War broke out, three German Witnesses were assigned to Shanghai by the Society's Swiss branch. "Since Japan became partners with Germany [the missionaries] had little trouble getting in" to China. [*Yearbook*, 1974, p. 44]

By 1956, although there was no official ban placed on Watchtower publications, supplies of literature had stopped reaching the country. Expediency had led the three German missionaries to leave; in 1958, two remaining European missionaries were, according to Watchtower sources, placed under arrest and labelled "reactionaries." One of them, the Society reports, served a seven-year prison sentence. No statistical reports of Watchtower activity have come out of China since 1958. The last available evidence is that there were, at that time, fewer than 150 Witnesses in all China.

Vietnam:

The Watchtower Society was officially recognized in South

Vietnam in 1973. [*KM*, June, 1973, p. 4] After the Communist victory, the Vietnamese branch of the Society was placed under supervision of the Paris branch. Watchtower sources estimate that there are 100 Witnesses remaining in Saigon.

Soviet Union:

The Witnesses are not permitted to organize; relationships with the headquarters organization have been severed.

> It is interesting to learn . . . [from] an extended denunciation in *Pravda*, that the sect of Jehovah's Witnesses had become almost as much of a headache to the rulers of Communist Russia as it was to the rulers of Nazi Germany. It seems that the Witnesses have been making converts all over the Soviet Union, even in such distant places as Siberia and Kurgan, and that they now constitute a formidable movement of underground resistance to the regime. [*The Washington Post*, March 21, 1959, p. A8; *JWDP*, pp. 280–81]

(Watchtower sources report that 300 Russians and Ukrainians were baptized, during World War II, in Ravensbrück concentration camp. Soviet dissident Pavel Litvinov has the impression that "Russian intelligentsia in the camps were drawn to an ecumenical Christianity, while non-privileged people were drawn to 'Jehovahists.'")

In 1956, from reports that reached Watchtower headquarters, the Society estimated that there were 64,000 Witnesses active behind the "Iron Curtain"; the number had grown to over 123,000 by 1959. In 1975, the official yearly report of the Society estimated that one-seventh of all the Witnesses active in the world were "behind the Iron Curtain."

In 1956, seven directors of the Watch Tower Society sent a petition, adopted at conventions by 462,936 Witnesses, to Soviet Premier Bulganin. The petition (which went unanswered) read, in part:

> There are or have been some 2000 of Jehovah's witnesses in the penal camp of Vorkuta; at the beginning of April of the year 1951 some 7000 of Jehovah's witnesses were arrested from the Baltic States down to Bessarabia and were then transported in freight trains to the distant region between Tomsk and Irkutsk and near Lake Baykal in Siberia; there are witnesses of Jehovah kept in more than fifty camps from European Russia into Siberia and northward to the Arctic Ocean, even on the Arctic island of Novaya Zemlya; and a number of these, especially of the 7000 mentioned above, died of malnutrition the first two years of their sojourn in Siberia. [*Ibid.*]

Petition requested

> that an objective government investigation be made and that the witnesses be freed and authorized to organize themselves according to the

way they are in other lands. Also that the witnesses in Russia be permitted to establish regular relations with their governing body in the United States and be allowed to publish and import such Bible literature as they need for their ministry.

The directors of the Watch Tower Society further proposed

a discussion between the representatives of the governing body of Jehovah's witnesses and those of the Russian [sic] government [and suggested that] a delegation of witnesses be permitted to proceed to Moscow for this purpose, as well as for the purpose of visiting the various camps where the witnesses of Jehovah are interned. [*Ibid.*]

There is no evidence that the petition was acknowledged by the Soviets.

East Germany:

Many of the same Witnesses who had been incarcerated in Nazi Germany were imprisoned by East German authorities. The Society's sources report that over 1,000 men and women have been sentenced to prison terms averaging six years. Fourteen were reported killed up to 1953. Nevertheless, the Witnesses seem to have more than a little mobility in East Germany: thousands of East Germans were able to attend assemblies held in West Germany. [*Yearbook*, 1954, p. 161; 1959, p. 126; *JWDP*, p. 278]

No statistics are available for Poland, Czechoslovakia, Yugoslavia, Bulgaria, Hungary, and Rumania—all countries in which the Watchtower Society's work is banned.

Latin America and Europe: Chile, Dominican Republic, Greece, Spain

Chile:

The Watchtower Society's accounts of its activities in Chile speak for themselves. This is how the Society describes the days of revolution, junta, and CIA activity (and, by omission, the death of Allende—which served the Witnesses well):

When the 1974 service year began, paralyzing strikes, violence, and unrest were part of day-to-day living in Chile. In every city there were long lines of people waiting to buy bread and other necessities; housewives spent an average of six hours a day in such line ups. Well, before the time for the "Divine Victory International Assembly" there was a change of government. . . . Although difficulties and trials of many sorts have pressed in on our Chilean brothers, they have felt secure because of their reliance on Jehovah. [*Yearbook*, 1975, pp. 22–23]

The tides of change have contributed to the spiritual catch.

For a long time, Chile enjoyed one of the most stable political atmospheres in all of South America. Suddenly this changed. In five years the Chilean people have seen three forms of government, each radically different from the others. The political turmoil has produced disillusionment. As a result, many people find the Bible's message about a perfect government in the hands of Jesus Christ both appealing and reasonable.

> . . . When the arrest of Communist activists in factories and industries left critical vacancies, witness employees were often put in key positions . . .
>
> Spot searches for firearms and the like were made of neighbourhoods at the break of dawn. Often, known witness homes were simply passed by.
>
> . . . Jehovah's witnesses in Chile . . . are . . . determined to take advantage of these swarming "waters" to continue in catching men alive so that these may gain life everlasting. [*TW*, Oct. 1, 1976, p. 591]

There are now over 15,000 Witnesses active in Chile.

Dominican Republic:

The fortunes of Jehovah's Witnesses have undergone many changes in the Dominican Republic. They were banned for a time under Trujillo; and then in the early 1960s, when the Church began to raise its voice against Trujillo—pastoral letters warning the government against excesses were read in all the churches—the ban was removed. Even when their proselytizing work was banned, the Witnesses were regarded as valuable workers on sugar estates. Imprisoned, they were model prisoners; they boasted of having had "the respect and trust of prison guards . . . the witness prisoners were allowed to enter the communications centre where Trujillo had equipment and recorders for monitoring other Latin-American radio stations. . . . [They were] trusted with jobs on which even soldiers were not used." [*Yearbook*, 1972, p. 153]

One sees, in the Dominican Republic, a familiar pattern. During the years of external hardship, the organization flourished. When the situation stabilized, "immorality and materialism" [*Ibid.*, p. 170] cost the Witnesses many members: "When violent methods fail, Satan tries other methods. . . . Materialism and immorality continue to raise their ugly heads, each contributing to the fall of some of the brothers who stood so faithfully through times of persecution." [*Ibid.*]

There are now approximately 6,000 active Witnesses in the Dominican Republic.

Greece:

The Witnesses have, at various times, been accused of being Communists, anarchists—and most recently, when George Papadopoulos was premier, of being agents of "international Zionism." "Jews control nine-tenths of the riches of the world," Papadopoulos' government is reported to have said; so, according to government sources, it followed that only Jews could afford to finance the work of the Witnesses. [*The New York Times*, June 4, 1970]

On November 13, 1970, the Ministry of Interior ordered the country's Registrars not to register marriages of Witnesses, or the children of such marriages, "because the religion of Jehovah's Witnesses is an unknown one." [*Aw*, June 8, 1975, p. 25] In 1974, when Constantine Karamanlis took power and civil liberties and a constitutional government were restored in Greece, the Witnesses were permitted to convene publicly for the first time in seven years; and in July, 1975, marriages between Witnesses were pronounced legal, and the children of those unions pronounced legitimate.

There are now 18,000 Witnesses in Greece.

They are subject to imprisonment for failure to join the military.

Spain:

In 1949, there were only 34 Witnesses active. [*Yearbook*, 1949] There are now 30,000. Legal recognition was granted to the "Association of Jehovah's Witnesses" in 1970. Observers in Spain have commented that the Church in Spain was for a long time obdurately opposed both to the Witnesses and to the Seventh-day Adventists, seeing in both sects a denial of true religion and a threat to patriotic values. The appointment of a liberal cardinal and the ascension of liberal bishops (even before the death of Franco) swung Spain in the direction of religious liberties.

In countries where the Witnesses are felt to be a threat to national security or stability, they are persecuted. In countries where the Church and the State are symbiotically joined, they are persecuted. Otherwise, they are tolerated.

Report of Activities of Jehovah's Witnesses Worldwide 1976 (adapted from the 1977 *Yearbook of Jehovah's Witnesses*):

Country or Territory	*Witnesses*	*Country or Territory*	*Witnesses*
Abu Dhabi	11	Argentina	33,503
Afars & Issas Terr.	7	Aruba	357
Afghanistan	9	Australia	29,101
Alaska	1,268	Austria	12,514
Algeria	23	Azores	248
American Samoa	89	Bahamas	519
Andorra	70	Bangladesh	2
Angola	3,822	Barbados	1,231
Anguilla	16	Belgium	19,745
Antigua	170	Belize	584

Country or Territory	*Witnesses*	*Country or Territory*	*Witnesses*
Benin	2,372	Guadeloupe	2,580
Bequia	25	Guam	136
Bermuda	217	Guatemala	5,259
Bolivia	2,476	Guinea	255
Bonaire	35	Guinea-Bissau	5
Botswana	283	Guyana	1,415
Brazil	106,228	Haiti	3,569
Britain	80,544	Hawaii	4,872
Brunei	2	Honduras	3,226
Burma	845	Hong Kong	576
Burundi	151	Iceland	165
Cameroon	12,269	India	4,687
Canada	62,880	Indonesia	4,264
Canary Islands	1,128	Iran	38
Cape Verde Rep.	60	Iraq	28
Carriacou	27	Ireland	1,891
Cayman Islands	27	Israel	276
Central Afr. Rep.	1,289	Italy	60,156
Chad	156	Ivory Coast	1,156
Chile	16,862	Jamaica	6,765
Colombia	16,286	Japan	38,367
Comoro Islands	2	Jordan	76
Congo	1,802	Kenya	1,973
Cook Islands	48	Korea	32,561
Costa Rica	5,104	Kuwait	18
Curaçao	681	Lebanon	1,827
Cyprus	846	Lesotho	672
Denmark	14,611	Liberia	1,060
Dominica	226	Libya	2
Dominican Rep.	6,540	Liechtenstein	21
Dubai	24	Luxembourg	819
Ecuador	5,995	Macao	7
El Salvador	6,010	Madagascar	805
Ethiopia	1,903	Madeira	252
Faroe Islands	82	Malawi	5,631
Fiji	640	Malaysia	433
Finland	13,402	Mali	32
France	65,827	Malta	91
French Guiana	200	Malvinas Islands	3
Gabon	344	Manus Island	9
Gambia	9	Marshall Islands	182
Germany, West	102,044	Martinique	1,105
Ghana	22,381	Mauritania	2
Gibraltar	87	Mauritius	380
Gilbert Islands	2	Mexico	84,356
Greece	18,711	Montserrat	29
Greenland	94	Morocco	188
Grenada	324	Mozambique	15,692

Country or Territory	*Witnesses*
Nepal	17
Netherlands	29,723
Nevis	47
New Britain	200
New Caledonia	359
Newfoundland	1,146
New Guinea	492
New Hebrides	47
New Ireland	51
New Zealand	7,442
Nicaragua	3,246
Niger	61
Nigeria	114,029
Niue	16
North Solomons	49
Norway	7,543
Okinawa	921
Pakistan	192
Palau	32
Panama	3,028
Papua	731
Paraguay	1,414
Peru	12,103
Philippines	77,248
Ponape	196
Portugal	18,119
Puerto Rico	16,620
Réunion	514
Rhodesia	12,951
Rodrigues	13
Rwanda	46
St. Helena	107
St. Kitts	147
St. Lucia	271
St. Martin	48
St. Pierre & Miquelon	2
St. Vincent	159
Saipan	26
San Marino	56
Saudi Arabia	4
Senegal	337
Seychelles	49
Sierra Leone	1,217
Singapore	344
Solomon Islands	610
South Africa	29,098
South-West Africa	349
Spain	34,954
Sri Lanka	545
Sudan	101
Surinam	911
Swaziland	689
Sweden	16,444
Switzerland	10,193
Syria	203
Tahiti	385
Taiwan	1,233
Tanzania	1,575
Thailand	732
Tobago	133
Togo	2,668
Tokelau Islands	4
Tonga	27
Trinidad	2,935
Truk	41
Tunisia	48
Turks & Caicos Islands	19
Tuvalu Islands	5
Uganda	166
U.S. of America	577,362
Upper Volta	65
Uruguay	4,771
Venezuela	13,749
Virgin Is. (Brit.)	83
Virgin Is. (U.S.)	479
West Berlin	5,620
Western Samoa	128
Yap	39
Zaïre	19,327
Zambia	57,885
196 Countries	2,058,241
14 Other Countries	190,149
GRAND TOTAL (210 countries)	2,248,390

Nathan Homer Knorr became the third president of the Watch Tower Bible and Tract Society in 1942. Unlike his flashy predecessors, he was a dull, rather plodding man, unfanciful—nothing like the lyrical con artist Russell, and nothing at all like the pugnacious, publicity-seeking "Judge" Rutherford. He had little flair, but a certain genius for organizing. Russell's sexual and monetary appetites were scandalous, and Rutherford's abrasiveness and litigious nature were legendary.

Knorr, the quiet president, had appetites of his own: "World-wide expansion was now the order of the day." By the end of World War II, there were three times as many Jehovah's Witnesses worldwide as there had been before the outbreak of war. Knorr saw to it that the varied parts of his empire became one united whole, under the tight control of Brooklyn headquarters. In order to do this, he set off on a world tour in 1947 to determine what was needed to strengthen and tie together the outposts of the Society. His personal observation of the varied activities of Witnesses in all branches gave him the insight and knowledge necessary to help them in whatever way was most useful, most especially in training those in the field.

In 1944, two years after Knorr became president, there were 128,976 Witnesses preaching worldwide [*JWDP*, p. 312; Yearly Reports, 1928–1958] There are now 2,248,390 [*Yearbook*, 1977, p. 30]

While the 1976 figures represent a 3.7-per cent increase over the number of proselytizers in 1975, there is this anomaly to consider: the number of hours spent preaching decreased, as did the number of full-time preachers. The Watchtower Society ascribes this to "economic pressures." I wonder if it might not have something to do with the fact that so many Witnesses expected Armageddon to come in 1975.

Missionaries, trained at the Brooklyn missionary school called Gilead (literally, "heap of witness"), are provided with a place to live and a cost-of-living allowance: $40 a month to cover all meals and transportation, all necessities (and probably very few luxuries). They are expected to preach 1,200 hours a year. [Information received orally from William Arthur, Gilead spokesman]

They don't have much time for sight-seeing, and they have neither the time nor the inclination to soak up local culture. When they get to their assignments, they must study the native language eleven hours a day the first month and five hours a day the second month (in addition to preaching from house to house with the minimal language skills they have brought with them). I once knew a missionary who'd been in Rome for three months and had yet to see the Fountain of Trevi or the Pincian Gardens; and I knew an American missionary in Delhi who'd been in India for six months without finding the time to travel the short distance to Agra to see the Taj Mahal.

Because of the restraints placed on their activities, the denial of opportunity to insinuate themselves gently and exploratively into foreign cultures (or to allow cultures to colour *their* perceptions), they remain, however long they stay in their overseas assignments, alien and *other*. They look lost and perpetually out of place.

Sometimes the unexpected happens—a child is born to a missionary couple, for example. I knew missionaries to whom this happened, in Guatemala, at a time when the Society made no provision for children of missionaries. They were—as are all missionaries to whom the unexpected happens—forced to fall back on their limited resources, and they lived in a wasteland of unhappiness and alienation. They had been obliged to leave the missionary home when their child was born. I met the wife one day. She was teaching at a private school run by an expatriate married to a Guatemalan. She was dancing—if such spiritless movements as she made could be called dancing—with little children in a circle: "Here we go round the mulberry bush/ . . . /This is the way we go to church/Go to church, go to church/This is the way we go to church/So early Sunday morning." For a woman who had come to Guatemala to tell people *not* to go to church, making a living this way must have been agony—and the agony was reflected in her listless, worn face. Her husband had a small jewellery-repair shop in their spartan house in one of Guatemala City's dreary downtown streets. It was sad. They must have come with very high hopes; and they were reduced to graceless lower-middle-class life in a strange country, doing things they did not love to do, among people they did not love and could not understand.

Sometimes desperation takes different forms. I knew another missionary, a Midwestern woman assigned with her husband to Rome, who rang a doorbell on the Piazza Navona one day and never came home again: a man answered, and she fell into his bed and into his life. The Witnesses said "the demons" had got her. (I think Italy, and perhaps happiness, had got her.)

When I lived in Bombay, Watchtower missionaries occasionally called on me—I was the only American living in an apartment building largely inhabited by Gujaratis. I offered them tea—which they accepted. They rejected my sympathy. They didn't like me very much, I could see, but I was the only person in the building who'd open the door to them. Their efforts were thankless: they wanted to give, and nobody received them. It didn't occur to them that someone—or India itself—might have had something to give *them*. But the Watchtower missionaries were there to *change* things they had never entered into or experienced, to alter people and cultures whose values they despised without understanding or feeling them. Hard work. Hard work to close yourself off from what you're obliged to influence: a kind of spiritual imperialism; they are spiritual colonialists.

(When the missionary women visited me in Bombay, I asked them what they thought of Mother Teresa, that extraordinary woman who sweeps the dying off the streets of Calcutta and gives them clean sheets, holds their hands, and comforts them and makes their dying a less brutally lonely thing. They had never heard of her.)

I'm not saying that many Watchtower missionaries do not feel fulfilled and happy to see their work flourish and to gain converts. I am only saying that a system that impels them to keep essentially aloof and remote from the people they proselytize is bound to produce casualties. There are casualties among missionaries of all denominations; but when Watchtower missionaries break down, it is, it seems to me, not because of any fatal flaw in their characters, but because it is the implicit *policy* of their governing elders to keep them estranged, detached, in no significant way related to the events that swirl around them. Their insularity sometimes works to protect them and preserve them; and it sometimes works the other way—their enforced alienation becomes anguish.

One day the Watchtower missionaries in India called on me just after I'd returned from a small village in Andhra Pradesh, where I'd met a priest who'd spent the best part of twenty years curing infants of roundworms. (A most unglamorous job; but roundworms are killers.) "Do you try to convert these people?" I'd asked him. "I baptise them," he said, "and I try to keep them alive, and I say Mass, and I pray for the grace of the Holy Spirit on us all. . . . It's hard to love God on an empty stomach." That day, the priest had another visitor—an Indian doctor (an atheist) who lived and worked in a nearby leprosarium. When they met, they embraced.

I told the Watchtower missionaries this story, not knowing myself exactly what the point of telling them was; and they said, "But the priest isn't preaching the good news of the kingdom. . . . And Jehovah will cure lepers in his New World." Across the way from the veranda where we were sitting, a new luxury high-rise building was going up. Tribal people from northern India had been brought in as construction workers. They lived—ate, cooked, drank, made love—on the girders of the building. The week before, a worker had fallen to his death before my horrified children's eyes. His widow had been given 25 rupees in compensation—just enough to cremate her husband. I told the missionaries that story too; and they said, "If we knew her language, we would tell her the wonderful hope of the resurrection." They had a cup of tea and talked about God's loving-kindness.

X

Leaving: 1955

To some, the world has disclosed itself as too vast: within such immensity, man is lost and no longer counts; and there is nothing left for him to do but shut his eyes and disappear. To others, on the contrary, the world is too beautiful; and it, and it alone, must be adored.—Teilhard, p. 45

Everything possible to be believed is an image of truth.—William Blake

One Sunday summer morning, as I left Watchtower headquarters to go out preaching from door to door, a member of a tightly huddled-together little group of fellow Witnesses, I saw two young women and two young men piling into a yellow convertible. They were all laughing. They carried picnic hampers covered with red-and-white-checked cloths, very full. One of the young men turned on the car radio—a Mozart quintet. I wanted to be with them. I wanted to *be* them. I longed for their world of colour and light and sound. My longing was so acute it was like a physical pain; and it was followed by an intolerable ennui: I didn't know what I was doing holding a satchel of *Watchtower* magazines, or why I was going to preach, or what I had to do with the Witnesses or they with me. I wanted to run away. I didn't, but I knew at that moment that someday I would.

The four young men and women had come out of a house on Pineapple Street, an old wooden house, white, with a forest-green door and forest-green shutters and dimity curtains and chandeliers that seemed to be lit even in the daytime. The garden of the house, with its cherry tree that had blossoms like crepe paper, was surrounded by a high white wooden fence, and set in the garden fence was a lime-green door with no doorknob on the outside. For days I imagined that if I knocked at that door, they would recognize me and let me in and we would sit in the garden under the cherry tree and I would never have to go back to the Watchtower Building again.

On the Saturday of that week, a Witness I knew and loved died. And the circumstances surrounding his dying made me understand that when I left, it wouldn't be because I preferred yellow sports cars and summer picnics and Mozart or jazz to God; it would be because God didn't live in my religion. If He lived at all, He lived somewhere else (not in my heart).

Mike died at a party at a Witness' house. Unlike most Witnesses, he never seemed to give a damn what impression he created on other people. He was funky and loving and flamboyant. He was an iceman; he drove an ice truck. When I was younger, I'd had a temporary job at the UN bank. Mike used to drive me up to the Secretariat building in his truck. We laughed at the incongruity of driving to the UN in a Sicilian-decorated ice truck, and he never used the occasion to preach about the evils of the "beastly United Nations" (which ranked second, in the Witnesses' chamber of Satanic horrors, only to the Vatican). He may have accepted the Witnesses' belief that the UN was the "desolation of desolations," but that didn't deter him from driving up gaily and irreverently to its portals. The fear and loathing such "devilish" places inspired in the Witnesses' hearts, and the repulsion and fascination, seemed entirely lacking in his.

But it was his heart that killed him. He'd had two heart attacks; on the morning of that party, he'd been out preaching for the first time since his convalescence. He was talking about his delight in being able to go from door to door again, talking with gusto about his pleasure in "sharing" (other Witnesses might "give the truth"; Mike shared), when he clutched his chest and began to gasp for air. He took the diamond ring he wore off his finger and gave it and his wallet to his wife (he knew he was dying; his last thoughts were for someone else). A few Witnesses went, spontaneously and generously and compassionately, to his wife to support her. A respected elder from Watchtower headquarters launched—as Mike's gasps began to sound, horribly, more like the final rattle of death—into an interminable story about the people he'd known who'd been taken unaware by death ("I knew someone else who died like that," he said, looking at Mike). Three-quarters of the Witnesses present set themselves to clean up the room in order to "give a good witness" to the police when they arrived. Mike was pronounced DOA. The cops were given a speech about our hope in the resurrection. Mike himself was ignored (except by the police, whose attempts to resuscitate him were heroic); grief was shelved (Mike's wife was sedated). The Witnesses congratulated themselves on the way the police had seemed to be impressed by their decorum and their calm; in their zeal to "give a witness," the actual fact of Mike's death seemed almost forgotten. I can't remember anyone crying out in love or horror—or praying.

The task of telling Mike's younger daughter that he had died was delegated to me. As an elder drove me to her house, he recited all the Scriptures I might use to comfort her. He might have been reciting the *Guinness Book of World Records.* I looked at the elder in a vain attempt to find some trace of sorrow or anger on his face as he continued to offer memorized words of comfort. He had already buried Mike in some recess of his mind; his concern was how to keep Mike's daughter from "going overboard with immoderate grief" (his words—she was 12 years old). I have hated very few people as much as I hated that man, then. "See if you can take Mike's daughter out preaching with you tomorrow morning," he said. "It'll keep her mind from selfishness."

Nobody had cried. Mike's daughter cried, and I couldn't find it in my heart to read a single Scripture to her.

I came to live and work at Bethel—Watchtower headquarters—in 1953, when I was 19. I left early in 1956.

I had over the years, since my baptism in 1944, little niggles of doubt (and a constant conviction of sin). My doubts terrified me.

Nobody ever told me that all believers doubt, or that the logical consequence of the possession of free will is to question, or that even mystics have at times felt abandoned by the God they adore; what a lot of misery it would have saved me if someone had told me. But the Witnesses couldn't tell me, because they themselves didn't acknowledge that it was true. To them, faith is total, unquestioning, uncritical, unwavering, and undemanding.

I regarded my irritable intelligence as a kind of predatory animal which, if not firmly reined, would spring on me, attack me, and destroy me.

Since to doubt at all was intolerable, the only solution that seemed possible was to submerge my doubts (to submerge myself) completely. I wanted to be eaten alive, devoured by Jehovah, to spend so much time in his service that my peevish spirit, humbled and exhausted, would no longer have time for querulous doubts. Women are good at turning their desolation to their advantage (or to what they think is their advantage); and what I was doing by entering Bethel was making spiritual capital out of spiritual despair, quelling my restlessness by giving it a death in a new life.

And I had other (baser) motives too: There was, for a woman, great spiritual prestige in being admitted to Bethel. It was both glamorous and holy. Men outnumbered women 10 to 1 at Bethel (although, among rank-and-file Witnesses, women outnumbered men 3 to 1). I had nothing against being surrounded by men. Part of the inner circle, circled about by men; I thought that part would be nice.

And I wanted to please my mother, whose standards I knew I never lived up to (I was never sure what they were) and whose ambition for me was boundless, at the same time that her competition with me was fierce. It was a foregone conclusion that all my boyfriends would be more charmed by her than they would by me, by her sacrificial gravity, her seductive saintly gaiety. Viewing me as a spiritual extension of herself, she would be pleased, I knew, if I went to Bethel. I believed, at that time, that I held the power to make her happy. It was not a good thing, I know better in retrospect, to feel. I wanted to make things good for her, to make up to her for all the things she didn't have, for whatever it was she wept for in my bedroom every night. I wanted to get away from that weeping, and from the acrimony that bound her and my unbelieving father together more closely than the most enduring affection.

I wanted to allay her pain, and I wanted her to stop passing her pain on to me. I really did believe that I was the agent of her happiness; I don't know through what subtle instruction or self-delusion I came to believe that.

And I wanted to get away from my father, whose bewilderment took the form of rage, who wept for me (not himself), and whose tears I rejected and despised. I was in alliance with my mother against him—an unnatural alliance: my inclination, till my mother and I joined forces against him, was to find him irresistible. It was an unholy bonding; and while, at the time, I dismissed my father as negligible or feared him as a monstrous "Opposer of The Truth," there must, I think, have been part of my nature that recoiled against the pitiless, hard person I was when I was with him. If my mother insisted on going out preaching Christmas Eve, I didn't want to be around to entertain my father's rages and then to defend her when she returned. I didn't want to fight with my father with her holding my hand, urging me on; I knew there was something sick and unholy about what we were doing.

I took the only escape route I knew. But if you had asked me then, I would have said, "I came to Bethel to serve the Lord." And I would have meant it.

I thought I loved God. I loved the idea of loving Him. I *knew* I loved Arnold; I had loved him since I was 15. Being at Bethel prevented me from walking down his street every day, hoping for an "accidental" meeting. But it didn't prevent me from fantasizing about him.

I told Nathan H. Knorr, then the Watchtower Society's president, about Arnold. He told me never to see Arnold again. If he had told me that I could never see my mother or father again, I might have obeyed him; but Arnold was my mother and father, and I couldn't not see him.

I'd call Arnold from one of the public booths when my craving couldn't be denied, and we'd arrange to meet. Once I got to his living-room and I heard his beloved Schubert *Trout Quintet* or one of the Beethoven quartets he always played for me, there was only joy. A guilt hangover the next day took the form of headaches, a steel vice around my head.

So I carried all this baggage to Bethel with me—my love for Arnold and my doubts; but I went in good faith. I meant to stay forever. Before I had been there two years, I knew I would have to leave.

One afternoon, as I sat working in the proof-reading department of the Watchtower plant at 117 Adams Street, a sudden black storm blew up, and two of the men whom I shared proof-reading tasks raced to the plate-glass windows and said, "Oh, boy! Maybe it's Armageddon. Wouldn't it be wonderful if it was Armageddon? Do you think it's Armageddon? Wow!" I laughed and laughed and laughed, because they sounded so much more like Batman and Robin anticipating a caper with the Joker than like decently awed men awaiting God's final judgement. And of course, my laughter infuriated them. Their little-boy glee gave way to sententiousness and censoriousness, and they silenced my hysterical laughter with glares, demanding to know what, exactly, I found so funny. I quailed—anything male and angry had the power to subdue me—and said "I don't *want* Armageddon to come."

It was the first visible crack in my defences.

I covered myself very quickly, and very transparently (that was the kind of remark, I knew from experience, that was not likely to go unreported to higher authorities): "I don't think enough people are saved yet," I said. It must have sounded as hollow to them as it did to me; and I felt hollow, as if the storm outside had blown through me, leaving my soul as dry as a whistle.

Then I began to cry.

I stayed at Watchtower headquarters—where I'd worked first as a housekeeper, then as a proofreader, for two and a half years—six months after that outburst. It had been temperate compared with what I was feeling; but it was the first time that I had revealed my spiritual duplicity nakedly, or heard myself say something unguarded.

At night I went out preaching, or to study classes in the Bethel residence. I smiled, talked, walked, sang hymns, conducted myself like a real person in a real world. But I didn't feel real. I felt as if everything were happening to someone else—as if I were both a character trapped in someone else's story and the person who "read" the character; I was both inside and outside of my own life (which was someone else's life). Nobody noticed. The most appalling thing of all was that I perfected my own part so well that nobody noticed.

At night I tried (as usual) to pray, and (as usual) could not.

Somewhere I'd read of an order of contemplative sisters who prayed till 5.30 every morning, to lessen the violence done in those dark hours after midnight. I thought of them when I couldn't sleep, which was most of the time. (I had travelled a long way in my mind since I'd been taught that nuns were whorish, wicked representatives of the Vatican—but nothing in the way I behaved reflected the way I was beginning to think.) There was some comfort in believing that they were keeping vigil during those long nights, when, for some reason, I always fell asleep at exactly 4.10 a.m. (I never knew why). I lay in bed picturing my body floating above itself; and my skin felt thin and crusty, like something dangerous and tender stretched across the mouth of a volcano. I felt as if my body were rent with enormous fissures, and that my skin was inadequate armour, no armour at all.

(The best thing anyone could have done for me then would have been to tell me I was going crazy. I envied crazy people because they *acted* crazy, and because there were names for them. I could not assign a name to the pain I felt. I smiled a lot. At one of my meetings with Arnold, to whom I did not confide my troubles—I confided in no one—he told me of a group of disturbed kids he was working with who screamed and flailed around and blindly struck out at things. I cried. He thought I was crying for them. But I was crying for myself. I thought they were lucky. My screams never got screamed; my rage was neatly contained.)

When I fell asleep, I dreamed. It was always the same dream: I am a little girl in a walled garden, full of old-fashioned flowers—freesias, sweet William, climbing roses, bachelor's buttons, and (with no regard to seasons) white and purple lilacs. At the end of the garden stands a creature of indeterminate sex, resplendent, dressed in cloth of gold, who extends his/her arms to me in a gesture both maternal and elegant, nurturant and magisterial. Will-less, I am drawn to the creature, who calls to me in a voice that is at once supplicating and commanding. And as I enter into its embrace, the voice (which I yearn for and fear) becomes tactile—it exists inside of me and outside of me; it becomes like molten silver pouring through my veins. Paralyzed (bloodless), unable to resist, I am swept away by the creature, who assumes various guises, some malevolent, some benign. Held tight in that icy embrace, I am swept out and over the garden walls, hurled into an empty sky, where, a Humpty-Dumpty of scattered parts, I hurtle through the void—and nothing puts me back together again.

I do not know the meaning of the dream. The bells wake me at 6.30 a.m. (they are like an extension of the dream), and, pregnant with the dream, cold and aching, I shower in the communal shower, while the voices around me intrude on my nightmare. I put on the face and the demeanour I hope will see me through the day, and I run down three flights of stairs to the artificial light of the yellow dining room, where I take my assigned place at a rectangular blue-metal table, waiting for the Bible discussion that precedes our breakfast to begin. I feel drugged; but even in this state—which is like sleepwalking through someone else's dream—I will myself to have control. I try to behave like other people—insofar as I can see other people: People lack definition at this time; faces blur. But objects are harshly, clearly defined, like objects in a hallucination. (I will never forget that dining room, its metal-topped surfaces, cold and slippery to the touch.) I prepare myself to spend a day among people who hate me.

I say that I spent my days among people who hated me. I don't think that's a crazy perception (though, God knows, I was not what could be called normal in those final six months). What *was* crazy was that they would in a flash have said (*did* say) that they loved me; and if asked why, they might have responded, "Because the Watchtower Society says we are a family and we must love one another," (Words all lost their meanings: *good, bad, crazy, love*—they meant different things in different mouths; and one was never sure whom to trust.)

Lara, the pretty girl who sat next to me at table, hated me. (The eight men who sat at the same table more or less ignored me, but I felt no ill will emanating from them; the worst they could do was make me feel lonely, and I was lonely already.) The first day I sat at that table, one of the men said, "Pass the coffee cream." So later I asked Lara to "pass the coffee cream." She said, her fork moving without a pause to her disdainful mouth, "It isn't *coffee cream*, it's milk." Maybe she thought I was trying to endear myself to the brother whose remark I'd parroted. She chose from that moment to dislike me. The only other sentence I can remember her saying directly to me in three years was "Your perfume makes me sick."

We were 450 men and 45 women at that time, and only a handful of the women were under 35; so to be intensely disliked by one young woman (who was herself cool and pretty and popular) was no small thing. My gratitude was always there, waiting, ready to spill over her if she ever once smiled at me. She never did. I could only imagine, from the way she looked at me, that she believed I was always on the point of committing some outrage (and perhaps her instincts were right). I did the worst possible thing anyone can do under these circumstances: I tried to model my personality on those of successful people—a most unprofitable and ridiculous undertaking.

I can't think of many things more awful and more corrupting than having to wake up each morning to the sure knowledge that you will be spending your time in intimate association with people who despise you. (When my own children went to school for the first time, and were immediate successes, I said seventeen Hallellujahs; I'd seen, in my imagination, their schoolrooms populated with Laras. I felt triumphant—and also vindictive: I recited a vengeful litany. I hoped everybody hated Lara's kids; I hoped they picked on them; I hoped they were the most unpopular girls in school; I hoped their stomachs ached every day from 9 to 3; I wanted Lara to know what it felt like. It is corrupting to be hated; I didn't know I could bear so much malice for so many years.)

Lara; and Stan Russell and Tom Whiting, who both felt that I had usurped their place in the printing plant and never let me forget it. They snickered and gossiped with each other and came all over pompous when I tried to talk with them.

Stan punished me according to the means he had at hand: he had me dismissed from the preaching cell of which he was the elder, because, he said, I didn't spend enough hours preaching. Whiting contented himself with telling me how the "brothers" thought I was becoming sick with pride, that they preferred the housekeeping sisters who made beds to me; and once, when someone in the proofreading department left Bethel abruptly, with no explanation, he said it was because I had "unmanned" him by red-pencilling his copy and that I might be responsible for his loss of faith. (Satan had used women before to undo good men.)

Actually, it strikes me as funny now: Could I really have prayed to Jehovah to forgive me for being presumptuous enough to undangle a brother's participle? I did. No wonder I'm superstitious about words: I spent two years thinking my eternal salvation depended on my approach to commas and split infinitives and dangling participles. It wasn't funny at the time.

The truth is, there were people who loved me, too. (Well, I say *love*: is it love if it can be—as it was, the moment I left—so easily aborted?) There were women who loved me. There were men who asked me to marry them. I never entertained the idea of marrying a Bethelite. I must always have known, on some unconscious level, that I was going to leave someday, that I would not stick it out. The men I was attracted to were not the men who cared for me; I denied physical attraction (if a man kissed me and it felt good, I immediately found reasons for not loving him).

I'm talking about my life at Bethel as if it were one of unrelieved gloom; and that isn't true. There were times when I felt absolutely high—stoned on God-talk (which, as it happens, can be a powerful aphrodisiac, among other things). Walking across the Brooklyn

Bridge with my friend Walter, holding hands and talking about God; learning to dance the tango with Walter and Peggy and Walter's roommate, Norman; dancing all night on the Society's missionary yacht in New York harbour; picnicking under the George Washington Bridge—there were easy, good times. And the best times were when we were in other people's homes, teaching them the Bible, and they offered us the intimate details of their lives and we felt enhanced and enriched and part of a loving community serving a higher cause.

But in the end, none of that was enough. In the end, my decision to leave had very little to do with people who loved me and people who didn't, with good times and bad times. In the end, it had everything to do with my feelings about the world, which I had been taught was reserved for destruction and which I nevertheless obdurately loved, though my ignorance of it was profound. It had to do with my feeling cramped and lonely and frightened; leaving was survival.

All of this is in the diary I kept the last six months I was at Bethel. When I read these diary notes now, they seem to be grossly self-conscious, not to say narcissistic (but I was, after all, writing as if God were peering over my shoulder—and it's hard to know how to play to that Audience).

I can barely decipher these notes, they are written in such a wild, erratic hand; and the urgency and pain that are missing from the words are in the handwriting. (There are, as a friend of mine says, no inanimate objects.) It looks like the handwriting of three different people; and I won't labour the reason for that.

> God can't kill Arnold. How can God kill Arnold? Arnold sends pepperoni to all the New Utrecht High School hoods in jail. The other day he bought three bikes for the kids of the Chinese laundryman. He spends his evenings listening to Beethoven quartets. (I wish he would kiss me.) He used to excuse us from English homework if we went to see a Marx Brothers film. Also he brought us chocolate-covered ants when we wrote good compositions. (Does Jehovah have a sense of humour? Why doesn't God ever laugh?) Once Arnold read an Archibald Macleish poem to me in class. To *me:*
>
> Not with my hands' strength nor with difficult labour
> Springing the obstinate words to the bones of your breast
> And the stubborn line to your young stride and the breath to your breathing
> And the beat to your haste
> Shall I prevail on the hearts of unborn men to remember
> (What is a dead girl but a shadowy ghost
> Or a dead man's voice but a distant or vain affirmation
> Like dream words most)

Therefore I will not speak of the undying glory of women
I will say you were young and straight and your skin fair
And you stood in the door and the sun was a shadow of leaves on
  your shoulder
And a leaf on your hair
I will not speak of the famous beauty of dead women
I will say the shape of a leaf lay once on your hair
Till the world ends and the eyes are out and the mouths broken
Look! It is there!

And why, for that matter, should God kill Archibald Macleish? How come all the people I love are going to be killed at Armageddon, and I'm going to live forever in the New World with Stan Russell and Tom Whiteing and Lara—who are *mean*?

I love going out on Bible studies and teaching people. It feels so good, I feel so elevated. But does this mean that this is the truth? It may mean only that when people are not dignified by exclusive devotion to a cause that demands more than their normal natures can supply, they are not extraordinary. And I'm afraid of ordinariness. At Bible studies we meet on the highest plane—we see each other in the most sympathetic light, as humans admitting our frailty and striving for beauty and order (for good? for the Divine?). But the relationship deteriorates when the mutual search is ended and we resume our daily lives. Then everything becomes flat. And off I go to new relationships, drawing strength from them. I feel like a parasite, battening on other people's needs and living off their hunger (I love their hunger); and teaching what I don't even know to be true. . . . One time a companion brought to my attention that I'd remarked to a couple with whom we were concluding a study, "We have to feel free to talk, to share. We can't be afraid of offering our feelings. We can be friends. Our religion doesn't matter." That was heresy. I hadn't even been aware that I'd said it.

Their only reality is otherworldly reality. They deny the world, and that denial is contrary to my nature. I can love Christ, but not Jehovah, and not the end of the world. Is that possible?

I can't judge or condemn—or be God's agent for condemnation. I can't bear to belong to a group that considers itself favoured. I can't accept the destruction of a child. I can't exclude from my love all the people who cannot believe. "He who loves the world is an enemy of God." I love the world. I will not allow my friends to be chosen for me: "We must love one another and die."

Brother K. came back from a round-the-world trip today. Told us about it at meeting. Said he was bored on the aeroplane—not enough magazines to read. I'd be bored on an aeroplane too. But I'm not a spiritual leader. Isn't God's spirit supposed to un-bore you? If you were really full of the Holy Spirit, would you be bored? Why couldn't he *think*? Or pray? Or meditate? Or contemplate? What would he do on a desert island? How can I trust a spiritual leader who would be bored on a desert island? . . . Why am I so harsh?

I can't give myself to a religion unless it is completely and without reservation. (I *may* not.) This religion demands complete dedication, submission, acceptance. I have reservations. I have always had.

Fromm says the whale was a symbol of the isolation and imprisonment that results from lack of love and solidarity: the whale is hell, the hell of not being able to love. I don't want to live my life in the belly of the whale. . . . I don't want to be contemptuous of weakness (including my own).

I've been sneaking into guest rooms to read, late at night: Emerson, Thoreau. Dead men are my comfort.

What scares me is how good I am at dissembling. I've learned to give back to others the view of themselves they ask for. I keep a central core of disbelief, but *I act as if I believe*. I don't know what to do, how to stop.

Sometimes I do love them. They transcend themselves. That's beautiful. But then they become rigid and dogmatic. The love they inherit from the teachings of Christ is narrowed and limited by their rejection of the world. Many of them were attracted by love and goodness to a life of giving. But their goodness is contradicted by their hatred of the world, their relegating all who will not listen to destruction —the "goats" who are against them. Their work satisfies the need to express themselves, and to give. It is better to give than to receive, and their need to give is fulfilled in their preaching work. But so stern and inflexible. (Why do I say *they?* If I say *they*, what am I doing here? They think I am one of them. *Them*.)

Brother Knorr wears terrible suits. . . . Also ties. . . . I got my $60 yearly clothing allowance today. Spent it on books and plants. So now will have to darn stockings, or ask my mother for money for clothes. Stupid, stupid, stupid thing to do. (Don't regret it.) Also bought tickets to *Death of a Salesman*. Three. Don't know whom to take.

Went for a walk in Greenwood Cemetery. Very comforting. The dead are very nice, like children, they can't do anybody any harm. Wouldn't mind being dead.

My favourite sentences in the Bible: "What is truth?" (Jesus never said.) And, "Jesus wept."

I am so ignorant. My father should have stopped me. He tried. Not hard enough. Arnold, too. The men I love never *force* me to do anything. I wish they would. I wouldn't thank them if they did. I want somebody to make this *stop*. Afraid.

Clearly, something had to give, break, bend: me. Inaction had become intolerable (I couldn't, in honour, stay). Action seemed impossible (I was as afraid to leave as I was afraid of the psychic consequences of not leaving)—*physically* impossible, as in those dreams where you try to escape and your legs refuse to carry out your commands; you are all motion and no movement, stuck. I couldn't tread water any more without eventually drowning in my own contradictions.

I was very, very lucky (what I mean to say is, Providence was divinely good. But that understanding came later; I'm anticipating): I shuddered and shook and cracked, but slowly and quietly, and not explosively; I broke down in stages, not all at once. And picked up the pieces as I went along. Everything that happened was terrible, but the terror went on for so long, I learned to live with it familiarly; I made pain my ally. Like an amusement-park horror-house ride: every time you turn a corner, you say, Well, that one wasn't so bad, and you steel yourself for the next one and think that maybe that one will be easier, and you know there's an end somewhere, if only you can hang on.

The first thing that went was my voice. Which probably got sick of itself: it had told so many lies; it was so many voices, all fighting for equal time. Towards the end, when I rang doorbells to preach, I opened my mouth and nothing came out. Nothing. As effective a paralysis as if God Himself had severed my vocal cords.

Then, next, the thing with the stairs. I was still going out in the evenings to Bible studies. Only I didn't talk to would-be converts about the Bible any more. I don't remember what we talked about (everything here gets blurred); I remember being fed a lot, plates of food and cups of tea, and holding children on my lap. (How good people were! I wish I could remember who they were, to repay them. This is the part of the horror ride where the tunnel is dark; I remember only their kindnesses. I don't know what they made of me. Did they think I was sane?)

But that, too, ended. First, I couldn't walk down stairs. Every house had stairs; the stairs were always narrow. After the doors were shut and the voices and the warmth were over, I hugged the banisters and edged down sideways like a crab. Sometimes it took me an hour to negotiate a flight of stairs. I couldn't walk *up* stairs. The paralysis was spreading. (I told Arnold, making light of it. He said, "Fear of going *down* stairs is a death wish. Fear of going up stairs must be a life wish. You're making progress.") I stopped going out at night to Bible studies. (I never said goodbye to any of those people. I forgive myself for this. I can't regret anything any more.)

Meanwhile, during the day, nothing had changed. (Everything had changed.) Except that I kept falling asleep. Every time I sat down, alone in my room, my eyes closed, and I slept, for what seemed to be five or ten minutes. Small blackouts. I didn't resist them. Delicious little secret deaths.

Then, one night, I was in the subway. (I don't remember what I was doing there, where I was coming from. My diary doesn't tell me. I'd stopped making notes in my diary, too enervated to write.) It was late at night. There were tracks on either side of me that seemed to stretch into black infinity. Marooned. I remember the subway walls—blistery with ugly wet patches—and a dim, sick light. A train pulled in, and I couldn't walk to it. And then another, and another—and I couldn't make myself walk. If I thought of anything at all, it was rats. Waves and waves of nausea. I began to think I was hallucinating this. But the sweet-sour smell of vomit, mine, was real. (As was the unlovely fact that I had wet my pants.) At 6 A.M., as if a spell had been broken, I walked to a train. I had been standing there for seven hours.

I got to Bethel in time to shower. Doused myself with perfume (Lily of the Valley). I remember the morning text for that day: "What are these wounds in thine hands . . . Those with which I was wounded in the house of my friends."

That night, I began to write in my diary again. I began to rehearse the speech I would give Brother Knorr when I told him I would leave:

> Dear Brother Knorr: I am not equal to demands, fatigued in mind and body. Can't think. Don't have proper motivation. No go-power. Need renewal, refreshment, need to overcome my own moods and sensitivities. Not fair to Jehovah, his organization, or myself if I stay. Feel close to breaking.
>
> They will think this is the easy way. To them it means no responsibility, no doorbells, not having to submit to authority. I know it is the hard way. To fight my way to my own truth, accepting nothing easily, to make my own decisions, to accept my aloneness and my loneliness and to have no one at night to thank for joy or to ask respite from pain, never to be really sure—always struggle and uncertainty. . . .
>
> I must leave a spiritual vocation because I have lost my spirituality. I know that I must leave to find myself. If I do not, nothing will ever be right again.

And still I couldn't leave.

Now this where the fairy Godmother (God/Father?) steps in. In the guise of a balding optometrist (charlatan or scientist or saint, he may have saved my life), in Greenwich Village, across the street from St. Joseph's Church (where now I sometimes go to Mass). Why did I go to Greenwich Village, to which I had never been, for glasses? The Lord knows. (I assume, so much have I changed, that

He does.) I don't remember the name of that eye doctor; his shop is no longer there.

He took an inordinately long time examining my eyes. He said: "I don't know your life or who you are or what you're doing. But whatever you're doing, you have to stop it. I've never seen anybody so rigidly controlled, and I've never seen so much strain. You're seeing things that aren't there, and you're not seeing things that are there. You may last six days or six weeks or six months, but you're headed for a breakdown, and it won't be pretty when it comes." Then he said, with a flash of insight that frightened me with it acuity, "I sometimes have to tell priests to take six months off. I'm telling you to take the rest of your life off, if that's what you have to do. If you want to live."

It was all I needed.

I ran down the subway steps. No terror. Somebody had finally told me I was crazy, or as close to it as made no difference. I told my roommate not to wake me up for breakfast, overriding her protests almost gaily (the release!): "The doctor says I'm killing myself." Also slyly (and merrily): "He thinks I'm cracked."

All I'd needed was someone to *tell* me. Another voice, a voice outside my own head.

I slept, on and off, for three days. The resident chiropractor stuck his head in once in a while and offered me cans of soup. My roommate looked frightened and didn't ask any questions. Margarita came in once to ask me if I wanted anything. "An apple turnover," I said.

When the three days were over, I made an appointment to see Brother Knorr. I was taking in great greedy draughts of air; I felt buoyant.

Brother Knorr thought I needed a rest. He suggested that I transfer to the Society's farm in upstate New York: manual work to bludgeon my brain cells into acquiescence. He addressed all his remarks to the Statue of Liberty. Or so it seemed: He sat with his broad back toward me, facing New York Harbour. His enormous desk between us. More than that between us. Worlds (the world) between us.

I said No, no rest. I didn't trust myself to say anything more.

He swivelled around in his chair (made to order in the carpentry shop).

"Weren't you high school valedictorian?"

"No."

"But you were smart."

"Yes."

"That's your trouble."

I was dismissed.

(I was glad he didn't offer to shake my sweaty hand. I thought, on the way down in the elevator, how long it had been since anybody had held me or touched me.)

I packed my suitcase. I called my mother. She came with a friend to collect me, my suitcase, and a driftwood lamp (my only possessions). I dropped off my key at the front desk. It was snowing. We drove back to Bensonhurst in silence. Back to the bedroom I shared with my mother, and to a silence that has remained unbroken between us: she has never asked me why I left.

I would like to be able to say that that was it—clean and finished and a final door slammed; courage exercised and rewarded. But I was back in the bedroom with my mother's weeping; and another charade began.

I went to local congregation meetings with my mother. I didn't know how to take the final step out. Three meetings a week. Was this what I had left for? I enrolled in a course at the New School. The course was on a Friday evening, a meeting only. Only two meetings to go now. No explanations to my mother.

But I never said out loud. *I don't believe.*

Spring came. "Breeding lilacs out of the dead land, mixing memory and desire," Arnold quoted—nourishing, indoors, old wounds and humiliations he would never share with me. But for me, a different alchemy: a thaw, and a release. The winter's hibernation was over (years of hibernation); there was an end to all the squirrelling around in my own brain—and a beginning: I felt open to nothing but pure feeling. I felt happiness rising up irresistibly, fiercely; why? Is it too simple to say that I had indeed grown bored with unhappiness? That a basically sanguine temperament had at last asserted itself? Of course it's too simple; but I don't know why the change came, except that I had youth and its regenerative powers on my side, and a determination to choose happiness, to throw everything bleak and wintry away.

I wanted to run away from the past. And in fact, that April, that May, I did literally run all over the place. Through Prospect Park; the Botanic Gardens, where the cherry trees were in bloom; up and down city blocks, as if some great source of energy had been unleashed. I spent long afternoons in the Gardens; sunlight had never seemed so sweet—not since I was a little child, a happy little pagan (before Jehovah came), hiding inside the overhanging branches of my grandmother's mulberry tree, loving the aqueous light filtering through the leaves, hugging myself in joy. A single cluster of lilacs was enough to intoxicate me, to send me into private raptures—and to send me running. (Sex, Freud would say: and he would be wrong. The thing about that time—when my love for the world was justified by the beauty of the world—was that nothing was a *symbol*: everything, simply and clearly and sweetly, *was*. And it was good.)

In the mild, disturbing air of that spring, even pain was an ally, an exquisite plaything. It was *my* pain. It belonged to me. And it cruelly excluded everyone else's pain. I fell into bed limp and exhausted every night, drunk on the beauty I saw everywhere; and my mother's tears moved me less that spring rain. They were *her* tears, not mine. I hardened my heart against them. And slept well.

There was still Arnold:

> The next time I see him I will tell him: *I love you.* Why should it be so hard to say! But it will have been said. I must. I can make him mine—by magic. Even if he doesn't know. I can become A. I can listen to the same music he listens to, hang the same picture over my bed that he has hung, so that it will be the first and the last thing I see each day as it is the first and the last thing he sees. ("Each day I salute the sun, the ocean and the land for your dear sake, my love.") The same Picasso print he has—not dishonest, I love the Picasso with the knowing, despairing, wise eyes. And frame it in white with a blue mat, as he has. I'll buy the records he loves, read the books he reads. If this is the only way I can have him, I want him.

The words are fake; the feeling wasn't. One has to be a greater person than I was not to make the truth sound like lies on paper.

The day I called him, to say the words, and hear the words (so foolhardy, also gallant), he didn't answer his phone.

I loved him till he died. I still do, and miss him very much. And frequently feel the irrational anger of the child abandoned by death, as if his death were something done to me. And I have thought until recently that all the passionate loves of my life were somehow grounded in my love for him, that all the intensity I have brought to other relationships derived from my unspoken love for him.

I feel now that my love for him was rooted in something greater (but that is another story); and I learned from him that men are both attracted to and frightened by the intense love of intense women, and that men do not require women to be passive so that they may be aggressive (it is not as simple as that, foil, counterfoil). They require women to be passive because passion/suffering frightens and alarms them. We see passionate, intense women as freaks, marked. We can only bear to read about them in books; in real life they make us uncomfortable.

Which is why, though it may not at first seem to follow logically, there is nothing so tender and thrilling as seeing a man in the posture of prayer and devotion; not at all because it gratifies women to see men humbling themselves, but because it offers us the sight of men who do not flee in manly false pride from passion and suffering, and because in houses of prayer (which are so often women's houses, places where women bring their passion), men in attitudes of devotion take the risk of belief and make themselves vulnerable—they share the climate of risk and vulnerability in which women live, and for which women are so seldom, in worldly terms, rewarded.

Knowing finally (I "knew" everything by instinct in those days) that Arnold would not be my lover—or never fully explain himself to me—saddened me. But not with a crushing sadness. With a dreamy bittersweet sorrow that cast only a faint shadow over my life, not an oppressive mass. (The truth was, I was in love with my sadness—with everything that belonged to me: I loved my mysteries.)

I have a snapshot taken at that time in my life: I am wearing a black leotard and a flared quilted skirt that ends mid-calf in delicious, provocative waves; my feet are shod in Capezio ballet slippers; my mouth is fixed in a Tangee (orange-in-the-tube, pink-on-your-lips) grin; my hair is tortured in an improbable arrangement that has even less to do with art than it has to do with nature; oversized five-and-dime gold hoop earrings graze my neck. It is my Greenwich Village uniform. But Greenwich Village is still largely a country of the mind; and my beauty-parlour perm and my Tangee Natural and my screw-on earrings mark me as ineffably Brooklyn. Everything, in fact, is hopelessly out of sync. I have created myself in the image of my fantasies, fantasies drawn from movies and novels of the Bohemian life: I look like a child's energetic drawing of something he has never seen—crude, imaginative, and unfinished. The look on my face, bewildered but insanely grinning, is the look I have seen on men's faces two seconds before they've fully understood that their flies are open in public.

Decisions began to make themselves. I stopped going to meetings, with no explanation to God, my mother, or myself. I got a job in Greenwich Village, that finishing school for my generation of energetic, imaginative, bemused young women. And my eccentric upbringing was in many ways a perfect preparation and a passport for my being alive-and-aware (we used the word *aware* a lot) in the Village of the 1950s. I fitted as sweetly into that decade as a nut fits into its shell. Because the thing about the '50s was that everybody—everybody being the people one knew or emulated or loved—felt out of sync with his time, and glad of it. We all cherished our idiosyncrasies and our neuroses; we would have laughed est, AT, Esalen, and all the '60s/'70s psychic-smoosh therapies to scorn. In spite of the somewhat paradoxical fact that practically everyone one knew spent his or her time on the analyst's couch, we couldn't imagine where we'd be without our disfiguring—but *interesting*—neuroses.

People were nice to me! I was constantly amazed by the goodness of people. I had repudiated everything I'd been taught: I had left Bethel and left the Witnesses precisely because I couldn't believe that "worldlings" were "wicked." But every time I saw evidence of kindness, it was with a kind of gratified amazement: I'd been right after all.

After a day at work, and on the weekends, I sat around in coffeehouses and bars, talking about Salinger and Camus, talking about "anguished awareness"—conversations that might have been tailor-made for my own concerns, my own hungers: Camus said "a subclerk in the post office is the equal of a conqueror if consciousness is common to them" (comforting words for a fledgling secretary); Salinger said that the Fat Lady sitting on her porch in the unendurable heat, swatting flies, cancer eating at her insides, was Jesus Christ. Where one registered *God*, the other registered *human:* for both, everything was hallowed by one's awareness of it. Both seemed to be living on the dangerous edge of the world. And we said, Whoopee! We'll go live there too.

And if, in our coffeehouses and bars and jazz clubs, we found not poets and artists, but dilettantes and poseurs, men who managed to be thoroughly absurd in the vulgar sense—that is, silly—without being at all noble, we did find plenty of lost causes. Women found men, that is, who spoke the language of despair and the language of ecstasy, and took them to their bosoms and to their beds.

What it amounted to was that we would accept any damned nonsense from a man, provided that it was haloed by poetic *feeling*. If our men were struggling and in pain—not to put too fine a point on it, they were losers—we brought them cups of consecrated chicken soup.

What we extrapolated from both Salinger and Camus was the message, perhaps unintended, that we were meant to be handmaidens to the gods. To the god-in-men. Camus regarded Don Juan as a great wise man who lived bravely without illusions of eternal love, a man for whom loving and possessing, conquering and consuming, were ways of knowing, means of provoking a nonexistent God. What good and faithful pupils we were! We invested every fast-talking faithless womanizer we knew with noble qualities. We lived to be loved, possessed, conquered, consumed.

I had left a consuming God—and fallen right into my generation trap: I longed to be a long-legged, cool, innocent young woman with an undiscriminating heart—a Salinger/Camus woman, to set off an ideal man's saintliness or heroism, to mediate between him and the harsh world, to console—to provide a backdrop for the essential deeds of an inspired lunatic.

And was nevertheless still a virgin, my search for an inspired lunatic frustrated by the fact that I lived at home. I had scruples about offending my parents' sexual morality while living under their roof and enjoying their protection.

My poor father: He had welcomed me home like a prodigal; and here I was confounding all his expectations all over again. Was I never to be a dutiful daughter? Head in his hands, he awaited my return every night (hymen intact; but how was he to know that?): "How can a pretty girl like you do these things?"

"I want to get my own apartment, Daddy."

"Don't say that—I'll faint."

"But Daddy, I really have to . . ."

He fainted. My father fainted the way other people sneezed: often, and at the slightest irritant. (I was his allergy.) As soon as I left the Witnesses, my father—his daughter returned to him—expected me to conform to his idea of what good Italian girls did (which was very little of anything). Good Italian girls didn't leave home, God forbid, except to get married.

Are our lives determined by a single throw of the dice? If I hadn't had Arnold to teach me to doubt, would I have learned how to doubt? (I think so.) If I hadn't gone to Mintons one night almost a year after I left Bethel, would I have found a reason to leave my mother's house and find my own, chosen life? (I think so.)

But that one night at Mintons determined the shape my life was to take for years to come.

Mintons was a jazz club on 128th Street in Harlem. Charlie Parker had played there: Billie Holliday still sometimes came in, after hours, with her phalanx of young men, her gardenias and her poodles, and her broken, heartbreaking voice. In 1956, it was still a place where two young white women could go unaccompanied. The night I went with my friend Rosalie from Queens, I fell in love with the sax player. In about the time it takes to say, "Will you have a drink with me?"

Now, at that time, when all the girls from Brooklyn and Queens who wore leotards and dreamed of moving to the East Village were in love with (men's) suffering, jazz musicians—if they were black—were high in the hierarchy of sufferers. I'm not saying that it was my Florence Nightingale temperament that made me fall in love with M.; but I'm not denying that that was a contributing factor. Chemistry did the rest. I went to bed with him in about the time it takes to say, "Yes, thank you, I'll have a drink with you."

He was wonderfully appealing: witty, wry, selfish, bitter, self-mocking, poor, married, a libertine who demanded total commitment from his women, a good and generous lover (when he was there). A perfect person with whom to break all the rules. And I was of course determined to break all the rules. Black jazz musicians were the inner circle of the Outsiders. Proximity to him guaranteed a place in that privileged circle. I joined a world celebrated by Beat poets. Paris had its existential chanteuses; I (and women like me) had the real thing: we lived next to the real cry of the heart.

Those musicians: they used women to sustain them (both sexually and financially); and we, I am afraid, played our part in this dicey game. We objectified them by loving their suffering better than we loved them. The truth was, most jazz musicians wanted with all their hearts to become safe studio musicians and to live on Park Avenue with German maids. It was we, their romantic camp followers, who thought the secular equivalent of the Holy Grail could be found at the Five Spot or Mintons or Birdland, we who thought their poverty was a mark of their noble not-belonging. Told to drain life to its dregs, where better could we do it than in smoky clubs, illegal after-hours joints, with wounded men who had lovers in other towns? Everything in that world gratified my hunger for experience; it was like being plunged into pure feeling unsullied by thought. We were chained to men we regarded, not without reason, as rebels and martyrs. The fact that these rebels and martyrs burned us up in the furnace of their own needs made everything all the more dangerous, hence all the more exciting. (And I was used to furnaces.)

That world was full of joy—those men were, after all, true creators, and they laughed a lot. But it was never really happy. To live in and for the moment is deadly serious work, fun of the most exhausting sort.

If I'd wanted a baptism of fire into the world (and I did!), I couldn't have made a better choice. (I've never regretted it.)

I had by that time been living in the East Village for four months. (I don't know what the actual geographical distance is from Bensonhurst to Dayton, but the psychological distance could have been measured in light years.) I had moved, not only because there was a limit to how much I was willing to outrage my family's sensibilities, but because I talked in my sleep. The morning my mother said (in the voice she reserved for the most awful, i.e. sexual, offences), "You said *terrible* things in your sleep last night" was the morning of the day I began apartment-hunting in earnest.

What amazes me most about the two years I spent with M. was the total absence of sexual guilt. I never for a moment thought what I was doing was bad. If I had any twinges of conscience at all, they had to do with M.'s faraway wife—and those twinges were few: love, I thought, created its own rules, transcended ordinary definitions of right and wrong.

The time I spent with M. burned (I thought) the past away. A year after I left Bethel, it was as if all those years had never been. M. was my exorcist, well chosen. I compressed a lifetime of learning and feeling and sexually loving into one year.

And so the Jehovah-less 1950s went. When my affair ended (I got *tired*, really), I tried on other lives. Another man, another life: I became a devoted practitioner of serial monogamy (and gave God not a thought), seeking nurturance and a way to live. I did not think of myself as marked by my religious experience, or as singular, or different from any other women I knew. The past had died without funeral rites. (I sometimes exhibited the corpse at parties: "I used to be a Jehovah's Witness." Calculated to amuse. Like saying, "I used to be a Teen-age Werewolf.")

I'm not saying it was altogether bad, that multiplicity of personalities. It was, if you didn't forget entirely who you were, exciting. If you did forget entirely who you were, you could have a '50s identity crisis—after which you usually got married.

I got married.

I had two children.

Dorothy Day has said that the birth of her daughter was so joyous it convinced her of the existence of God. My births were joyous too—orgasmic; I did not, however, as a consequence praise God.

And I thought of God only when my husband, in casual conversation, stated his beliefs; which were that he didn't know if there was a God, but if God existed, God had to be good. Which provoked me to rage: I thought it was stupid, sentimental rubbish and maddeningly devoid of logic, and somehow smug (I couldn't bear his taking the word *God* casually in his mouth, along with his martinis and his gin-and-limes). How could one infer from the fact of God's existence the fact of God's goodness? It didn't follow.

It particularly didn't follow in India, where my husband had gone to work and where we lived. Where was the evidence of God's goodness? In the poverty and degradation that forced one either to cauterize one's senses or to curse one's own impotence every day of one's life? In the rats that bit off the deadened fingers of lepers while they slept? In the deformed beggars who dogged our path every time we set foot in the bazaar with our fat American purses? In the bland carelessness of the very rich who pronounced blessings over quadruple amputees on their way to tea parties where they discussed endlessly whether it hurt a fish to be pierced by a hook? In the bloated bellies of children who stuffed their mouths with mud to satisfy their hunger? In the blind *saddhu* who died outside our kitchen door, naked and erect? Once, when my husband came back from an inspection tour of a leprosarium, I taunted him: Do you still believe that if God exists He is good?

This is the worst fight I ever had with my husband: My son (born in Libya, where evidence of God's goodness didn't seem too manifold either) had been diagnosed (incorrectly) as having leukaemia. We wore living in Bombay; we got the diagnosis on Christmas Eve (and lived with it for thirty-six hours); I was eight months pregnant with my second child, my daughter. My husband said that he would pray for our son. I few into an earsplitting rage, wild, demented: He had never, in good times and in fair domestic weather, prayed; how dare he pray now? My husband, in his great grief over our son, hardly knew how to answer the fury I had become. He said, mildly, "Do you mean you're *not* going to pray for Josh?" "Never," I said. "I wouldn't ask a crumb of Him, that bully."

My rage should have taught me something. I persisted in believing that all my ties to God had been severed, that my feeling for God was as moribund as I believed Him to be. I didn't understand how fraught His absence was, how significant.

When I lived in Tripoli, I loved to hear the high sweet call of the *muezzin*, calling the faithful to prayer.

On frequent visits to Rome, I spent most of my time in churches, some of it on my knees.

When I lived in Guatemala, I surreptitiously made the sign of the cross when religious processions passed.

Once, in Warangal, in central India, I entered (as a sight-seer—Eastern religion had little appeal for me) a temple no longer used for worship, set in a wooded hollow in a dry plain. The cool, dry temple smelled of bat dung, a sick-sweetish odour, and of old flower offerings and of centuries of bodies and time. I approached the Shiva altar and immediately felt what I can only describe as a presence—like the rushing and reverberating of great wings. I fled to the Land-Rover outside, words of self-mockery already forming on my lips.

But what was all this but aesthetics, architecture, and aberration? It had nothing to do with God. I would have been outraged at any such presumptuous suggestion.

I was lonely, and purposeless. I was not in love with my husband. (I remember, just before I married him, thinking, "I will never love his body"—and marrying him nevertheless. I thought marriage would be restful; I thought he was good. I was tired. We wanted to love each other; I thought that would be enough.) My children, nourishment and joy, did not provide what I felt I lacked: a central core to my existence. But, I told myself, most overseas wives were purposeless—unless they were able to regard a series of distractions as a life; and most, uprooted, were lonely—unless they were very much in love with their husbands (and sometimes even then).

I remember sitting in the ruins of Leptis Magna, tracing my fingers over mosaics thousands of years old, sitting under a bougainvillea tree (thousands of glorious purple clusters), gazing at the blue-green turquoise Mediterranean, everything fresh and clean, ancient and formal—feeling that nothing could ever dazzle or surprise me again.

There is an amphitheatre that rises out of the desert in Tunisia, larger than the Colosseum at Rome, and a traveller comes upon it unprepared. It is suddenly, breathtakingly there. Except that it didn't take my breath away. If I had read about it in a book, I would have been thrilled and enraptured. When I saw it, it seemed unremarkable. Everything seemed unremarkable.

When people asked me what I did in India for four years, I say lightly, "I arranged flowers in vases." But of course I did, and felt, much more in that vast, maternal landscape, which is not so much a country as a state of mind. I was loved by two men, and I loved a third—all loves ephemeral, but all forcing a wedge between me and my husband.

I wanted to go home, to America: Listening to Martin Luther King say, "We shall overcome" on the U.S.I.S. overseas radio wasn't quite the real, exciting thing; deploring the war at cocktail parties in Guatemala City (where the Embassy's First Secretary considered Senator Fulbright a traitor) was an exercise in shrill futility. I'd acquired a taste for political activism. I wanted to go home.

We came home. I kept up with the times: came to New York, bought a Brooklyn brownstone, got a divorce, sent my children to a progresssive school. It was 1966: civil rights, protest marches, consciousness-raising.

My life was centred around my work, my children, my friends, and an occasional (but never enduring) lover.

What more could one ask for? My life was a chosen one; I was luckier than most. It would be a betrayal of my children, of the men and women who have loved me, and a betrayal of self, not to say that it was a good life. But the impulse to praise when there is No One to praise makes the heart sore. I did not, could not, praise the Word.

My experience with the Witnesses—more accurately, the experience of *leaving* that stale, dry religion (which was a form of servitude)—had created a hunger for words unsatisfied by a secular society; unfashionable words: *good, evil, love.*

When I left the Witnesses, it was to discover the world, which I was prepared to find beautiful. I found what everybody finds: It's as good a place as any to work in, beautiful and ugly in equal measure; there are moments of transcendent joy, and times when the world (like one's heart) is dry and weary.

There are temporary refuges; there are (it seems to those who live without God's grace) no "covert from the tempest," no refreshing river in the dry places, no shadows in which to hide.

When I left the Witnesses, I told myself that if I had to spend the rest of my life alone (believing that in all the important things, I would always be alone), the leaving would still have been worth it. I could not foresee the consequences of leaving; but I knew that the act itself was necessary, that I must not try to anticipate the consequences, and that the consequences of not acting would be worse that anything that might happen to me afterward. In all the years that followed, I never found reason to regret my decision, even through all the inescapable desolations and humiliations, the hurts and wounds that life inflicts upon us all. I vowed to accept as truth only that which I knew to be true, and to live—"convinced of the wholly human origin of all that is human"—with only that which I knew to be true. I expected to live and die without certainty, without the absolute, and without absolution.

(Sometimes there was pure joy in remembering why I had left. Crossing the Brooklyn Bridge at night, seeing that skyline burning hot and icy, the skyline that defined and was a symbol for the world—"This is mine, all mine"—I rejoiced; I had chosen it; I loved it (I love it). And sometimes when making love. Or decorating the Christmas tree with my children—squabbling, hassling, but alive and juicy, in love with whatever was human and whatever was magic. At those moments, I remembered the years of deprivation, but only to exult in the riches of the present. The past was like a bad dream.

I was (am) often false, frivolous, silly, negligent. I read, when I was 35, the diary of a 17-year-old girl who swore "never to compromise," and I loved her: I was that girl, and I had compromised, and had been compromised. But I had never expected it to be easy. And I could tell myself that I had performed one tremendous, courageous act: I had left a religion that was small and peevish and meretricious to take my lumps and my joys where I found them. Where *I* found them. Nothing further I might ever do would equal that one deed; but it had been done. It was the source of my pride, and my self-love.

And there were lovers and friends and comrades, brothers and sisters, along the way.

And that is where the story ought to end.

I thought, in fact, when I began to write this book, that (barring pleasant, but not earthshaking, surprises) the story had ended.

I was wrong.

This is the hardest part to write. Perhaps the best way is just to set down the facts.

When I began this book, I was a theological illiterate.

Words like *redemptive* and *sacramental* crept into my vocabulary, nonplussing my friends and vaguely disturbing me. I couldn't find their secular equivalent. I loved saying them.

A magazine asked me to interview Dorothy Day. In the course of a phone conversation, she talked about the Hell's Angels outside one of her Houses of Hospitality and how they were raucously threatening her peace. She said she was going to pray for them at Vespers; and would I join her? I said I was afraid I was unable to pray. She said, "Well, then, dear, I'll pray for you and the Hell's Angels at Vespers." It tickled me to be thrown in with the Hell's Angels; I thought, You wouldn't catch the Witnesses praying for Hell's Angels; and I loved the word Vespers.

Later that week, a friend sent me a crucifix—a tiny pewter Jesus, warm and soft with age. "Why did you do that? I'm not religious." "Guess again," she said. (I'm not claiming to have seen the hand of God in this; one of the things I despised about the Witnesses was their ability to make supernatural hullabaloo about every natural occurrence if they were involved in it; I am saying that I cherished both the call and the present; and I began to carry the crucifix with me.)

Halfway through writing this book, I had a bitter experience with a man, the long and short of it being that I grew to hate him with a hatred so corrosive I felt I could not survive its toxin. I did not know what to do with these feelings. I did not feel I could live with them. No admixture of pity—just pure, venomous hatred. I couldn't bear myself. (I have spoken of my mother in terms that are less than endearing. But I want to say: I have always wanted to love her; I have always wanted her to love me. And in fact I do love the person she was before she became what it was perhaps impossible for her not to become. It grieves me that what I've written will grieve her, that my necessities overcame my scruples.) Where he was concerned, I had no grief, no pity, no scruples.

Obsessed, I wrote him letters every day for six months, calling him everything vile and hateful and loathsome. I didn't mail them. They did not act as a catharsis; they made me hate him all the more. In desperation, without calculation, I asked God—in Whom I did not believe—to take my hatred away, to exorcise it.

I do not believe in magic.

I woke up the next morning, and the hatred was gone. From which I drew no conclusions.

I was a theological illiterate. I was faced, some time after the incident I have just described, with the task of comparing the doctrines of the Witnesses with the teachings of traditional Christianity. Providentially, I read Teilhard de Chardin. And fell in love with Teilhard; and—even I could not escape drawing the conclusion this time—with God.

Not with the *idea* of God, and not with the little, punitive Jehovah of my youth. With the Triune God of love and mercy who calls us to Him in spite of our calloused hearts, "unto whom all hearts are open, all desires known, and from whom no secrets are hid"; with that God Who is "the shadow of a great rock in a weary land," "Begotten of his Father before all worlds, God of light, Light of Light, Very God of very God; Begotten, not made"; with the God Who asks us not to desert the world, but to join our works in the world to His, to be co-creators of the Kingdom of Heaven on earth. I fell in love with the God Who, made flesh, bore the anguish of man (by virtue of which nothing is profane); with the God Whose love brings us back to the things of this world, Who, knowing that the world can be terrifying, blind, and brutal, nevertheless commands us to be happy; with the God Who invites us to believe in the communion of saints and to share in the mystical totality of Christ.

(And don't ask me about the origins of evil, or about rats and bloated bellies and earthquakes and why He permits them. I don't know. When I was a Witness, I had the answers to all those questions, or thought I did. What I did not have was faith in the ultimate goodness of God. Now I don't have answers; I have faith. "For now we see through a glass, darkly; but then face to face: now I know in part; but then shall I know even as also I am known." I only know that I will know. And I know that leap into belief was not an escape into passivity or resignation or withdrawal from the world; it was the beginning of a truly human struggle to realize God in the world.)

In the end, whether or not one is a Christian has almost nothing to do with persuasive intellectual argument: it has to do with whether one has experienced God; it has to do with the grace of God—a mystery. It has little to do with how "good" a person is.

> The committed believer and unbeliever then have much in common. Both are dedicated seekers of truth. Both seek in darkness—to both God is an absence, one who is not there, for he is an object to be found. Yet he is there, for both believer and unbeliever have an objective in their lifelong striving—though called different names, conceptualized differently, by each. To both, then, God is a presence and an absence, one who is there, and one who is not there.—Anthony Willhelm, *Christ Among Us* (New York: Paulist Press, 1975)

I could not believe in a Church, or in a God, that required me to believe that the goodness and the idealism of the believer surpassed the goodness and the idealism of the non-believer. When I left the Witnesses, I said, "God can't kill Arnold." I am not required now to believe that Arnold is damned. I am not obliged to believe that anyone is damned. Which is not to say that evil is not given the name of evil: Blake says, "To love thine enemies is to betray thy friends/ That surely is not what Christ intends." That is something to think about: the Church demands that we think and that we listen to the imperatives of our conscience, even when, especially when, the imperatives of our conscience go against the authoritative teachings of the Church. The law is not written on stone; it is written on the heart; that is something the Witnesses—in their literalism—do not understand.

That summer, the summer I read Teilhard and fell in love with God, I had an absolute conviction that He was present, that He was adorable, and finally that His wish to be known was as great as my wish to know Him. That is what I mean by "experiencing" God. I was not, like Paul, blinded by a sudden light, nor, like Saint Teresa, pierced to the quick by the arrows of His love. I did not swoon. My conversion, if it can be called such, did not feel like a sudden fall or a sudden flight. It didn't feel "sudden" at all. It felt like a coalescing, a culmination, a unifying, a knitting together of everything that had ever happened to me; and most of all it felt like a sweetness, sweeter than anything I had ever experienced before. It also did not feel like the end of a road; it felt like the beginning of a walk out of a tunnel into light. It was rapturous. The tears I cried that summer were tears of release, as if something frozen had shattered into a pinwheel of kaleidoscopic light.

I was living at MacDowell, an artists' colony in New Hampshire. I am an urban person; when I think of "Nature," I think of it as something other people do, involving mosquitos and unidentifiable objects and gibberish noises in the too-dark night. Given a post-card-pretty New England green, I register "lovely"—and feel homesick for a New York bag lady and a bopping Puerto Rican with a transistor radio.

But that summer for the first time, the Country held no fears for me. The physical world had lost its menace, its threatening and overwhelming other-ness; it had never looked so beautiful.

When I compare the Church with the Witnesses, I think: The Witnesses explained everything, and explained everything legalistically. The Church does not attempt to explain everything: triumphant, militant, glorious, it is humble enough to get on its august knees and say "We do not know"; "We have committed grave errors." (I do love the paradoxes of the Church. With all the great art and music of the world at its disposal, the church in Peterborough, New Hampshire, alarms the Sunday-morning air with recorded electronic bells—which drives the local good-taste Episcopalians wild, and which I think is funny.) The Church has room for everything, including God knows, vulgarity. That is what I love about it—that it is catholic, universal.

I sometimes wish, with the nostalgia of all recent converts who revere what they have never known, that the Church would return to its ancient, formal aesthetic ways. The vernacular does not thrill me, nor do folk masses; and—while I know I am guilty of hopelessly objectifying them—I wish that contemplative nuns would go back to contemplating and praying for me instead of throwing pots (there are enough bad potters in the world, and there is not enough prayer). But I know that I am being silly. Because along with all the changes in the Church (some of which I can't help deploring) has come a great openness, an embracing. The Church is in ferment, yeasty and alive. To enter the Church now is to become part of a living organism; choices are required of us all—and to choose prayerfully is harder than to worship by rote.

Mostly when I compare the Witnesses with the Church, I think: To be a Witness meant not to give, but to give *up*; whereas the Church says that not to use one's talents to join one's efforts to God's is "a serious wrongdoing." The Church says that to be godly is to be fully human, and to be fully human is to be godly.

What I fell in love with was the Mass, the mystery of the Sacraments, the liturgy. What I love is God.

I alarmed people in New Hampshire by being religious in what they perceived to be an unreligious way. I tried to steal a Book of Common Prayer (the beauty of that language—*And let our cry come unto Thee!*) from the local Episcopal church (which was beautiful, and where I attended Communion). I didn't think God would mind; my fellow colonists thought the minister would. (It is interesting to me how people who profess not to be religious are always telling people who profess to be religious *how* to be religious.)

I alarmed my friends at home more seriously: When the passage of time had convinced them that this wasn't an aberration, they expressed fear, bewilderment, cynicism ("Are you looking for an ending to your book?")— and worst and most painful, betrayal. They thought my intellect would take a vacation. They thought all my moral values would change (they have not; they have just been given a context). I found it difficult to convince my friends that I was still a feminist, still politically radical, only something had been added: God. In which case, they invariably responded, if nothing has changed, why do you need God? The answer is, of course, that while nothing has changed, everything has changed. I know what the internal changes are; the external changes are still revealing themselves. And when one's conscience propels one in the direction of the Church, there is very little one can do about it; nor would I wish to do anything about it.

It is a source of great joy to me that praise and doubt are not mutually exclusive, that I can question the hierarchy and not be regarded as a reprobate or a bad child; that I can engage in loving arguments with members of the Church and still be part of a loving family, a living community whose voices frequently clash with one another's, but who are united in love of God, united at the Mass.

I do not feel that I have given up intellectual or moral responsibility for my life. I have questions that have to be answered. But I think the answers are to be found within the framework of the Church, and the struggle has to be fought within the framework of the Church—which does not despise questions or questioners. My New Hampshire friend was right: to be a Catholic and a feminist and a leftist sometimes appears to be a fantastic juggling act. I think of the hierarchy's position on abortion, and the Church's statements about sexuality, and of the position women in the Church—all vexing and painful issues. I am not concerned with the gender of the Deity—Who seems to be to be a living flame, and that takes care of that—and furthermore, if God had come to earth as a woman, no one would have listened to Him/Her. When I learn more about the historical context in which Paul, that maddening, saintly man, wrote, I will be able to come to terms with him, talking about female submission in one breath, saying "In Christ there is no slave, no freeman, no male, no female" in the next. That can come later. In the meantime, I am patient. I have never been so patient in my life.

My father says: "Oh, my God, you're doing God-talk again."

I say, "It's different this time, though, isn't it?"

"We're not enemies this time," he says; and, "you're happy." Then he says, "Explain to me why God sent the bears to rip the children who mocked Elijah."

"I can't."

"When you were nine years old, you knew all the answers. And the answers separated us. It's different now."

Everything is different now.

Abbreviated Codes for Sources Frequently Cited

CODE	SOURCE
	BOOKS
Aid	*Aid to Bible Understanding* (New York; Watchtower Bible and Tract Society, 1969, 1971)
All Scrip	*All Scripture Is Inspired of God and Beneficial* (New York: WB&TS, 1963)
Babylon	*Babylon the Great Has Fallen!* (New York: WB&TS, 1963)
Children	Rutherford, J. F., *Children* (New York: WB&TS, 1941)
Cole	Cole, Marley, *Jehovah's Witnesses* (New York: Vantage Press, 1955)
Faith	Macmillan, A. H., *Faith on the March* (Englewood Cliffs, N.J.: Prentice-Hall, 1957)
FPL	*From Paradise Lost to Paradise Regained* (New York: WB&TS, 1958)
Hoekema	Hoekema, Anthony A., *Jehovah's Witnesses* (Grand Rapids, Mich.: Eerdmans, 1974)
JWDP	*Jehovah's Witnesses in the Divine Purpose* (New York: WB&TS, 1959)
LGBT	*Let God Be True* (New York: WB&TS, 1946, revised 1952)
Life	*Life Everlasting in Freedom of the Sons of God* (New York: WB&TS, 1966)
NPC	Conway, J. S., *The Nazi Persecution of the Churches* (London: Weidenfeld and Nicolson, 1968)
NWT	New World Translation of the Holy Scriptures (New York: WB&TS, 1961)
Qualified	*Qualified to Be Ministers* (New York: WB&TS, 1955, revised 1967)
SS, vol.	Russell, Charles T., *Studies in the Scriptures*, Volumes I–VI (New York: WB&TS, 1886–1904)
Teilhard	Teilhard de Chardin, Pierre, *The Divine Milieu* (New York: Harper & Row, 1960)
This Good	*This Good News of the Kingdom* (New York: WB&TS, 1954, revised 1965)
TMSG	*Theocratic Ministry School Guidebook* (New York: WB&TS, 1971)
Truth	*The Truth Shall Make You Free* (New York: WB&TS, 1943)
Yearbook, date	*Yearbook of Jehovah's Witnesses* (New York: WB&TS, 1927–)

Z&L Zaretsky, Irving I., and Leone, Mark P., eds., *Religious Movements in Contemporary America* (Princeton, N.J.: Princeton University Press, 1974)

PERIODICALS

Aw *Awake!* (New York: WB&TS)
KM *Kingdom Ministry* (New York: WB&TS)
TW; TWT; ZWT *The Watchtower* (New York: WB&TS); previously *The Watch Tower* and *Zion's Watch Tower*

Additional Sources

Beard, Charles A. and Mary R., *The Rise of American Civilization*, Vol. I (New York: Macmillan, 1927)

Camus, Albert, *The Myth of Sisyphus and Other Essays* (New York: Knopf, 1955)

Gaylin, Willard, *In the Service of Their Country: War Resisters in Prison* (New York: Viking, 1970)

Küng, Hans, *On Being a Christian* (Garden City, N.Y.: Doubleday, 1976)

Zahn, Gordon, *In Solitary Witness: The Life and Death of Franz Jägerstätter* (New York: Holt, Rinehart and Winston, 1964)

Index